# ChaRIOT

*The New Cultural Conversation*

K. Edwin Bryant

**Type of Work:** Text

**Registration Number / Date:** TXu002286329 / 2021-10-26

**Application Title:** ChaRIOT: The New Cultural Conversation.

**Title:** ChaRIOT: The New Cultural Conversation.

**Description:** Electronic file (eService)

**Copyright Claimant:** K. Edwin Bryant, 1974- . Address: 70 Birch Alley, Suite 240, Beavercreek, OH, 45440, United States.

**Date of Creation:** 2021

**Authorship on Application:** K. Edwin Bryant, 1974- ; Citizenship: United States. Authorship: text, artwork.

**Copyright Note:** Regarding authorship information: Deposit contains only copyrightable text.
Full Media Publishing

**Names:** Bryant, K. Edwin, 1974-

## DEDICATION

*For Kohl, Kaleb, and Kye*

It is my hope that in time you join me as a
ChaRIOT for your generations.

## Table of Contents

## Foreword

So much is being said and written in contemporary America about "the culture wars" and how they impact our lives and self-understandings as a nation—socially, intellectually, politically, economically, and otherwise. The problem of race remains at the root of such cultural conflicts, and it surfaces in every conversation about the nation's past, its present, and its future. It is the one problem that still sharply divides Americans of all backgrounds and walks of life, and that figures into the enduring debates about how to define America historically. This helps explain in some measure the importance of *The ChaRIOT: The New Cultural Conversation,* which highlights the critical need for what K. Edwin Bryant envisions as "the new cultural conversation."

*The ChaRIOT* is quite unlike the many books on history and culture I have read up to this point. Bryant carefully combines history and biography as he traces the unfolding drama surrounding race and racism in America over time. He not only offers a panoramic view of the long history of Black America's encounter with and struggle against racist oppression, but also shares many of his own personal experiences with the scourge that is systemic and institutionalized white supremacy in this land. Covering issues as wide-ranging as the Middle Passage, the historical and structural roots of white supremacy, the Black community's deadly encounters with law enforcement, Black Lives Matter protests, the Black experience in corporate America, and the call for reparations, Bryant sets the stage for "the new cultural conversation," which, as he describes it, should involve not only a serious reckoning with America's racial past and present, but also a careful reimagining, rethinking, and reshaping of the cultural landscape of the nation for future generations.

The word "ChaRIOT," which Bryant describes as "a transformative new concept," drives the content of this book. The word is synonymous on some levels with the word "agent," which means one who acts or becomes a special instrument in a particular cause or mission. Bryant calls himself "a ChaRIOT," which means that he not only takes sides with the oppressed, but that he has also chosen to become a prophetic voice and an activist in the continuing crusade to dismantle personal, systemic, and institutional racism in America. He challenges other freedom-loving persons to join him in this "ChaRIOT movement," which could not be more important at a time when white supremacists are resurfacing with a boldness, passion, and sense of pride and purpose that are hard to fathom in this 21$^{st}$ century. Bryant's sense of the "ChaRIOT Movement" is grounded in essentially the same vision that sparked Martin Luther King Jr.'s struggle for the beloved community, and it encourages sustained resistance to the kind of fragmented and tribalized America advocated by hatemongers and right-wing extremists.

Bryant has given us what I would call a timely book, or a book that is meaningful or relevant for this time in our history. It resonates with gripping force in what scholars are calling this "post-truth age," when politicians, especially at the state levels, are passing laws designed to whitewash history or to shield the ugliest parts of the nation's history from school children. As evidenced by the vicious attacks on Critical Race Theory and *The 1619 Project*, historical truths and facts are no longer cherished as a part of this nation's educational processes, and all too many are claiming, directly or indirectly, that bringing critical-analytical thinking skills to bear on its history and culture will do far more harm than good. Bryant's book is useful for engaging this type of thinking, and his call for "the new cultural conversation" is really a rallying cry for a new cultural consciousness that moves us beyond the shortcomings of who we are as a multiracial democracy to the fullness of what we can and should become.

Bryant's book should appeal to a broad readership. There is something here for academics, especially those in history, religion, politics, and cultural studies. Social and political activists will find here much food for thought and inspiration. The highly readable content will also make this book appealing to many in the public square, especially average churchpersons who are looking for ways to translate the fruits of their faith into social and political efforts that transform society and culture for the better. Apparently, Bryant set out to write a book for the people, irrespective of their backgrounds or stations in life, and he has succeeded. He has demonstrated that rare ability to speak to and reach people at every level of the social ladder.

I close with comments about how this book has impacted me personally. I appreciate very much Bryant's critical-analytical reading of the whole of American history, his reflections on his own personal journey and life experiences with racism, and his stirring call for "the new cultural conversation" and "a ChaRIOT movement." He urges us not simply to read history, but to understand history and culture in new and challenging ways, while also moving from the theoretical to the practical in our search for a new historical and cultural reality.

*Lewis V. Baldwin*
*Emeritus Professor of Religious Studies*
*Vanderbilt University*
*March 2022*

# The ChaRIOT

## Preface

The most remarkable events of 2020 brought forward a focus on race and structural racism. More precisely, it was the year that no matter where you turned, Americans were forced to face reality: America was the epicenter of a watershed moment on racial reckoning. Our country was thrust headfirst into reconciling its past, present, and continues to ponder how race in America will shape its future. 2020 is distinguished as the year that the injustice experienced by Black communities forced America to confront systemic racism and its Confederate symbols.

During this watershed moment on race, an opportunity has been given to Americans to dismantle the implicit biases and systems that sustain racism. It has not been since the Civil Rights Movement began in 1955 that the public climate for change has been so ripe. Yet many Americans are skeptical that this moment of racial reckoning will lead to significant changes in the United States. The moment of reckoning demands that people who benefit from privilege *own* that the privilege of being White comes with benefits that being Black does not offer.

Four hundred years after the first slaves were brought to this country, Black people are still often the targets of oppression, macroaggression, and microaggression by fellow Americans–Americans who are White. The key to deconstructing racism in America involves uniting with people who courageously and temporarily suspend the benefits of (privilege) to acknowledge that these acts against Black men, women, and children taking place in our country must discontinue. The conversations we need to begin the dismantling of systemic racism demand an acknowledgment that Black and Indigenous People of Color are human and equals.

# INTRODUCTION

## The ChaRIOT

When The White House announced it would support a study on reparations in February 2021, it reopened an unhealed wound in the hearts of Black Americans. The announcement also set off yet another round of media stories, conversations, debates, anger, and even denial from some about America's racist history, the legacy of the chattel slavery industry, and how much, if any, monies should be paid to Black people for centuries of enslavement. Discussions about reparations date back to the period just after the Civil War and have always been a subject that prompts angst, hurt, push back, and a revisiting of the unrelenting racist systems that are ingrained in every fiber of the nation.

In 1989, Rep. John Conyers (D-Michigan) introduced the H.R. 40 Commission to Study and Develop Reparation Proposals for African-Americans Act and brought it before each Congress until he retired in 2017. The bill proposed examining slavery and legalized discrimination in the colonies and the United States from 1619 to the present and recommend appropriate remedies for Black people. More than 150 years after the topic was first brought forward post-Civil War and more than 30 years after H.R. 40 was introduced, the reparations remain as far from coming to fruition as they were during Reconstruction.[1] *New York Times* bestselling author and journalist Ta-Nehisi Coates took the reparations controversy to new heights in 2014 when he wrote, "The Case for Reparations," published in *The Atlantic*. The content is rich in history and facts about the legacy of racism in the United States of America and the price the country is paying for refusing to confront it. Though the entire country is impacted by

---

[1] Congressional Research Service, "H.R.40 - 117th Congress (2021-2022): Commission to Study ..." Congress.gov (Rep. Jackson, Lee Shelia [D-TX-18], January 4, 2021), https://www.congress.gov/bill/117th-congress/house-bill/40.

historic and systemic racism, Black people have always paid the highest price of anyone. And they still do.

If we examined just one year in the life of Black Americans, the events in 2020 paint an undeniable picture of vast disparities and inequities along health, social, economic, political, educational, and justice lines.

The events of an unforgettable year began on Sunday, January 26, when we heard in disbelief that Kobe Bryant, his 13-year-old daughter, and seven other people died when the helicopter they were riding in crashed in the hills of Calabasas, California. Within three weeks of the tragedy, we began hearing chatter that a mysterious virus originating in China had made its way to the States and was infecting people in a few nursing homes in the Northwest. The coronavirus spread quickly across the United States, and by March 13, the unthinkable happened: the country shut down, and people began contracting the virus and dying in sweeping numbers. Black, Indigenous, and People of Color (BIPOC) were succumbing to the disease at three times the rate of White people due to a myriad of factors, and not the least of them was and are longstanding racialized disparities.

On Tuesday night, May 26, protests erupted in the streets of Minneapolis, Minnesota for a man whose name was soon known all over the world as being a victim of a merciless police officer. The evening before on May 25, a 46-year-old Black man was choked to death by a White Minneapolis police officer as he begged for his life on Memorial Day. The entire 9:29 second murder was captured on a video that went viral and caused unprecedented outrage among people from all walks of life, from A-list celebrities to pastors to the everyday Joe and Jane. There had been Black Lives Matter protests before May 26th, but an image of the helpless George Floyd pinned to the ground under the knees of three White officers and the life drained out of him on camera rocked America. By May 27, streets in cities around the country were filled with thousands of people participating in Black Lives Matter demonstrations for racial justice. Black people felt free to voice their rage, frustration, and extreme pain unchecked in the streets and in their workplaces. Apprehensions about speaking truth to power and suppressing how they feel about being the target of racist

2

behaviors and daily microaggressions were off the table. Black people were calling out racists and the racism they keep alive. I observed how the news media gave extensive coverage to the protesters and what they had to say about how living in America as a Black person adversely affects their psyche, physical health, and emotional wellbeing. What we saw was the anguish Black people usually only feel safe expressing to one another in the privacy of their homes and with families, friends, and neighbors who look like them. What we witnessed as Black people were having their say was the bottled-up frustration from not being able to advance at work despite being more than qualified or from suffering the indignity of a White retail associate assuming that because you are Black, you must be monitored in a store lest you steal something. We heard the cries of people who knew, but for the grace of God, the same fate that befell George Floyd could be visited on them at any time for doing nothing more than being a member of the Black race. We heard from parents who were anguished and weary from worrying about their children having a fatal encounter with police every time they left the safety of home. And then we watched one Black parent after another describe the ritual of having "The Talk" with their kids about what to do to make it home safely if the police stop them. Interestingly, some of the parents recited stories of how their parents gave them the same cautionary talk decades earlier.

As more and more people joined the 2020 Black Lives Matter marches and numbers peaked at 500,000 on June 6, celebrities used their platforms and influence to call attention to racial injustice.[2] Several CEOs pledged to do a better job of increasing diversity hires and promotions within their companies, while others admitted or claimed they did not know about the daily bouts with racism that Black people have to endure. Moreover, many of the encounters that Blacks are having with racial bias and microaggressions are taking place

---

[2] Larry Buchanan, Quoctrung Bui, and Jugal K. Patel. "Black Lives Matter May Be the Largest Movement in U.S. History." The New York Times. The New York Times, July 3, 2020.

inside the walls of the very companies that those CEOs lead. The actions emit biased perceptions, stereotypes, and instances of essentializing Black people.

One CEO of a global financial services corporation convened a special meeting with a group of the company's Black executives to hear about experiences in their daily lives and at the office. He admitted to not ever giving much thought to how they feel and what they experience as Black Americans. That CEO is no different than most White Americans, as they generally do not consciously think about race or the Black experience. They do not think about the pain and anguish of living in the country of your birth and being subjected to experiences of inequity, injustice, and intergenerational racism from fellow Americans.

There are certain realities in America that highlight the plight of Black Americans and the privilege of White Americans. These realities have polarized America, and that division persists and is kept fertile generation after generation because racism is predicated on a system embedded so deeply in our society that it is a norm, a taken-for-granted assumption that Whites do not think about or even acknowledge.

When I was in high school, I came into my own concerning how race divides people. As my White childhood friends, whom I had grown up with, came of age with, and made memories with, began to separate themselves from me, and began clinging to other White teens, I soon began to understand. The irony is that I spent my entire childhood and teen years being exposed to diverse people, never knowing those experiences would prepare me for my work as a diversity, equity, and inclusion consultant to corporations. As I work as a faith leader and consultant, I am struck by how little has changed since I was in high school more than 30 years ago. A case in point is what one of our children experienced. Our youngest son, who is under the age of 9, is playing on a sports team with other boys his age. Not long ago, he told his mother and me that one of the White boys on the team used the N-word when talking about Black teammates. As I listened to my son recount that story, I was reminded of how Dr. Martin Luther King Jr. lived a life that exemplified his belief that giving honor to all God's creations was obligatory and a debt we owe to other human beings. I thought about how that young boy was carrying the ball of racist intolerance that had been passed to him by his elders, and because of that act, intergenerational racism seems to never wither and die.

Therefore, pent-up frustration and rage spilled into the streets during the 2020 protests. It seemed that no city, town, or village in the United States was untouched by the events. In my predominately White hometown of Elyria, Ohio, a forum, "Time of Listening," was hosted by the mayor, YWCA, and Lorain County Urban League to give residents of color a safe space to share their experiences with racism after a week of demonstrations against injustice.[3] Four hours away in Dayton, Ohio where the church I pastor is located, I was particularly watchful of the protests. Hundreds of people were still demonstrating peacefully in Dayton days after Floyd was killed. Unfortunately, tempers boiled over and clashes between groups of protesters and police took place one evening, including protesters blocking streets and people throwing rocks and bottles at police cruisers.

Black people have been marching in the streets for decades to demand civil rights, justice, and equity. The history of injustices that Black people endure and that I describe in this book have been articulated and recounted by historians, scholars, faith leaders, educators, and everyday people witnessing and experiencing acts of racism. I must drive home the point again the intergenerational nature of racism and how what my son heard from a White boy his age happened in 2020 but Black people were subjected to being called racial epithets in 1920, 1820, 1720, and 1620 when they arrived here in chains.

Sadly, we have not overcome as a nation. Systemic racism is still part of the everyday lived experience of Black people. Racial inequities and disparities continue to serve as barriers to creating a country where one's race no longer determines socioeconomic

---

[3] Ryan Haidet. "Time of Listening: Elyria Residents Invited to 'Experiences of Racism' Forum." wkyc.com. WKYC, June 2, 2020.

outcomes and where the imbalanced system we know today is replaced with systemic balance and justice for all of us. Until then, the epidemic of racial injustice, noxious beliefs, and systemic oppression will be with us, and we all will continue to pay the price for a lack of commitment and progress in putting forth the effort needed to save ourselves.

We cannot rest now. We cannot sit back and think we are done because millions of people marched in Black Lives Matter protests. We cannot be satisfied that the state of things is turning around because Derek Chauvin was sent to prison for murdering George Floyd or three White men in the South were sentenced to life in prison for hunting the unarmed Ahmaud Arbery and gunning him down. We should not think we are on our way to creating a country where equity for all is imminent because a Ketanji Brown Jackson is on track to make history by becoming the first Black woman to hold a seat on the U.S. Supreme Court, or because in 2020, CEOs pledged the largest amount of money in U.S. history to fight racism. This centuries-old disease is a constant in our workplaces, retail stores, schools, academic institutions, communities, and in encounters with police. In the case of Ahmaud Arbery, his encounter with three White male "Citizen Joes" in a South Georgia town resulted in him being shot and killed on a street near his home for the crime of jogging while Black.

We saw Arbery's name and image plastered on signs carried by Black and White marchers during Black Lives Matter nationwide protests. White allies and accomplices have been joining Blacks on the front lines of the fight for civil rights and justice since the 1950s, and many gave their lives to support the cause. However, I must say the number of Whites who joined Black Lives Matter marches during the 2020 protests was staggering and *who* joined the marches was at times surprising. Many people did a double-take when they saw Republican Senator Mitt Romney marching with protesters in Washington, D.C. *The New York Times* reported 2020 as drawing the largest and most diverse group of protesters in American history. But to what end?

If we let this moment pass, we would have lost one of our best opportunities to start a new movement for equity, one like this country has never known. No one can do this for us. No one is coming to teach us, lead us, or save us from ourselves. No chariot is coming to carry us to the America, where everyone has what they need to thrive and live well. We must be the ChaRIOT. We must be the ChaRIOT that takes us to *that America* after we put in the work required to create *that America*.

*The ChaRIOT: The New Cultural Conversation* is a research-informed book that offers a glimpse into the history of Black Americans' journey from their Motherland through the brutal Middle Passage and to the shores of America, where they were enslaved into a system of racial oppression and inequity. I chronicle my journey with race and lived experiences with racism as a Black child, Black man, faith leader, and diversity, equity, inclusion, and justice expert. I have included statistics, results of studies and polls on race, events from history, key figures in the civil rights movement, and the Black Lives Matter movement. I use facts, figures, and stories to illustrate the state of Black Americans historically and currently and why no one in America should be content waiting for change.

I outline the complexity of racism by examining its historical roots and how it became systemic and structural. The book looks at cause and effect relationships and systems that support and feed racial inequity, oppression, and disparities. Two major events, the COVID-19 pandemic and the racialized violence against Blacks that led to the massive protests in 2020, provide a backdrop to a broader discussion on how Black trauma is linked to pervasive racism and its intergenerational grip on the United States of America. Black people's hearts and minds retain the pain.[4] They keep count. Simply put, it is time for a New Cultural Conversation.

The central focus of the book is a transformative new concept I introduce called "The ChaRIOT." I am a ChaRIOT, and in my book, I urge others to join me by becoming one as well. We must build a ChaRIOT community, a ChaRIOT Nation.

As a ChaRIOT, I stand for the oppressed. I am a messenger offering a calm voice but one that is not afraid to contest and to speak

---

[4] Resmaa Menakem. *My Grandmother's Hands: Racialized Trauma and the Pathway to Mending Our Hearts and Bodies*. Illustrated edition. (Las Vegas, NV: Central Recovery Press, 2017).

loud enough to be heard. I will be a voice reminding everyone to pay close attention to the issues on race happening in our world, and more importantly, how to deconstruct and dismantle the systemic racism and biases that exist in our country for persons who are non-white.

The ChaRIOT is also an advocate for persons who share in or benefit from privilege but can admit, "I do benefit from White privilege, but I am not on a scale that you could call a racist." I think there needs to be a space for those persons to reside in, and I believe my vision for it provides or grants that space for them to acknowledge and to own the fact that events stemming from racism are happening. That vision allows them room to admit they share in particular privileges but can hold those inherent advantages in balance and allow that balance to encourage them to advocate for persons who have borne the burden of historical exclusion. This is how we build an inclusive community.

The message and the work of the ChaRIOT are simple: it is the type of action that requires completely dismantling systemic racism in America. Being a ChaRIOT and building a movement also requires an upsurge of the human spirit unlike that we have ever seen. We must build something we have never built before to take us to a place we have never been before. It involves a federation of people who unite in a "zero degrees of belonging," a point at which people can divest themselves of their corporate titles or designations or academic degrees and share a similar space with someone who does not hold the same station in life, yet still see them as human beings and equals.

In the ChaRIOT Movement, the basic principle of dismantling a system of racism means each of us acknowledging the contribution of one another. It requires us to acknowledge that an ideal human society is built on a division of labor and acceptance that everyone has a contribution to make, and for efforts to work together for good, we must all honor, respect, and appreciate the diversity of contributions.

The ChaRIOT leads the work needed to dismantle racist systems, pursue equity, and make certain that people can share in the ability to live out the so-called "American Dream," while negotiating the issues of race in America so they can live a life that is pleasing to themselves and others.

# The ChaRIOT

I offer the ChaRIOT as a solution to the various social ills that stem from racism existing at multiple levels: systemic, institutional, overt, covert, explicit and implicit bias, and microaggression. I challenge us to reimagine a new way of being—one in which the long arc of the moral universe Dr. Martin Luther King Jr. so aptly described begins to bend away from racial injustice towards justice.

The chapters of this book outline a roadmap for what we must do to build a movement of many movements within the broader ChaRIOT Movement. In Chapter 10, I offer a specific plan for the radical action needed to ensure this period of inflection is not wasted in meaningless transactional moments but is spent transforming racist systems and the dominant culture into a culture of equitable outcomes.

White people must stop denying, deflecting, and defending racism, racist systems, and racist behavior. They must reject the idea that Black people should stop talking about racism, stop protesting, and stop demanding equity. White people must cease their accusations of Blacks "playing the race card," because it is easier to be dismissive of their experiences than work alongside nonwhite people to find solutions. Whites must use their power, influence, and wealth to dismantle White supremacy and institutionalized racial systems, as Blacks do not have the means to do so. It is not the responsibility of Black people to demolish systemic racism; this charge belongs to Whites and White power structures.

The oppressed cannot remain so; they must and they will rise. In his acclaimed 1963 book *Why We Can't Wait,* Dr. King wrote, "It is an axiom of social change no revolution can take place without a methodology suited to the circumstances of the period."[5] I believe the sentiment of Dr. King's assertion still holds. The ChaRIOT and its radical action approach to change align with this period in our country's history. However, it will take an awakening of the human conscience to lead the equity movement with the ChaRIOT spearheading the effort.

---

[5] Martin Luther King Jr. Essay, In *Why We Can't Wait* (New York: Berkley, 1963), 27.

## The New Cultural Conversation

Judging from the outcry for allyship and accompliship from the descendants of colonizers and oppressors heard around the world in 2020 and today, this way of life is more than possible, it is desired. But we must work collectively and collaboratively and *with urgency*. The time is now to change the future. This gift of time is ours to lose or make a difference like no other generations before us. I strongly believe we can make this moment of reckoning on race transformational if we grasp the opportunity to create a New Cultural Conversation and a new equity movement. I believe that without this change-work, history is doomed to keep repeating itself. I believe that together, we can do something so special that we can change America for the better. I know we can. I am a ChaRIOT.

## Chapter One

## No Chariot is Coming, We Must Be The ChaRIOT

As a diversity, equity, inclusion, and justice (DEIJ) consultant to global private industry companies, I see firsthand how organizations often struggle with the steps needed to translate their stated commitments to diversity into intention and intention into action. This includes those companies that have invested considerable time, monies, and energies into creating a diverse environment where all employees feel included. Even those companies operate with the undercurrent of tension that comes with racial diversity. As a faith leader and senior pastor of Mount Pisgah Baptist Church in Dayton, Ohio, my vision is for humankind to strive towards equity and justice for all people. The reality is we live in a world where equity is not pursued equitably. Those of us who live in the United States of America make our lives in a country that was built on racism and chattel slavery, a country that has never confronted its history in either state of being, though racism has been embedded in the fabric of America for more than 400 years.

I am sharing part of my story and experiences as a Black man, faith leader, executive, husband, father, and son to help illustrate how racism continues to operate at every level of every system in the United States. This book explores how the "land of opportunity" is structured to primarily serve White people through the oppression of Black, Indigenous, People of Color (BIPOC), which sustains systemic inequities, disparities, exclusion, and injustice, and why it is imperative we use hearts and minds to create a radical vehicle of change for the oppressed: We need a ChaRIOT.

I conceived this new mode of transportation, the ChaRIOT, to take us from where we are today—functioning in a system that is broken for BIPOC people in America—to a state of revolutionary war for the soul of this nation.

## My First Experience with Exclusion

My first real encounter with racism and exclusion came when I was just seven years old. Like most people in America, my perspective on race, racism, and justice was shaped by my childhood and upbringing. I was born and raised in Elyria, Ohio, a small, predominantly White retirement community west of Cleveland, Ohio. As a Black boy growing up in a city where people who looked like me made up only 10 to 12 percent of the total population, most of my first friends were White. The schools I attended were predominantly White. My teachers were White. The neighborhood where my parents, brothers, and I lived was almost exclusively White. I had a few friends of color but because of where I grew up, my exposure to Black people and Black culture did not happen in any significant way for me until I went away to college.

Elyria, a city of some 53,000 people, is nestled at the two forks of the Black River six miles from Lake Erie and 20 miles from Cleveland. The summers are hot and rather humid, and the winters are cold. But it is the beauty of the city that stands out. Many people describe it as stunning: picturesque waterfalls, nearly 400 lush acres of parks, and a city square that attracts families from miles away for annual festivals and celebrations.

It was in a classroom that I first experienced racism, but I did not recognize it at the time. I was in the third grade. I can remember vividly that something just did not feel right to me but as a youngster, I could not quite identify what made me feel so uncomfortable and slighted. I was in Ms. McClelland's class where we had a spelling test on Fridays. I remember that day like it was yesterday. I took the spelling exam and had only missed two words.

Three white kids right next to me had taken the same test but missed some words. Our teacher asked, "Who wants to make up their quiz to get a perfect score?" I raised my hand. Three White students next to me raised their hands. Ms. McClelland let them come up and retake the test but did not allow me to participate. I could have left my hand raised in the air all day, but Ms. McClelland was not going to allow me the same opportunity she so freely gave to the White students. I went out to recess and played with my classmates like I always did. As a kid, you kind of shake things off. Recess usually kind of gets things out of a kid's system. By the time lunch comes, you have forgotten. But that experience subconsciously was in my spirit.

When I look back at the incident, I now know Ms. McClelland's decision was an act of racism. Allowing some students to do better because of the color of their skin and denying others that same opportunity because of the color of their skin is a conscious act of racism or at least, unconscious bias. Exceptionally few Black people in this country have not had a brush with racism, a racist act, or implicit bias. It may come in the form of being watched intently by an overly attentive sales associate in a supermarket or department store. It may mean being denied a business loan when you have checked all the boxes needed to show you are a good risk. Or you may experience the inability to move beyond a cubicle even with an advanced degree and having twice the experience as a White co-worker. The bottom line: It is virtually impossible to not be touched by it if you are of African descent or a person of color.

Systemic racism and racial injustice are among the most pressing issues in the United States today because they are killing us. This country is being asphyxiated by the mental health crisis of racism, nationalism, and polarization. There is no doubt that the Proud Boys, Qanon followers, and White supremacists who masqueraded as patriots and violently attacked our Capitol on Jan. 6, 2021, were goaded by then-President Donald J. Trump. But the deeply embedded embers of disdain for BIPOC people were burning within them long before they were stoked by years of racist and seditious rhetoric from the leader of the free world. The embers were there when some White Americans felt they had lost ground to people of color under the leadership of the country's first Black president, Barack H. Obama.

Black people living in America, no matter their station, class, or condition, are being smothered under a blanket of injustice and inequities that are institutional, multigenerational, multilayered, and unrestrained. Whether White people recognize or acknowledge it, the fact is, they are suffocating too. Not in the same way as Black Americans, but Viola Davis' character in the 2011 motion picture

"The Help," perhaps said it best when she delivered a powerful line as she confronted a racist young housewife during a pivotal moment in the film. "Ain't chu tired Ms. Hilly?" Davis's character asked the White woman regarding her relentless campaign of oppression against the Black maids in the community, who were treated as nothing more than modern-day chattel slaves.

Racism is in the threads that make up the fabric of America. This disease did not begin in 1619 when a ship carrying 20-30 enslaved Africans arrived in Point Comfort in the English colony of Virginia. It did not begin when thousands more Africans were stolen from their homeland and brought to America in chains to be owned by other people and classified as property. It did not begin when chattel slavery became a norm in this country, especially in the Southern states.

The origins of racism by White-skinned people can be traced back to Christopher Columbus and other colonizers landing on the shores of land they are credited with discovering, even though Indigenous peoples were there long before their ships arrived.

On August 3, 1492, European Christopher Columbus and his crew sailed from Spain in search of pearls, precious stones, gold, silver, spices, and other riches. They made landfall on one of the Bahamian islands and Hispaniola (Haiti and the Dominican Republic today) two months later where they sailed from island to island in what is today known as the Caribbean. Columbus' racism and implicit bias were well documented during his first voyage—by his own hand. The journal, written between August 3, 1492 and November 6, 1492, recorded his opinions of the Indigenous people of the region. Most troubling was the White-skinned man's argument for why dark-skinned people should be enslaved, including their well-built muscular bodies, good looks, peaceful dispositions, and what he described as "ignorance."

He penned his thoughts that with 50 enslaved men, he and his crew could rule and gain even more riches.[6]

Though widely taught in public schools for generations, Columbus never set foot on North American soil, which of course was inhabited by Native Americans. But he was a brutal colonizer and governor of the Caribbean islands. He committed atrocities against native peoples on the islands, decimated their populations, and pilfered the resources of the land, according to the biography *Columbus: The Four Voyages* by Laurence Bergreen.[7]

Systematic European colonization began in 1492 upon Columbus' arrival to the land of people of color. It is estimated that from his arrival to the end of the 19th century between 2.5 and 5 million Native Americans were forced into slavery. To further extract as much gold as possible from the toxic gold and silver mines, the Europeans required all males above the age of 13 to work for free and give slaveholders the gold they found in an oppressive practice known as "encomienda," which granted free land and free labor to Spanish rulers.

Slavery is one of America's "original sins" and among the most enduring and destructive systems in America's history and its effects are still with us. They simply morphed and continue today as the multigenerational enslavement of an entire segment of the American population through oppression, disparities, and exclusion. It was not solved by the framers of the U.S. Constitution because the framers never considered Black people to be human beings but property. It was not resolved by four years of the Civil War in which more than 600,000 Americans were killed. It was not resolved when slaves were freed by President Abraham Lincoln signing the Emancipation Proclamation on January 1, 1863.

---

[6] History.com Editors. "Christopher Columbus." History.com. A&E Television Networks, November 9, 2009.

[7] History.com Editors. "Christopher Columbus." History.com. A&E Television Networks, November 9, 2009.

The Proclamation declared "that all persons held as slaves" within the rebellious states "are, and henceforward shall be free." More than 165 years later, America is still in the grips of what Texas A & M University social scientist Eduardo Bonilla-Silva described in 1997 as a "racialized social system."

Systemic racism was not resolved even when the Civil Rights Act of 1964 and the Voting Rights Act of 1965 appeared to be turning points for Black people. Every generation of Black Americans must endure the hopes and dreams of overcoming the pain of so many disparities that continuously—and without the needed disruption of race-based inequities—keep them from truly being free. And that dream rises and falls with each event that stops short of the promise to deliver justice and equity to Black lives.

I am reminded of an event Dr. King wrote about in his book, *Why We Can't Wait. Brown v. Board of Education of Topeka* was a landmark 1954 U.S. Supreme Court case in which the justices ruled unanimously that racial segregation of children in public schools was unconstitutional. Dr. King described how the United States Supreme Court retreated from its position by approving the Pupil Placement Law, which permitted states to determine where children could be placed by virtue of family background and other subjective criteria. The law fed into limiting the integration of schools, which meant that technically the High Court reversed itself.[8]

Dr. King described the "deep disillusion" of Black people and their conflicting emotions of joy at the 1954 ruling but also the disappointment that followed when the Pupil Placement Law was introduced. He went on to describe emotions as a pendulum swinging between elation and despair when Black people realized no real progress would be made.

We experienced this seesaw of hope and letdown in November 2008 when America did what many Black people thought

---

[8] King. *Why We Can't Wait* (New York: Berkley, 1963).

was the impossible and elected the country's first Black president. I saw Black people shedding tears of joy and relief in the days that followed and on Jan. 20, 2009, when he was inaugurated. It was a magnificent sight to see as President Obama and the first Black First Lady walked hand in hand down Pennsylvania Avenue on Inauguration Day.

I suppose some Black people felt hope like they never had before. Many felt, as we sometimes say in the Black community, "Like we had arrived." Hearts were soaring and some minds dared to dream of the possibility that racism could be dismantled and that a post-racist society could emerge. But that hope was soon dashed when Black people realized nothing changed or would change in their daily lives even though tens of millions of White Americans voted for a Black man in two presidential elections. Black people were just as far from racial equity as they were before the 2008 election that made Obama the 44th president of the United States.

Before the election of her husband as the first Black president, Michelle Obama stirred anger and public castigation from some in White political and conservative circles when she made a statement in an unguarded moment at the 2008 Wisconsin primary. She said that for the first time in her adult life, she was very proud of her country and felt like hope was making a comeback. Once Mrs. Obama's comment was covered by the media, she became a target of White Americans who took issue with what she said and accused her of being the proverbial angry, Black woman.[9]

What those in the dominant culture did not seem to understand is how someone who graduated from prestigious universities like Princeton and Harvard Law School and won a job at a high-paying Chicago law firm could sound so disenfranchised and disconnected from the very country that gave her those opportunities. What White people failed to understand was that Michelle Obama was speaking

---

[9] Evan Thomas. "Michelle Obama's 'Proud' Remarks," Newsweek. Newsweek, March 12, 2008, https://www.newsweek.com/michelle-obamas-proud-remarks-83559.

from the one place they could never go: Her experience as a Black person living in America.

Twenty-three years before making the statement that drew so much ire, Mrs. Obama was a student at an Ivy League college. In her thesis on the subject of "Princeton-Educated Blacks and the Black Community," she wrote a passage that in part read, "my experiences at Princeton have made me far more aware of my 'blackness' than ever before. I have found that at Princeton no matter how liberal and open-minded some of my White professors and classmates try to be towards me, I sometimes feel like a visitor on campus; as if I really don't belong. Regardless of the circumstances under which I interact with Whites at Princeton, it often seems as if, to them, I will always be Black first and a student second."[10]

Far too many accomplished Black men and women have had that experience, whether on a majority White college campus or in corporate America or at a predominantly White law firm or a myriad of other settings. Mrs. Obama went one step further and suggested that even if she does what White America expects Black people to do and assimilates into White society, she will always be on the "periphery of society: never becoming a full participant." It was through that lens she made the statement about being proud of America for the first time in her adult life. However, that moment of hope she expressed in Wisconsin in 2008 would be tested in ways unimaginable to previous first ladies or presidents.

As President Obama moved into his first term, he faced unprecedented criticism, challenges, voices from racists, and one blatantly disrespectful episode after another. One of the most high-profile incidents of impertinence during President Obama's time in office occurred at a live televised address to congress outlining his health care reform proposal on Sept. 9, 2009. U.S. Representative Joe Wilson (R-South Carolina) took the outlandish step of standing and shouting at the President of the United States, "You lie!" After being

---

[10] Thomas. "Michelle Obama's 'Proud' Remarks." Newsweek. Newsweek, March 12, 2008. https://www.newsweek.com/michelle-obamas-proud-remarks-83559.

rebuked by Democrats and Republicans, he issued a half-hearted written apology that same night but refused Democratic House Majority Whip Jim Clyburn's (D-South Carolina) call to apologize on the House floor.[11]

There was no shortage of evidence and incidents that having a Black president had ushered in any significant advancements in race relations. On the contrary, some have a valid argument that it may have even done just the opposite. Three years and one month after Barack Obama was sworn into office, tragedy struck in a Southern town that would serve as a flashpoint in igniting a new movement in the fight against racism and injustice.

Sanford, Florida, a city of roughly 59,000 residents, sits on the southern shore of Lake Monroe, in a state with a long history of being racially charged. When barrier-breaking baseball great Jackie Robinson first took the field to play as a member of an integrated baseball team, the toxicity of racism in Sanford reared its head in the form of Robinson being denied lodging and the Sanford police chief threatening to cancel the game if he played.

On a rainy Sunday night in late February 2012, a teenage Black boy was visiting his father in a gated community in that same city where Jackie Robinson suffered racialized indignities. The teen was watching a ballgame on television before leaving to go on a mundane trek to a nearby convenience store and satisfy his sweet tooth. He never returned.

Trayvon Martin was walking home alone, carrying a grocery bag of Skittles and a can of Arizona tea. It was still misting and cool, and Martin had pulled the hood of his jacket onto his head. As he neared his home, a 28-year-old man, a self-appointed neighborhood watch "captain," approached the boy and demanded to know what he was doing in the neighborhood. George Zimmerman, the son of a White male judge and Peruvian mother, told police during a 911 call

---

[11] "Rep. Wilson Shouts, 'You Lie' to Obama during Speech." CNN. Cable News Network. Accessed November 17, 2021.
https://edition.cnn.com/2009/POLITICS/09/09/joe.wilson/.

right before stopping Martin that the young man looked suspicious and like he was "on something."

It is still unclear exactly what transpired or how things escalated. Only two people know what happened for certain and one voice has been forever silenced. What we know is that within minutes after calling the police, who told him to stop following the unarmed teen, Zimmerman had pulled a gun and shot Martin in the chest, mortally wounding him. He died face down on the wet ground with his arms underneath him. On Feb. 26, 2012, three weeks after his seventeenth birthday, Trayvon Benjamin Martin became a symbol of racial injustice.

It took six weeks of intense protests in Sanford and around the country and the constant barrage of media stories to finally pressure police to arrest Zimmerman and charge him with second-degree murder. Sixteen months later, a nearly all-White jury of six women acquitted Zimmerman. His defense team used a school suspension for a small amount of marijuana to paint Martin as a troubled youth and unabashedly used Martin's race to convince jurors that Zimmerman felt his life was threatened by a violent Black teenager. On July 14, 2013, one day after the trial ended, the media released a picture of one of Martin's hands littered with wet grass that had clung to his knuckles as his body laid on the ground.[12]

Martin's murder and the police's refusal to arrest his killer set off a vortex of media stories, social media posts, commentaries, and discourse on race, class, and justice. He became the face of injustice in America with a closeup of his youthful features appearing on posters, t-shirts, and other items such as hats and cups. In a twisted slice of popular culture, a photo of Martin's face also became one of the bestselling items purchased by White males for use in target practice on the firing range in 2012.

---

[12] Trymaine Lee. "Analysis: Trayvon Martin's Death Still Fuels a Movement Five Years Later." NBCNews.com. NBCUniversal News Group, February 27, 2017.

# The ChaRIOT

The killing of Trayvon Martin served as the genesis for a new kind of movement to honor the lives of unarmed Black men, women, teenagers, children, and members of the lesbian, gay, bisexual, transgender, intersex, asexual, and nonbinary communities (LGBTQIA+), who are killed by police or in police custody. Much like 14-year-old Emmett Till's 1955 murder by two White men who were later acquitted by an all-White jury helped prompt the civil rights movement, the killing of Trayvon Martin ignited a new movement for social justice. In 2013, immediately following news of George Zimmerman's acquittal, three Black women, Alicia Garza, Patrisse Cullors, and Opal Tometi, introduced #BlackLivesMatter. More than a hashtag, Black Lives Matter is activism, and in the words of some Black athletes, a "lifestyle statement more than a movement."

Martin's death and Zimmerman's acquittal also once again led America to a place it had been countless times before: a reexamination of racism, Whiteness, injustice, and how to bring the races together. Political pundits, bloggers, professors, and race experts appeared on news networks to talk about America's shameful history and how we must use this incident to have a real conversation on addressing racism. For all the discourse, pontification, and rehashing America's racist past, the country found itself back in an all-too-familiar place: conversations that lead to no substantive or even nominal progress towards eradicating oppressive systems of racial inequity. Here are a few reasons why.

First, some White people will never willingly stop being racists. Their belief system is so ingrained with bias, prejudice, and in some cases downright disdain for people of other races, their unwillingness or lack of desire to stop being racist simply is not within them. It is comfortable for them to live in a racist society and to be racist. In fact, they would not have it any other way. Their behaviors run the gamut of spewing racist language to physical manifestations, including violence and murder.

A case in point is one of the most horrendous acts of racial violence in modern U.S. history. Emanuel African Methodist Episcopal Church, known as "Mother Emanuel" is the oldest African Methodist Episcopal Church in the Southern region of the United

States. Founded by slaves in 1817 Charleston, South Carolina, the church represented nearly 198 years of Black history. White supremacist and neo-Nazi Dylann Roof entered its sacred space on June 17, 2015 and executed nine unsuspecting people during a Bible study to which he had been welcomed by the very people whose blood he spilled. He later said that even though they were nice people and he considered not going through with his plan, he decided he had to kill them because "Blacks were taking over." At only 21 years old, Roof was so infected by the disease of racism, that he had become detached and demented. He has since been tried, convicted, and sentenced to death but has shown no remorse.[13]

This is not to suggest that all racists are violent or murderers. On the contrary, most are not, and therein is the second major reason why racism continues to be part of every system and sector of America. There is a segment of the White population that do not consider themselves racist—and in fact, are likely to become highly defensive if someone called them racist—but they have unconscious and implicit biases that manifest or show up in their daily interactions with Black people. This group of people is often the most difficult to reach because while they are complicit in perpetuating racism, they do not recognize it or are apathetic or insensitive to their contribution to suppression and oppression.

Before she called police to falsely report that a Black man was threatening her and her dog when he simply asked her to leash the pet as the New York City Parks Department requires, I am sure Amy Cooper would have emphatically denied she was racist or had ever committed a racist act. As an executive at financial services company Franklin Templeton, Cooper probably lunched with Black colleagues and engaged in friendly interactions with Black people in her everyday life. However, Cooper knew that as a White woman, she could exploit her position on the social hierarchy and law enforcement would

---

[13] Mark Berman. "'I Forgive You.' Relatives of Charleston Church Shooting Victims Address Dylann Roof." The Washington Post. WP Company, October 26, 2021.

presume she was telling the truth. What happened in Central Park that day—coincidentally the same day George Floyd lost his life in what can only be described as an execution – was not an isolated incident. Rather, the sad reality is that Black people have these kinds of experiences daily in this country due to racism, bias, and privilege. More about Amy Cooper's and other Whites' White privilege later.

In the lobby of a New York City hotel, another White woman, Miya Ponsetto, physically attacked the 14-year-old son of Grammy-winning jazz artist Keyold Harrold by shouting a baseless claim that he had stolen her phone. The hotel manager, taking Ponsetto's claims at face value, began demanding to see the boy's phone. Minutes into the incident, an Uber driver returned to the hotel and gave workers Ponsetto's phone, which she had left in his car. Ponsetto did not apologize and denied her behavior was racially motivated. The December 26, 2020 incident made international news and ultimately led to her arrest for attempted robbery, grand larceny, acting in a manner injurious to a child, and two counts of attempted assault.

At the heart of these two incidents, which took place in 2020, is the fact that a system provided the platform for those women to feel comfortable summoning law enforcement and using their Whiteness as weaponry. In doing so, they brought down the weight of a law enforcement agency that has a long and violent history of racist behavior toward Black Americans, beginning with the slave patrols.

Racism is America's most enduring legacy, and in many ways, the most visible and visceral remnants of slavery persisting today. Amy Cooper and Miya Ponsetto are extreme examples. Most White people with bias practice it in their daily lives, often without being conscious of it. Assumptions about what and how Black people think, how they live, how they worship, how they raise and relate to their children, and how they love their children are part of their unconscious bias, as are ways White people interact with Blacks in workplaces, schools, colleges, supermarkets, and in their communities.

But there are White people—many White people—who want a shift, a change, a transformation. People who have grown tired of hearing the same metanarrative about race that our news cycles repeat in a never-ending loop. There are people weary of participating in conversations on race that peak with promise but then fizzle. They are looking for a way out and to something they have never experienced before.

No longer are they satisfied or placated with transactional or transitional moments but want transformational change on race. There is no shortage of people who want change and are searching for a place where people realize and accept they are more alike than they are different and that there does not need to be an erasure of differences for there to be uniqueness. At the same time, people can participate in the community with others that do not look like them or have a culture that is similar to them; yet, people can interact in ways that are healthy while maintaining their sense of identity. This new community has eluded America since White people came to this country and began erasure of the Indigenous people and their culture.

Most people who want to see change have the mistaken idea that a magical vehicle will appear—a chariot—and transport us all to a new community where there is zero degrees of belonging. French philosopher and sociologist Jean Baudrillard stated that this state of being is when people can divest themselves of their titles and their degrees, their economic prowess and their bank accounts, their networks and social gatherings and just participate in the community without needing to emphasize who they are, how they are honored, or what privileges they have. I see the rise of a new community, of a new movement, of a new way of being on the horizon through an upsurge of the human spirit.[14]

This new community has a requirement: the deconstruction and dismantlement of racism in America. Not everyone wants this new way of living in America. Even after George Floyd's cries to breathe while he was being asphyxiated under the knee of a White police officer led to the largest and most diverse group of protestors in American history has this country ever been willing to work

---

[14] Andy McLaverty-Robinson. "Jean Baudrillard: Hyperreality and Implosion." Ceasefire Magazine, September 7, 2012.

collectively to end systemic racism. But it can. The time is now. We are at a precipice. This watershed moment on race we are having in America presents a new but urgent opportunity to resolve an old problem that brought us to a place of Civil War in 1861. We are now in a new war prompted by this moment of inflection: a war for the soul of the United States of America.

*I am a ChaRIOT*

By the time I was in the 9th grade, I was a preaching minister and a bit of an anomaly. My perspective on the world was a little bit different from most people my age. I took a deep interest in Jesus and how he dealt with people. I saw that Jesus was someone who welcomed others. He had conversations that others did not want to have. I found myself gravitating more to people who just had a respect for humans, not necessarily White or Black people. My peers, both Black and White, observed my genuineness. They came to revere me as *The Young Preacher*.

There was continuity in the way in which I involved myself with everyone, regardless of who and what they were. Because I remained unwavering in my morals and views of the world, I eventually came to garner respect from everyone. I was the ChaRIOT within that ecosystem of young White and Black people coming of age and becoming ever aware of their differences, diversity, and that race relations in America would ensure the friendship they shared before could not move forward into the future.

No one really understood why their perspectives in high school had changed. What made me different was my awareness, and whether I agreed with it or not, my exposure to the *why* that drove how they had come to see me and people who look like me, those hidden transcripts.[15]

---

[15] James C. Scott. *Domination and the Arts of Resistance* (United Kingdom: Yale University Press, 2008).

## Chapter Two

## Injustice and Justice and the

## Extraordinariness of Ordinary Days

*The phone rang. It was a lawyer. In under two minutes, I went from being seen as a highly recognized academic to the accused. Two minutes. That is all it took for my life to shift. I share this information not as a spectator but as someone writing from a lived, shared experience.*

*In 2012, I was accused of violating someone sexually. What made the accusation suffocating was the court enforced gag order. And worse, the accusation came from a woman with whom I had no meaningful interaction—social or otherwise.*

*Were my family and I confident she was lying? Absolutely, 100 percent! Justice was supposed to be my advocate; perhaps the blindfold got in the way. I felt alone, isolated, and misunderstood. Worst of all, I felt violated by the lie. Through that experience, as horrible and senseless as it was, I became acquainted with the arc of accusation as well as that of justice.*

*In October 2012, I was declared innocent of all accusations on all accounts. I was declared free, but my truth was still locked up— choking on a gag order. It only took one accusation to disrupt my life. My life was broken; however, now the pieces are reassembled.*

*I was supposed to be innocent until proven guilty. This was not my reality. Indeed, it is not the case for most Blacks in America. An accusation is a violent tool used by unsympathetic humans to strip away the presumed innocence of Black Americans.*

*Black brilliance is our reality separate from an unsympathetic regime. We cannot allow how Blacks are treated in America to remain a spectacle. The time to respond is now so that our perseverance is not subverted by panic.*

I include this painful chapter in my life as a call to action for faith leaders and others in a position of influence. It is time to sound the alarm about our intolerance for injustice. A convenient case of prophetic laryngitis is not acceptable. If you are anxious about what you will lose, then remember the gospel message: 'what does it profit to gain the whole world and lose your soul.'

## Power Relationships and Justice

I want to offer a viewpoint on power and justice that may be out of kilter with the mainstream opinion, but I believe power relationships do not control or support justice; they impede justice.

There is a dichotomy we must recognize in the sphere of injustice and justice: For justice to be lived out, it must seek to find injustice.[16] And that is where the power relationships lie, how laws are structured, and how those laws influence social systems within our society.

Baudrillard argues that the "Zero Degree is a null space of indifference within the identity of the system, neither an integrated inside nor safely outside of the system, and yet, totally indispensable."[17]

The American consciousness needs elevating about injustice and how power relationships impede people who need justice from attaining it. We must cross the 'invisible line' and reach the point of zero degrees. What can be expected when that line is crossed? A temporary 'extraction' from privilege. A new human experience that allows a person to feel the pain of 'the other.'

The center of the story of culture at this present moment is Blackness. Blackness is the protagonist, and its antagonist is the blight of racism and injustice. It reaches back to Emmett Till, heads north to

---

[16] Johan Christiaan Beker, *Paul's Apocalyptic Gospel: The Coming Triumph of God* (Minneapolis: Fortress Press, 1982).

[17] McLaverty-Robinson. "Jean Baudrillard: Hyperreality and Implosion." Ceasefire Magazine, September 7, 2012. https://ceasefiremagazine.co.uk/in-theory-baudrillard-9/.

The Central Park 5, dips South and attacks Trayvon Martin and Sandra Bland, pivots upward and evokes melanin mayhem in the Midwest, annihilating Michael Brown, Tamir Rice, and John Crawford III. For added measure, it makes one more sweep South and cuts down a jogger named Ahmaud Arbery, then makes a stop in the home state of the iconic brand Kentucky Fried Chicken and takes the life of Breonna Taylor late one night in her own home. The blight of racism, not done yet, heads to the upper Midwest on Memorial Day to set off the most notable lynching since 14-year-old Emmett Till was pulled from the Tallahatchie River in 1955: The blight of racism lynched George Floyd on a Minneapolis street as he begged to take a breath, setting off social justice protests around the world.

America, persevere with us. Help us reach the arc of justice. To participate in a shared suffering 'hollows out[18]' space for us to explore a new type of humanity, a federation bound by a collaborative fight for justice.

Dr. Martin Luther King Jr. said it best: "The arc of the moral universe is long, but it bends towards justice." The arc of injustice may want to take notice that the day of justice, the zero degrees, is on the horizon.

I often read some of the many books authored by Dr. King and keep one in particular, *Why We Can't Wait*, by my bedside for insight and inspiration. I make reference to it in this book often. I also read books and articles about his life and was struck by a comment he made on the discussion of justice in a 1966 interview with CBS' Mike Wallace.

Dr. King said, "And I contend that the cry of 'black power' is, at the bottom, a reaction to the reluctance of white power to make the kind of changes necessary to make justice a reality for the Negro."[19] He made that observation more than half a

---

[18] Stanislas Breton. *A Radical Philosophy of St. Paul* (New York: Columbia University Press).

[19] Lily Rothman. "Baltimore Protests: Behind 'A Riot Is the Language of the Unheard.'" Time. Time, April 28, 2015. https://time.com/3838515/baltimore-riots-language-unheard-quote/.

century ago, and it is just as relevant and factual today as it was in 1966.

In 2020, several pivotal events occurred for the first time in America, and they led to the current watershed moment on race relations and a reexamination of injustice in America. Some believe it was destiny. Others believe a perfect storm ushered us to this precipice of change. Whatever brought us here, not since the civil rights movement was ignited by the savage beating death of Till in a racist attack, have justice and injustice been thrust into the national dialogue.

These are the events that drive the capacity for injustice and justice to be seen. Having people who are non-black march with people who are Black, to me, is not necessarily a reflection of justice. Or, honestly at that point, social justice. That, to me, is nothing more than an upsurge of the human spirit. It does not become justice until those same persons—Black and non-black—assemble and decide to be strategic and commit a principal act of protest.

A global pandemic that began in February 2020 unearthed a dearth of food security, financial security, and socioeconomic equities. The pandemic set off fear, a national shutdown, and a recession all at once, resulting in record filings for unemployment benefits. We saw people who had never sought public assistance standing in food lines that stretched as far as one could see. With schools and colleges moving to online learning, many Black children and Black college students around the country who did not have computers and high-speed internet experienced a new kind of digital divide. Children who depended on school breakfasts and lunches to ensure they at least had two meals a day were pushed further into food insecurity.

We heard the news reports of more and more people contracting the coronavirus and dying. By mid-April, more than 23,000 Americans had died from the novel coronavirus , and nearly 600,000 people had the disease. The virus was mysterious, highly contagious, and taking a lot of lives; disproportionately those lives were BIPOC. The disease was ravaging communities of color throughout the country. Black people in states with racial data available showed higher contraction rates and higher death rates from COVID-19. This continued through 2020 and 2021 with Black deaths occurring at three times the rate of White deaths. Experts attributed the deaths to multiple factors linked to the injustices that evolve from being poor and Black: lack of access to health care, health disparities, medical racism, food deserts, holding "essential" frontline service-oriented jobs, and living in subpar neighborhoods due to the legacy of disinvestment and redlining in American cities.

Amid the pandemic, the murder of a Black man on a Minneapolis street by a White police officer was captured on a video that went viral. America erupted with protests. People outraged by the event were demanding justice. Anger bubbled over as millions poured into the street despite the pandemic. Some of the changes Black people had demanded for years suddenly and effortlessly came to fruition. For example, the first time, we saw many symbols of racism be torn down or banned. Statues of Confederate Civil War generals were defaced and toppled. NFL Commissioner Roger Goddell seemed to be contrite as he made a public apology to Colin Kaepernick, who was ostracized and ousted from his role as the San Francisco 49ers quarterback for kneeling during the national anthem in protest of police violence against Black people. NASCAR, long a sport that disproportionately attracts Southern White men and women, banned the Confederate flag at its races and all venues after it had flown over stock car competitions for more than 70 years. NASCAR had been urged to abandon the offensive flag by its lone Black race car driver Bubba Wallace in the wake of the protests.

Multiple Fortune 500 companies issued public statements condemning racism and committing to "do better" by their Black employees and Black communities. To date, tens of billions of dollars have been pledged by corporations to address racial inequities and end disparities.

These unprecedented steps toward progress appear to be a breakthrough, but are they? People do not usually fight to hang on to things that are not meaningful to them; so, just how effective and impactful is tearing them down? Even people who are lukewarm about the Confederate flag, statues, and buildings named after Confederate "heroes" were not willing to stand with Black people who saw them as symbols of racism and hate. How people see justice is often divided along party lines, and this can advance or impede justice.

My point is that justice is political and social. Justice is complex. As we reflect on what happened in 2020, we must ask ourselves if we are really any closer to dismantling the systemic racism than we were in 2019? Will the protests, removal of racist symbols, a lackluster apology from an NFL commissioner who seemed to be tone-deaf about racism, and pledges of money eliminate a cultural hierarchy that has placed Black people at the bottom since their arrival to American shores? Are we now a society where Black people who experience injustices in the workplace, housing, banking, voting rights, and during police encounters, can get justice?

The gestures we are seeing are grand, but what about changes in policy and legislation? Will any of these actions disrupt the power structure that houses injustice and justice?

How did we get here and what needs to happen next to ensure justice is afforded to everyone? We need a ChaRIOT Community to build a ChaRIOT Movement.

### *"Hey, You!"*

Black Americans have been conditioned to expect to be suspects and experience injustice no matter how far inside the law they live. Living under a constant awareness of racism can cause damage to a Black person's psyche and threaten their ability to move about freely in society without constantly being concerned about things that White people never have to give a second thought.

Let's say a young Black man is walking down the street window shopping and minding his own business. Suddenly, he hears someone whose vernacular sounds different from his, cry out with urgency, "Hey, you." Even if there is a White person walking alongside him, what the French Marxist philosopher Louis Althusser argues is this: That Black person will more than likely be the one to turn around and answer the hail because they had been socially conditioned to do so.

# The ChaRIOT

What I am arguing is that some Black people have answered the hail when they hear a White voice yell out with urgency. They have caved to the subjectivity of what we see on the news, and that is Black people are constantly under suspicion of wrongdoing. Blacks live with the knowledge and the anxiety that if something goes wrong, we are usually and more likely to be blamed. And when something happens and there are Whites or other persons of different ethnicities or cultures around, based on how society sees Black people, they are conditioned to think that non-white people will suspect them of wrongdoing. Perhaps that is how many Black men and women feel when they are shopping and a White store associate follows them and scrutinizes their every move, which is what happens to me at a Kroger supermarket I shop at every day after my morning run. Perhaps that is how they feel when a police officer pulls them over for no reason. Is it any wonder that the country is at this moment of reckoning on race?

Being stereotyped as a suspect and hearing the accusatory "hail" of a White person is an injustice that is part of the social reality of life in America for Black People. One "Hey, you" from a White person to a young Black man who was a victim of their unfounded suspicion led to tragedy.

The deaths of three Black people at the hands of White police officers within the first five months in 2020—a trifecta of trauma—that led to the watershed moment on race relations in America began on a Sunday afternoon in late February when a young Black man heard a "Hey, you," that proved fatal for him. On Feb. 23, 2020, a 25-year-old Black man got dressed in running clothes, laced up his running shoes, and left the home he shared with his mother for a daily jog through a coastal South Georgia neighborhood near his home. Though now in his middle 20s, the former high school football star had been meticulous about maintaining physical fitness since his teen years. Friends said he liked to stay in shape, and he would often be seen jogging past the Spanish moss trees that lined the streets in neighborhoods, including streets in the predominantly White suburban community of Satilla Shores.

Ahmaud Marquez Arbery ran every day along the same route, which took the former high school athlete down the long street toward

Fancy Bluff Road and onto a two-lane road. His route took him across four lanes of Jekyll Island Causeway and into the subdivision of Satilla Shores.

That Sunday afternoon was sunny and clear and Arbery undoubtedly felt it was picture-perfect for an avid runner like himself. He was dressed in a white T-shirt and light-colored shorts, clothing one could not comfortably wear in February in most Northern states. But in Glynn County, which boasts of the three most prominent sea islands in the state and was immortalized in the poem "Brunswick Georgia," the weather on this winter day was warm enough for Arbery to be comfortable in summer wear.

"Ahmaud Arbery was out for a jog," Lee Merritt, an attorney representing Arbery's mother, told *The New York Times*. "He stopped by a property under construction where he engaged in no illegal activity and remained for only a brief period. Ahmaud did not take anything from the construction site."[20]

While he can be seen on video inside of a home under construction in Satilla Shores, Arbery merely walked around inside and did nothing more than look at the beams and wood that would frame doors. Friends said he was interested in construction. He briefly walked out of view of the surveillance camera before reappearing and continuing to admire the progress of work on the house. Authorities would later say he had bent down to refresh himself with a sip of water from a faucet that was already operational.

At the very moment that he was admiring the site, unbeknownst to Arbery, a Satilla Shores resident was calling 911 to tell a dispatcher that a Black man was inside a house that was under construction. The caller implied the Black man was doing something wrong and that the site was under a threat of some sort of crime from the young man even though the surveillance camera had captured

---

[20] Richard Fausset. "What We Know About the Shooting Death of Ahmaud Arbery." The New York Times. The New York Times, April 28, 2020. https://www.nytimes.com/article/ahmaud-arbery-shooting-georgia.html.

images of several White adults and children entering the construction site for a look at the new home.

Moments after that call, White former police officer Gregory McMichael and his son Travis McMichael stood in their front yard and watched Arbery run by as he continued his exercise ritual through the Satilla Shores neighborhood. The father and son grabbed their guns and hopped into their white pickup truck to pursue what they later described to police as a "burglary suspect" whom they had the right to stop and apprehend in a citizen's arrest. It was just before 1 p.m.

Gregory had a .357 magnum and Travis was armed with a shotgun as they pursued Arbery and unsuccessfully try to cut him off. Within two minutes, a second pickup driven by a neighbor of the McMichaels, William "Roddie" Bryant, joined the pursuit. According to Gregory's account in the police report, he and his son gave the 'Hey, you' by yelling, "Stop, stop, we want to talk to you!" They then pulled up to Arbery and Travis McMichael got out of the truck carrying his shotgun and approached the young Black man, while the elder McMichael, holding a .357 magnum, yells from the bed of the truck for Arbery to stop or he would "blow your fucking head off." A video shot by Bryant shows Travis, shotgun still in hand, approach Arbery and the two men engage in a fight as Arbery defends himself in a struggle for his life. He fights valiantly even after being shot once by the shotgun and then two more times at point blank range.

After a third bullet from Travis' gun tears into the former athlete's body, Arbery stumbled a short distance and fell forward. The unarmed Black man lay sprawled face down in a growing pool of his own blood, while the man who shot him looked down on his bullet-riddled body. A gasping, gurgling sound can be heard on the video as Arbery's blood poured onto the street and ran unchecked. It was a street Arbery had jogged along almost daily.[21]

---

[21] Associated Press. "New Body Camera Video Shows Moments after Arbery Shooting." 90.1 FM WABE, December 16, 2020. https://www.wabe.org/new-body-camera-video-shows-moments-after arbery-shooting/.

Though the judge in the trial against his killers would not allow the jury to view it, the video captured Travis McMichael standing above Arbery and calling him a racial epithet as his victim lay bleeding to death from three shotgun blasts to his body. Travis's arms were covered in Arbery's blood from their struggle over the gun. Minutes later, he was still holding the shotgun that he used to take Arbery's life for no reason but the color of his skin.

The time was just after 1 p.m., a mere seven minutes after Arbery left the construction site to continue his jog along the tree-lined streets that would take him back to the safety of his home.[22]

Some people may be wondering why he did not stop when he heard the hail of the White voices yelling at him. Maybe he knew it would not lead to a good end for him. Maybe, like many Black people, racism had conditioned Ahmaud Arbery to believe he would be accused of doing something wrong, even when nothing could be further from the truth. After all, he was just out for a run on an ordinary day that became extraordinary for him and his family and friends.

**Trauma Number Two**

Seven weeks after Ahmaud Arbery was hunted down and shot to death, a hard-working 26-year-old Black woman was looking forward to some time off after a four-day stretch of working overnight shifts as an EMT in Louisville, Kentucky. In a city where the chances of becoming a victim of violent crime are 1 in 139, Breonna Taylor's job as a first responder sometimes took its toll, mentally and physically. Despite the long hours and emotional challenges of her job, family and friends said Taylor loved her work. She loved to help people and had plans to enter nursing school.

Taylor and her long-time boyfriend, Kenneth Walker, made plans for a date night on a rare Friday when she was not working. They enjoyed a meal at a steakhouse and headed to Taylor's home where

---

[22] Richard Fausset. "What We Know About the Shooting Death of Ahmaud Arbery." The New York Times. The New York Times, April 28, 2020. https://www.nytimes.com/article/ahmaud-arbery-shooting-georgia.html.

she baked chocolate chip cookies and served them to Walker with ice cream before watching a movie in bed.

Inside Apartment 4, as the fatigue of working four all-night shifts overtook her willingness to see the movie to the end, Taylor began drifting off to sleep. She asked Walker to switch off the television. It was just after midnight on Friday, March 13.

What the young couple did not know was that several police officers had been outside surveilling Taylor's apartment after obtaining a no-knock warrant, based on an unfounded tip that drug money was inside. When they could no longer see the glow coming from the television screen, police punched in the front door with a battering ram, shattering the young couple's peaceful slumber in the most intrusive way. In the confusion of believing an intruder had invaded the apartment, Walker later said he fired one shot towards the ground as a warning.

Another officer began firing a barrage of bullets blindly through the patio door and windows in the back of the apartment, tearing through walls, soap dishes, and cereal boxes inside the cupboard. The apartment was literally torn apart by police gunfire. Within seconds, Breonna Taylor was shot at least five times and bled to death in her underwear on the floor of her own home, never knowing why.[23]

It would be revealed that Taylor was never rendered aid by the police on the scene.

Her mother, Tamika Palmer, arrived at the scene about 1 a.m. after being alerted by a frantic call from Walker. It would be nearly 11 hours of uncertainty as officers first told Palmer two ambulances had left for a nearby hospital. She went in search of her daughter. Having been told her daughter was not at any of the hospitals she visited, two hours later Palmer went back to the apartment but was still told she must wait outside. She stayed in the apartment building's parking lot

---

[23] Rukmini Callimachi. "Breonna Taylor's Life Was Changing. Then the Police Came to Her Door." The New York Times. The New York Times, August 30, 2020. https://www.nytimes.com/2020/08/30/us/breonna-taylor-police-killing.html.

as one detective after another at the scene tried gaslighting Palmer and deflecting blame from the reality of what happened by asking her questions about her daughter being in "some kind of trouble" and whether Taylor and Walker ever fought with each other. [24]

Finally, at 11 a.m., nearly 12 hours after receiving a call from Walker in the middle of the night telling her that her daughter had been shot, Palmer learns from the police that her loving and vibrant daughter was dead

Taylor became the new face of the #Say Her Name campaign launched in 2014 to draw attention to Black women that died at the hands of police or are victimized by racist law enforcement officers, as those women are often overlooked by media organizations and the broader public. These women include Alberta Spruill, Rekia Boyd, Shantel Davis, Shelly Frey, Kayla Moore, Kyam Livingston, Miriam Carey, Michelle Cusseaux, and Tanisha Anderson. Sadly, on March 13, 2020, Breonna Taylor's name was added to the long list of Black girls and women who were killed by officers who had sworn "to serve and to protect" them.[25]

To this day, no charges against the police officers who wrongfully and apathetically took Breonna Taylor's life have been filed and one of the officers has just received a book deal to tell his story about the night he participated in her killing.

## Trauma III

On Memorial Day more than 700 miles from where Breonna Taylor was gunned down by police, an event took place on a busy Minneapolis street that shocked America and the world. The irony of it occurring on Memorial Day was poetic because memorials honoring

---

[24] Ta-Nehisi Coates and Photography by LaToya Ruby Frazier. "The Life Breonna Taylor Lived, in the Words of Her Mother." Vanity Fair, August 24, 2020. https://www.vanityfair.com/culture/2020/08/breonna-taylor.

[25] "Say Her Name." AAPF. The African American Policy Forum. Accessed November 29, 2021. https://www.aapf.org/sayhername.

George Floyd were erected all over the world in the days after his death.

It was the plaintive cry of a Black man that would be heard around the world as he was pinned to the ground with a police officer's knee on his neck that seared into the hearts and consciences of anyone with a thread of humanity.

"He was crying out for his mother and that really touched me," said a teary-eyed White mother being interviewed about what she saw captured on video. "I heard him as a mother. All mothers heard him."

Lonnae O'Neal, a senior writer for *The Undefeated*, penned an essay about the tragedy in the publication that spoke to and for Black mothers. She concluded it with this: *To call out to his mother is to be known to his maker. The one who gave him to her. I watched the Floyd video, for us, the living. It's my sacred charge. I am a black mother.*[26]

George Floyd's "Hey, you," began around 8 p.m. on May 25, 2020, when a teenage clerk called police to report a Black man possibly passing a counterfeit $20 bill in the neighborhood store Cup Foods, which is located in a heavily trafficked predominantly Black community. Within seven minutes of the call, two police officers arrived and began questioning the man as he sat behind the wheel of his silver Mercedes-Benz SUV. One of the officers drew his weapon and ordered George Floyd out of his car and then pulled him out. Floyd, though distressed, was cooperative after he was handcuffed. Six minutes later when officers tried to put him in their squad car, a struggle ensued, and events escalated very quickly and tragically.

As Floyd repeatedly explains that he is claustrophobic, he was forced into the backseat of the police car. He continued to struggle, proclaiming his claustrophobia.

---

[26] Lonnae O'Neal. "George Floyd's Mother Was Not There, but He Used Her as a Sacred Invocation." The Undefeated. The Undefeated, June 24, 2020. https://theundefeated.com/features/george-floyds-death-mother-was-not-there-but-he-used-her-as-a-sacred-invocation.

Two more officers arrive and join the first two officers. Derek Chauvin, a White officer who had arrived on the scene, roughly pulls Floyd out of the backseat of the car and forces his face down onto the pavement.

Witnesses began to gather and capture the incident on their cell phones as it grew in intensity. Three cops held Floyd face down on the pavement: Chauvin with a knee pressed to Floyd's neck, J. Alexander Kueng's knees on Floyd's back, and Thomas Lane holding down Floyd's legs with his knees. The man was paralyzed under the weight of the three officers. A fourth officer, Tou Thao, held the growing crowd back as they begged officers to allow Floyd to stand.

What happened over the next 9 minutes and 29 seconds was a slow, torturous public lynching. As Floyd begged, pleaded, called for his deceased mother, and repeatedly wailed, "I'm going to die today," Chauvin casually put his hand in the pants pocket of his uniform. Helplessly being slowly asphyxiated, Floyd said he could not breathe more than 20 times. Chauvin continued to ignore Floyd's cries that he could not breathe and bore his knee down into Floyd's neck and held it there until his victim's voice was silent. The 46-year-old father died on 38th & Chicago Street, the same Minneapolis street that he walked upon freely and frequently as recently as minutes before his life was cruelly taken by someone who did not see him as a human being.[27]

Floyd is one of a long list of Black people whose lives were stolen by police officers protected by an American justice system that is not blind.

Amir Locke, 2022. Daunte Wright, 2021. Andre Maurice Hill, 2020. Corey Christopher Goodson, 2020. Rayshard Brooks, 2020. Daniel Prude, 2020. Elijah McClain, 2019. Atatiana Jefferson, 2019. Stephon Clark, 2018. Botham Jean, 2018. Philando Castille, 2016. Alton Sterling, 2016. Michelle Cusseaux, 2015. Sandra Bland, 2015. Freddie Gray, 2015. Janisha Fonville, 2015. Eric Garner, 2014. Tamir

---

[27] Evan Hill, Ainara Tiefenthäler, Christiaan Triebert, Drew Jordan, Haley Willis, and Robin Stein. "How George Floyd Was Killed in Police Custody." The New York Times. The New York Times, June 1, 2020. https://www.nytimes.com/2020/05/31/us/george-floyd-investigation.html.

Rice, 2014. Oscar Grant, 2009. Sean Bell, 2006. Amadou Diallo, 1996. Rodney King was severely beaten by Los Angeles police in 1991, which was recorded and seen by millions of Americans on a highly televised video. He sustained life-changing injuries from the beating and died in 2012 in a drowning accident. [28]

These Black Americans and so many more were going about the activities of daily living when injustice interrupted their lives and robbed them of a future. Driving home from the supermarket, returning home from a dental appointment or a job interview, staying up late on a Friday night playing board games with family, and sitting in one's living room enjoying a bowl of ice cream. They had families and friends who loved them, but love—no matter how fierce—could not protect them from the unjust oppression that awaited them.

Even after approximately 26 million people participated in the historic 2020 protests for racial justice, these injustices did not stop. A 42-year-old Black homeless man was out for a walk in Los Angeles on September 23, 2020. As irony would have it, he was stopped by two homeless outreach police officers and accused of jaywalking. Shortly after stopping him, the video shows the two police officers pushing Kurt Reinhold as he asked them not to put their hands on him. The shoving continues until Reinhold begins to defend himself. The officers attacked Reinhold, and the three entangled bodies scuffled on the ground until two very loud and unmistakable sounds pierced the air. Reinhold—a son, brother, father, and friend—went limp with death. He was shot to death by one of the officers less than two minutes after the intrusion on his routine errand. The officers claimed self-defense even though they escalated the encounter by name-calling, shoving, and pushing Reinhold. His family is suing the Orange County Sheriff's Department for wrongful death and racism.[29]

---

[28] Alia Chughtai. "Know Their Names: Black People Killed by the Police in the US." Al Jazeera Interactives. Al Jazeera, July 7, 2021. https://interactive.aljazeera.com/aje/2020/know-their-names/index.html.

[29] Brandon Pho. "What Does the Released Footage around OC Sheriff Deputy Killing of Kurt Reinhold Show?" Voice of OC, April 8, 2021.

Technology and television raise the visibility and vibration of these injustices and create the perception that Black people being profiled, assaulted, and killed by police officers and vigilantes is new, but it is not. Relations between Black people, police, and violence have a long and complicated history.

There are many incidents before the killing of Trayvon Martin that brought the Black Lives Matter movement forward. We must look farther back than the beating that left Rodney King broken and bloody in 1992; further back than 1965 when Marquette Frye's beating by Los Angeles police on a hot summer afternoon set off the Watts Riots that left 34 people dead; and further back still than when in 1955, White law enforcement in Money, Mississippi looked the other way for a month before they arrested Roy Bryant and his half-brother J.W. Milam for Emmett Till's murder—only to be acquitted by an all-white jury. The pair shamelessly gave intricate details of the killing to *Look* magazine one year later and were paid $4,000 to tell their story.[30]

I am a faith leader and researcher who focuses on issues of race, class, inequity, and justice. Through my research, role as a senior pastor, and diversity consultant, I know that the roots of racism in American policing began centuries ago and are still pervading throughout Black communities. Understanding just how long and unjust these roots are takes us back to the time in America when Black people were enslaved.

### Black People and the History of American Policing

First, Black Americans were never a consideration when the framers of the U.S. Constitution created it or when it was ratified in 1788, becoming the official framework of the government of the United States of America. Article I, Section 2 of the Constitution states

---

https://voiceofoc.org/2021/04/what-does-the-released-footage-around-oc-sheriff-deputy-killing-of-kurt-reinhold-show/.

[30] Shaun Michael Mars. "Marquette Frye (1944-1986), April 7, 2020. https://www.blackpast.org/african-american-history/frye-marquette-1944-1986/.

that any person who was not free would be counted as three-fifths of a free individual to determine congressional representation. This was known as the "Three-fifths Compromise" and increased the power of slaveholding states, but the Article made no effort to ensure that the interests of slaves would be represented in the government.

The view of Black people in the same capacity as White people in terms of being a human being was not considered in the framing of the Constitution or this nation. As a result, the authoring of the very document that holds supreme control for this land, and influences the world, created a system that overrides any attempt to impart justice for the suppression of the Black community. Black people had to be written into the document that frames the subconsciousness of Whites and how they see Black people in America. Whether White people know it or not, this document is an important source of their perspective.

In addition to the Constitution, two historical narratives foreshadow the strained relations between Black people and law enforcement today: the slave patrols and the Black Codes, which evolved into the Jim Crow laws.

Southern capitalism relied almost exclusively on enslaving Black people. Slave owners had an irrational fear of mass slave escapes or uprisings, as they would interrupt the economic status of the region. To ensure they maintained their way of life, slave owners had to hold on to their property—enslaved Black men, women, and children who had no agency over their bodies or lives. They were the epitome of human beings being objectified.

Slave patrols were established in the 1700s as an early form of American policing. They were made up of White male volunteers who had the power to enforce laws related to slavery. According to historian Gary Potter, slave patrols served three main functions: (1) to chase down, apprehend, and return to their owners, runaway slaves; (2) to provide a form of organized terror to deter slave revolts; and

(3) to maintain a form of discipline for slave-workers who were subject to summary justice, outside the law.[31]

The now-dismantled citizen's arrest law in Georgia that Arbery's killers used to justify having the right to chase him down has roots in the slave patrols. Slave patrols were sanctioned to use violence and any other means they deemed necessary to ensure escaped slaves were returned to their owners. Slave patrols were also created to beat back slave uprisings. On the plantation, slave patrols were empowered to dole out harsh punishments to slaves determined to have violated the rules or laws outlined by slaveholders.[32]

White people were not exempt from slave patrols invading their homes. Members of slave patrols could enter anyone's home suspected of harboring people who had escaped the plantation. Those who gave protection to escaped slaves paid a steep and often harsh price for doing so, including physical assault.

When the Civil War ended in 1865, so did slave patrols, but they were replaced very quickly with Black Codes.[33]

In some states, these laws required Black people to have written evidence of employment for the upcoming year or they would be forced to forfeit wages or risk arrest. Black Codes aimed to keep Black families working for White farmers by dictating how, where, and when they could work as well as limiting the amounts of their wages. They also stipulated where Blacks could live.

The 14th Amendment outlawed Black Codes in 1868, but subjugation did not end for Black people. They were still denied civil

---

[31] Gary Potter. "The History of Policing in the United States, Part 1." EKU Online, August 20, 2021.

[32] Connie Hassett-Walker, Assistant Professor of Justice Studies and Sociology. "The Racist Roots of American Policing: From Slave Patrols to Traffic Stops." The Conversation, October 13, 2021. https://theconversation.com/the-racist-roots-of-american-policing-from slave-patrols-to-traffic-stops-112816.

[33] History.com Editors. "Black Codes." History.com. A&E Television Networks, June 1, 2010. https://www.history.com/topics/black-history/black-codes.

and human rights and were abused by law enforcement officers and the criminal justice system.

By the early 1900s, formal police forces were formed, and assaults and unjust treatment of Black and vulnerable people continued along with Jim Crow laws that mandated "separate but equal public spaces" for Black people. Police and sheriffs were used to enforce Jim Crow laws and violators were subject to brutal treatment. Law enforcement officers were often accomplices and accompaniers of the Ku Klux Klan and other White racists who committed crimes against Black people. Law officers' crimes included conspiring with racists, refusing to stop violence against Blacks, and active or passive participation in lynching, whether it was done under the cover of darkness or at public events in the full view of Black and White citizens.

At the same time, the justice system did not punish perpetrators or police when Black Americans were violated. The system did not hold them accountable for harming or murdering Black citizens. We see this still playing out America today as an infinite circle of names and faces become hashtags and police officers are acquitted in their deaths, or in most cases, are never charged.

In my opinion, all these factors—White officers with racist views, racially biased laws and justice systems, racist hearts, and origins in slave patrols—are among the feeders that created conditions for modern-day police violence in Black communities.

While we all recognize that police violence is but one of many injustices that continue to plague Black people and communities, it is most often the circumstances in which the family is least likely to receive any real justice.

## The Secret Solidarity of Injustice and Justice

We cannot have a conversation about the Black people whose lives have been taken during police encounters without talking about injustice. We cannot have a "new cultural conversation" about injustice without examining its intricate ties to justice. We cannot make progress in building a ChaRIOT that ensures justice for Black and vulnerable people without disrupting the White powerbase upon which injustice is built and sustained.

We must not ignore that the way power is organized is manipulative, mishandles identity, and seeks to make people who are non-white maintain a particular space.

I define justice as a divine concept that disrupts how power is organized. For me, justice is not about righting a wrong because justice understands at its core power relationships define how people interact with it or how people are impacted by it. To go after the act, in and of itself, is insufficient. The pursuit of justice must seek to undermine how power relationships and social rules deconstruct Black people or any other excluded group of people in America and makes them subjects and objects. As I see it, one of the touchpoints or tentacles of the change matrix is to reclaim people from the subjectivity that they have endured and the identities that have been imposed upon them and do not represent their authentic identity.

When Jesus came out of Nazareth, he sought out John the Baptist, who is baptized, and then the heavens opened up. Most people miss a small phrase that Jesus makes, and what he says is that 'I have been called to preach and heal and raise the dead, heal the sick, and give sight to the blind.' And the word he uses to describe that is 'kingdom.'

At first glance, most people generally think that he is either using some form of Arabic, Latin or Greek, but he is drawing from what we as scholars call the 'Masoretic Text.' The word that Jesus is using for kingdom means, revolution, in Hebrew.

For Jesus, the concept of kingdom that he brings forward in these small Mediterranean-based cultures is designed to help unseat or unpack or be revolutionary and disrupt how power exists and how it is structured.

The ChaRIOT views justice as the use of power to make subjects or to assign prescriptions or to force an identity upon someone who is not in power. Power relationships do not control justice, they impede justice. It is only when those who embrace the banner of justice in the way I see it, take hold of it, and seek to contest injustice, will we be even marginally positioned for transformation around race and social change.

This is how the dichotomy of the secret relationship between injustice and justice emerges. For justice to be lived out, it must seek out injustice. Justice must seek out the power structures that enable a police officer to be judge, jury, and executioner of Black people because he or she has determined that their lives do not matter. It must search out and right the system that expects Black forgiveness but not White accountability.

Consider how the grand jury refused to indict the White police officers that killed Breonna Taylor in the one place she should have been safe: her home. The $12 million paid to her family in a lawsuit against the Louisville Metro Police Department was not justice or even restitution for callously taking Taylor's life, stealing her future, and essentially robbing family and friends of her love, and the world of any contributions she would have made to society as a nurse and a human being. The power structure that allowed officers to recklessly and wantonly fire into Taylor's home without care or regard for life must be sought and deconstructed by a bloodhound named "Justice."

Justice must seek inequalities and injustices such as the failing public education system that continues to keep Black children from being at educational parity with White children. The bloodhound named Justice must seek out the injustice that allows a Black child's zip code to determine what opportunities they have in life. Justice would remedy disinvestment in Black communities, the lingering racial wealth gap, barriers to accessing home loans and investment capital, and health disparities that have taken Black lives at three times the rate of White lives during the COVID-19 pandemic.

For the ChaRIOT, it is these realities that drive the capacity for justice. Having people who are non-Black march in allyship with Black people, as we saw in an unprecedented way in 2020, is not necessarily a reflection of justice. Or, honestly at that point, social justice. While it is allyship, it does not become justice until those same persons, Black and non-Black, assemble and decide to form their own federation—the ChaRIOTS—in an upsurge of the human spirit that cannot be denied by the state, that no one can ignore.

# The New Cultural Conversation

Until this federation is formed by a connection between persons who do not look like one another have assembled, the ChaRIOT will not be that transformative vehicle we need, and the circle of dialogue and metanarrative would continue leading us nowhere.

It is time to work toward the deconstruction of how people see themselves within the conversation on race and injustice and race and justice. This would begin to form the New Cultural Conversation required to begin dismantling systemic oppression. The ChaRIOT seeks to dismantle the institutions and processes that promote implicit biases and use them as a means of separating one group from another. Seeking justice alone will not bring about lasting change. Justice remedies situations. Seeking to go after the wrong action in and of itself is insufficient. Complacency with monetary restitutions for killing a Black person is not justice.

Invoking a forceful change and legislative in the system that provokes and encourages the slaying of Blacks is Justice. We can see and feel a change in this manner as it drastically lessens the chances of a particular malicious behavior ravaging Black communities.

Justice and injustice can be considered a set of interrelated parts that turn inputs (racist acts) into outputs (injustice). Systems must be viewed holistically; one piece is not the system. The whole is more than the sum of its parts. We enact change and affect the whole system when we manipulate the right levers. We know there is a cause-and-effect environment fostered into every system. If the right levers are manipulated, then there will be systematic change.

The system that governs the United States regards itself as a teacher. This eliminates its ability to learn. The system that governs the United States references unfashionably antiquated laws as justification for injustice. Thus, the 1863 citizen's arrest law that the McMichaels and Bryant used to take Arbery's life. This speaks to the system's gross neglect to renew contracts of justice.

Exactly what levers affect the Black community? What can we manipulate to bring about real change? The system. Legislation. The laws that govern this land.

The system allowed officers to legally obtain a no-knock warrant to execute a search for drugs inside Breonna Taylor's home with no evidence of her doing anything wrong. No drugs or monies were recovered but the unarmed Taylor was killed by five bullets from a police officer's gun. Taylor's death sparked global protests and unrest. Chaos ensued and the system was challenged by Challengers. On June 11, 2020, 13 weeks after Taylor was shot to death, Louisville Kentucky Metro Council unanimously passed "Breonna's Law" banning "no-knock" warrants and requiring body cameras be turned on before, during, and after every search. In Taylor's case, police officers' cameras were turned off. One Kentucky legislator said she left the country a policy legacy, as states across the country began considering versions of Breonna's Law to ban or restrict no-knock warrants.

Ahmaud Arbery was murdered by three White men while exercising his right to run freely down a neighborhood street or any street in America if he was not hurting anyone or breaking the law, which he was not. When the story broke of how Arbery was hunted down, many Black people were reminded of the slave patrols. As his name was added to the signs carried by protesters and as more marches erupted across the nation, it was not the screams for restitution that were heard. We heard the cry for justice.

We began to demand change as true ChaRIOTS for justice. We know that even if the three white men who murdered Arbery were not arrested, the law that allowed them to hunt and kill a Black man in the first place would have to be challenged. Georgia Governor Brian Kemp (R-Georgia) took swift executive action to repeal the citizen's arrest law that the McMichaels tried to use as a shield to defend killing Arbery. Gov. Kemp signed House Bill 479 on May 9, 2020, repealing the Civil War-era law that allowed bystanders in Georgia to arrest someone if a crime is committed in their presence.[34] Georgia became

---

[34] Jeff Amy. "Georgia Gov. Kemp Signs Repeal of 1863 Citizen's Arrest Law." ABC News. ABC News Network, May 10, 2021. https://abcnews.go.com/Politics/wireStory/gov-kemp-set-repeal-georgias-1863-citizens-arrest-77601118.

the first state in the country to repeal the antiquated law, which left open too many opportunities for racist behaviors to exercise the law's original intent. When the law was approved in 1863, it was enacted to track down escaped slaves. Later, racists used the citizen's arrest law to justify lynching Black Americans. [35]

The chaos created by Arbery's case resulted in Black people and White people coming together, which prompted a move for legislative change. This is one small step towards justice. Justice is the courage to resist the injustice deed by focusing on the use of the law for change; that is *organized power.*

## Injustice Requires Justice

In June 1963, the Southern way of doing things like overt discrimination and preserving segregated schools that kept Black children at a disadvantage was being threatened by the power of the civil rights movement. Medgar Evers, NAACP's first field officer in Mississippi, was an outspoken and passionate activist for Black people being treated unfairly and inhumanely in the wake of decades of Jim Crow laws and a myriad of injustices.

Civil rights demonstrations were accelerating in Mississippi, and Whites targeted Evers with intensity after he led a boycott against merchants. Within days after he gave a televised speech on the goals of the movement in Mississippi, Evers pulled into the driveway of his home and was gunned down in view of his family when he exited his car on the night of June 12. He was just 37. It took three trials and exhumation of his well-preserved body to finally bring his assassinator, Byron De La Beckwith, to justice in 1994.

There is a delicate balance requiring there be acts of injustice for people to reclaim the concept of justice. It is difficult for some to

---

[35] Tariro Mzezewa. "The Arbery Murder Defendants Say They Were Attempting to Make a Citizen's Arrest. Is That Legal?" The New York Times. The New York Times, November 22, 2021. https://www.nytimes.com/2021/11/22/us/citizens-arrest-arbery-murder-trial.html.

possibly embrace, but I believe it's true: Medgar Evers' assassination was one of the many unjust tragedies that pushed us to a certain place, as the Civil Rights Act became law in 1964, just one year after his murder.

People in the South went through those demeaning acts of injustice, and the rise of broadcast television let the world see it. Those images broadcast into the living rooms raised the vibration of the movement. There was a call to action for people to stand up and confront the hatred springing forth from racism. Then America saw White people and people of different races and ethnicities in accompliship with Blacks as they all marched to cross the Edmund Pettus Bridge in Selma and march in other protests throughout the South. Because injustice requires justice. The justice requires injustice. They are two sides of the same coin. One feeds the power of the other.

## Chapter 3

## A Nation Polarized by Race

Whether a Black person was born into 1619 America when the first slave ship landed on American soil after it was seized from the Portuguese by English pirates who took it to Point Comfort, Virginia—or born into 2019 America—the irony is that a 400-year difference did not change one important fact for Blacks: Since the first Black woman gave birth to a baby on American soil, Black people have been born into a nation divided against itself by race.

The Trump administration captured the hearts of a broad cross-section of Americans by demonstrating the courage to 'rule on the exception.' Two salient examples of this were zero tolerance of BIPOC people was Trump's revocation of asylum for people of color fleeing less than ideal living conditions in their countries and his inhumane proposal to rescind birthright citizenship, which is a policy that guarantees any child born in this country has American citizenship at birth regardless of the status of their parents.

I hold lawmakers, politicians, and Christian faith communities in contempt for criminalizing persons who are escaping violence in pursuit of the courageous act of seeking asylum. This is but one example of how the former president created a new rule, an exception, that not only ignores values that helped to build our society but also lights the wick to propel America back towards the principles, prescriptions, and patterns that birthed the Antebellum South.

Racial polarization in our country is not new. It did not just develop in the four years that Donald Trump was in office, though many people seem to think that to be the case. It is not a phenomenon that happened organically, as many people seem to believe. Polarization has been cultivated, nurtured, and furthered throughout four centuries of America's complicated racial history, including relations with Native Americans. I believe we must examine the origins of racism, how it became systemic and how polarization continues to serve as a barrier to the United States ever living up to its promise.

Racism serves a dual purpose: It has always divided people in America and has always been used to *keep* them divided. White against Black. Black against White. Black against Black. White against Native Americans. Black people against Brown people. Blacks and Whites against Asian Americans. White brother against White brother if we consider that the issue of ending slavery divided families to the point that even some brothers shed blood on opposite sides in the Civil War. Even today Whites are divided: White allies against Whites who condemn the Black Lives Matter movement.

My experiences with race as a Black boy in a state where African Americans comprised such a small percentage of the population helped shape my lens on race in America. As Black children on the North side of Elyria, we had maybe one other person that looked like us in our classroom. In elementary school, I did not think much about it. It was the way it was. Elyria was divided into four quadrants, as most cities are. South and west sides of the city were your predominantly African American sides. Your east and north sides were predominantly White, although you did have some diversity.

Some of my most vivid early memories of interacting with people of other races are experiences that took place right outside my front door. In my neighborhood, the kids I played with were of Indian descent, some were White, and others were mixed race. I developed a good touchpoint on diversity by just playing with my friends, having fun, and not seeing people's colors or backgrounds, or cultural differences. Those experiences were enhanced by spending summers running around the community with friends or at the pool swimming, which is one thing I still love to do. My family lived on the north side of town, which was in some ways considered the well-to-do area for the Black families who could make it out of lower-income communities. Most times, I would be the only one who looked like me. Later, I began bringing my extended family members from Black neighborhoods over to experience the difference between their pool and my pool, and even to 6-year-old children, it was abundantly clear that the contrast in the facilities was stark.

My grandparents, who were fervent believers in seeing something of the world beyond the borders of one's community, traveled frequently, often in their RV. From the time I was five years old until my grandfather passed away in 1987, every summer and every time there was a break from school, I would be with him on the road. I was well-traveled as a child, which gave me many opportunities to see different cultures and different people, even if it was by way of just meeting people at gas stops or seeing people in restaurants or parked in the RV trailer camps. I would talk with people and play with kids that were at the camps. Over years of road trips with my grandparents, I learned a lot about travel but even more about people. I observed and took note of different speaking patterns, traditions, backgrounds, behaviors, and social norms. I was always intrigued by diversity.

When I was not traveling around the country in an RV, I could be found having fun with my friends, most of whom were White due to the racial makeup of my community. From my perspective, we all were on a level playing field. We were just kids being kids. It was all good times—until one day, it wasn't. I cannot recall the exact moment that things shifted, but when I got to the fifth or sixth grade, I began to see a change in the relationship between myself and my White friends. Some of the relationships I thought were solid, first weakened, and then they broke. However, I now understand that possibly their parents had negative or stereotypical views and perspectives about Blacks and the interaction of their children with us. White children I normally played with or walked to and from school with every day each day began to put some distance between us. Suddenly and without warning, they no longer were interested in hanging out. They no longer wanted to ride bikes or play baseball with me.

I have always loved sports of all kinds and was an avid baseball player on the north side of town where I was generally the only Black person on the team. I loved the game but also thrived on the social interaction and camaraderie of sports. I saw these friendships fade as well. I built relationships with some of the athletes who were kind at baseball practice but did not have much conversation with me at school. Around seventh or eighth grade, I began noticing that people were choosing whom they wanted to be with versus just connecting and laughing together and having fun without regard for one another's race. By the time I was in ninth grade, I saw friends with whom I had shared affectionate friendships in elementary school and early middle school, greatly distance themselves from me.

Having never experienced the kind of behavior from my friends, I initially thought it was me. It was a bitter and sobering lesson when I finally understood what had happened. Elementary school and junior high school were predominantly composed of White kids with only a few Black students mixed into the population. When I went to high school, there were children from the south and west side who converged in one high school. Some Black students were used to Whites avoiding them, but then you had a lot of White students who were not used to being in school with so many Black students and felt uncomfortable or even fearful of them.

I lived on the north side of town, but my grandmother lived in the heart of the south side of town. I spent all my summers and most weekends there and already knew all the Black kids that I eventually saw in high school. Since I knew them already, it was not a big shocker or challenge for me when they showed up at high school.

It was challenging to authentically hold in balance the White friendships that I loved and valued, and then give space for the new relationships and partnerships that I had found and loved with Black peers. One of the most surprising points of contention that emerged was some Blacks who wanted me to disassociate with the Whites and vice versa. I learned how to hang with my Black friends and hang with my White ones. I found myself gravitating more to people who just had a respect for humans and not necessarily a preference for a White or Black person. These experiences are why I have never been afraid to share friendships with either side, and that is what shaped me as a young adult in college.

I was in college before I really understood the enigma of why so many White kids who grow up playing with Black kids suddenly pull away when they reach their teen years. Distancing themselves from Black people is what America teaches White children. This rite of passage in the White community is how and why racist views are handed down from generation to generation, creating an ever-evolving cycle of division and racial polarization that have framed the American story for more than 400 years.

## Dear White People: Please don't say 'I am not a racist'

Four words in the English language usually evoke one of three very primeval responses from White people when they hear them: denial, disgust, or anger; sometimes all three. Those four words are "You are a racist."

In July 2018, the Brookings Institute published the findings of a Census survey about the changing demographics in America. The U.S. Census Bureau projects that White people or people of European descent will be the minority race by 2045, indicating that African Americans, Latinos, Asians, and other racial and ethnic minority groups are projected to become the minority-majority.[36] The survey found that nearly two-thirds of the people polled (64%) believe that the ongoing demographic change will have a mostly positive impact on the country. However, one-third (31%) of the public said these changes will impact the country negatively. According to figures published by the U.S. Census Bureau in July 2019, 328.2 million people live in the United States, which means that about 109 million Americans likely have an unfavorable view on most of the country being comprised of non-white people.[37]

What is most striking about the survey findings is that the question was not about immigrants or crime or jobs or welfare. The 31 percent of people who responded negatively to the survey were

---

[36] William H. Frey. "The US Will Become 'Minority White' in 2045, Census Projects." Brookings. Brookings, September 10, 2018. https://www.brookings.edu/blog/the-avenue/2018/03/14/the-us-willbecome-minority-white-in-2045-census-projects/.

[37] Bureau, U.S. Census. "Drops in Natural Increase, Net International Migration Resulted in 0.5% Annual Growth to 328.2m." Census.gov, October 8, 2021. https://www.census.gov/library/stories/2019/12/new-estimates-show-us-population-growth-continues-to-slow.html.

addressing a question that was solely about racial diversity. Of those, how many would consider themselves to be racist? For certain, not very many; perhaps none at all.

One thing is certain: White American people fervently object being called racist. Another certainty is that there is a moral and perceptual divide between White Americans about what it is to be racist.

Racism is a dirty word and to call someone racist is considered an egregious insult. How many times have we seen people at a demonstration marching in the name of White supremacy but deny being racist when asked or labeled? Today, they are more likely to add that they are being "a patriot" and are there to support their country.

A *Politico* article published in July 2019 cited how White attendees of a recent Trump rally in Cincinnati vigorously defended themselves against accusations of being racist by stating how they had donated money to help Black foster children, how they loved their Black and mixed-race grandchildren, and how they liked their Black co-workers.[38] One of those same rallyist made ethnically insensitive remarks about the religious beliefs of Rep. Ilhan Omar (D-Minn.), a Muslim who came to the United States as a Somali refugee.

People who make racist remarks or tell racially insensitive jokes but do not see themselves or consider themselves to be racist contribute to the problem as much as people who are blatantly racist. Some might argue they add to the problem even more so.

Trump often denied being a racist and self-proclaimed to be the least racist person in the world. In addition, he repeatedly claimed to have done more for the Black race than any other president in U.S. history. At the same time, he has shown time and again that he can traffic in racist language, tropes, and character assassination.

---

[38] Bianca Quilantan and DAVID Cohen. "Trump Tells Dem Congresswomen: Go Back Where You Came From." POLITICO, July 14, 2019. https://www.politico.com/story/2019/07/14/trump-congress-go-back-where-they-came-from-1415692.

# The ChaRIOT

One of the most harmful and racist campaigns engineered by Trump was the birther controversy. In 2011, Trump began giving interviews to the media in which he purported the lie that Barack Obama was not born in Hawaii or any state in the union. He turned the comment into what became known as the "birther movement," which he led for more than five years. The lie spread throughout the country and abroad. Even after Obama released his long-form birth certificate, the birther movement picked up momentum and also fueled several other unfounded racially-charged conspiracy theories.

We often heard the former president call Rep. Maxine Waters (D-Calif.) an "individual of low intelligence." He has frequently made xenophobic statements such as Black and Brown immigrants come to America from "shit hole countries," and that four Democratic Congresswomen of color should go back to the countries from which they came. Ayanna Pressley (D-Mass.), Alexandria Ocasio-Cortez (D-New York), Ilhan Omar (D-Minn.), and Rashiba Tlaib (D-Mich.) did nothing to provoke Trump's racist attack—nothing but be people of color. Not that it makes a difference, but only Rep. Omar was born outside of the United States. However, she is an American citizen.

While president, Trump routinely made racist comments but at the same time, tried to make the connection to his supposed non-racist stance by dropping names of his Black celebrity friends like Kanye West and NFL Hall of Famer Jim Brown.

Being a racist or even being called racist implies the person is evil, hate-filled, intolerant, and prone to committing heinous acts against people, based exclusively on race.

The act of denying racism exists almost equally problematic and inherently racist in and of itself. This consistent denial feeds and fuels polarization and division while providing the very structure that houses inequities, disparities, and oppression. Denial is the action that continues to normalize the mistreatment of Black people and further divides the nation. Given the climate of the country in this moment of reckoning on racism in America, it is impossible to be oblivious to bias, prejudice, stereotyping, and the systems in America that continue to make the country a fertile place for the pervasiveness of racism.

What is racism? Why do we need to recognize it, and why is its significance important in America and American life?

There is no one definition of racism. Most of us cannot come to an agreement on what it is exactly but nearly every Black person says they know it when they experience it or when they see it.[39] Racism is one of the most complicated and divisive issues in American history and it is the most profoundly important issue in our country.

Even as a senior pastor, faith leader, New Testament scholar, and corporate diversity consultant, my view on racism is just as complex as any other American's view. If I were to define racism, I would say that it is an action, attitude, or institutional structure that subordinates or oppresses a person or group because of the color of their skin or their ethnicity. In America, it is most often the visibility of one's skin color that attracts racist acts or evokes racist attitudes or thoughts from White people who subordinate members of minority groups. Racism is also the marginalization or oppression of people of color based on a socially constructed racial hierarchy that privileges White people. My point is that racism for me is rooted in the capacity of one race to rule on something that the other cannot. And given that the framers of the U.S. Constitution did not have Black people in mind, as they were considered property, the lingering effect of that omission is still very much part of the American story.

---

[39] Les Back and John Solomos, eds., *Theories of Race and Racism: A Reader*, Second edition., Routledge student readers (London ; New York: Routledge, 2009), 330–331. In the chapter entitled, "The Fact of Blackness," Fanon defines, " It [color prejudice or racism] is nothing more than the unreasoning hatred of one race for another, the contempt of the stronger and richer peoples for whom they consider inferior to themselves, and the bitter resentment of those who are kept in subjection and are so frequently insulted. As colour is the most obvious outward manifestation of race it has been made the criterion by which men are judged, irrespective of their social or educational attainments. The light-skinned race have come to despise all those of a darker colour, and the dark-skinned people will no longer accept without protest the inferior position to which they have been relegated." This definition was borrowed from Sir Alan Burns, *Colour Prejudice* (London, Allen and Unwin, 1948), 16.

Racism in America is not just actions or behaviors of a few people or even the masses. Racism in America is pervasive. It is systemic and institutionalized and emerged from a foundation of White supremacy, which is why polarization is still so much a part of America. Systemic racism is a combination of systems, institutions, and factors that provide White people with advantages but cause extensive disadvantages in access and opportunities for people of color.

## America's Racist Roots

There are several facts White Americans must fully understand about systemic racism and why it has polarized our nation for centuries. First, it is rooted in the history of our institutions, systems, and specifically, laws that support the White race dominating other races.

Equity and justice for all Americans have eluded our country since the first White settlers began encroaching on Indigenous people's land in the early 1600s before the first slaves arrived. Over some 200 years after the early settlers arrived in approximately 1607, Whites took more and more of the Native people's land. The Indian Removal Act was signed into law by President Andrew Jackson on May 28, 1830, authorizing the president to grant lands west of the Mississippi in exchange for Indian lands within existing state borders. A few tribes went peacefully, but many resisted the relocation policy. In the winter of 1831, more than 125,000 Native Americans that lived on millions of acres of land in Georgia, Tennessee, Alabama, North Carolina, and Florida–land their ancestors had occupied and cultivated for generations—were ordered off by the federal government and on to what became known as the "Trail of Tears."[40]

---

[40] History.com Editors. "Trail of Tears." History.com. A&E Television Networks, November 9, 2009. https://www.history.com/topics/native-american-history/trail-of-tears.

# The New Cultural Conversation

The journey to the specially designated Indian Territory, which the Native people were forced to walk to, was hundreds of miles long. It was heavily riddled with disease, grief, and despair, and many men, women, and children died along the way. The irony of the Indian Removal Act was that the White settlers were also voracious capitalists who wanted the Indigenous people's land to plant more cotton for the slaves they owned to chop and pick. At its core, the "Trail of Tears" was created by White entitlement, racism, privilege, white centering, and greed. The erasure of Native Americans and their history, culture, customs, and contributions to America began with taking their land, and it has continued for some 414 years.

The history of American laws sanctioning and supporting racist acts such as the Indian Removal Act also includes the infamous Black Codes, forerunners of Jim Crow laws, which were a group of state and local statutes in the South that legalized racial segregation. These so-called laws forbade Black people to enjoy the same basic human rights as Whites such as ordering and eating inside of a restaurant or drinking water from the same fountain as White people or not having to relinquish their seat on a bus if there were no empty seats for a White person. Jim Crow laws, named after a Black minstrel show character, were created post-Civil War and existed for nearly 100 years—four years after the Civil Rights Act of 1964 was signed into law by President Lyndon B. Johnson.

The second destructive nature of system racism is manifested through speech, media images, actions, language, verbal and nonverbal communication, and behaviors that sustain a system of inequality and inequity, based on race.

Third, how the institutions are structured in society – banking, housing, criminal justice, law enforcement, education – are historically permeated with bias, racism, discrimination, privileged identities, and prejudice. They do not allow for equal opportunities and serve to marginalize and oppress Black, Indigenous, and other people of color.

Fourth, systemic racism is endemic and deeply entrenched in every layer of American systems. Its cause and effect are evidenced in a multifaceted trove of inequities and disparities, including health, housing, wealth, education, incarceration, employment, career advancement, and entrepreneurial opportunities.

The COVID-19 pandemic is one of the most visible examples of how systemic racism and inequities wreak havoc on Black people, Indigenous communities, and Latino people. In the United States, at the height of the pandemic and for a protracted period, Black people were contracting and dying from the coronavirus at a rate that outpaced that of White Americans three times over. This is due to issues of disparities such as access to health care, pre-existing chronic diseases, and Black people's disproportionate placement in frontline service-oriented jobs.

During a White House coronavirus task force briefing, Dr. Anthony Fauci, Director of the National Institute of Allergy and Infectious Diseases and Chief Medical Advisor to President Joe Biden said, "Health disparities have always existed for the African American community…[coronavirus is] shining a bright light on how unacceptable that is because, yet again, when you have a situation like the coronavirus, they [Black people] are suffering disproportionately. We will get over coronavirus, but there will still be health disparities which we really do need to address in the African American community."[41]

The fifth reason our nation has been polarized for centuries is that institutionalized racism means segmented or pocketed or random racism simply do not exist. It is vast and intertwining; it infiltrates and saturates the entire country and has extended to every system in America since the Trail of Tears.

Africans were brought to this country to fill a need to address a so-called "state of emergency." The early White settlers from

---

[41] "Dr. Anthony Fauci on Health Disparities" in … YouTube. YouTube.com, April 7, 2020.
https://www.youtube.com/watch?v=Q8eDzI4MiYQ.

England needed people to help jumpstart the economy, as we saw in the case of Native Americans, who were pushed off their land by settlers catering to their capitalist hearts. Those in power created a state of emergency to forcibly impose Africans into a system support their false emergency without anyone stopping them or interfering in their plan, lest those folks risked their physical safety, up to and including being harmed by slave owners determined to protect ownership of their most important property: other human beings.

We must recognize the complicit role our government played in creating and maintaining the system of slavery. There have always been manufactured states of emergency established that give governmental officials legal rights and reasons to mistreat Blacks.

When I think about how "states of emergency" were used by the settlers and our government, I lean into the concept introduced by German political philosopher Carl Schmitt, who said this: "He who is sovereign is the one who has the power to rule on the exception." By "exception" Schmitt meant the appropriate moment for the power holder to step outside the rule of law in name of public interest and public good. *In the case of slavery as a system, the people who built and sustained chattel slavery were willing to shake up the order of things—which is what a state of emergency does—to create a system of bondage to protect their financial interests.*

There will continue to be manufactured states of emergency to address what some Whites in power consider to be a problem or an opportunity. Black Codes are a good example of this, as they were created to address the "state of emergency" when slavery was abolished after the Civil War. Whites were afraid of free Blacks running rampant and wanted a way to control them while ensuring White Americans maintained their positions at the top of the social and economic hierarchy.

More recently, former President Trump manipulated the U.S. Postal Service to ensure Blacks in particular areas could not vote or at least, would have great difficulty voting. His strategy was to use gerrymandering and orchestrate states of emergency to give him the authority to rule on the exception because he and his administration were insulated by legislation, as were slave owners.

# The ChaRIOT

## The Origin of Systemic Racism

To understand how systemic racism evolved and why we have been a divided country because of it, we must examine its origins in slavery. Structural racism and greed are why Black men, women, and children were stolen from their homeland and brought to America. If we are committed to the ChaRIOT being the vehicle that will eclipse this moment of racial reckoning in America and create a transformative shift, we must delve deeply into what took place at Point Comfort, Virginia in 1619 because it forever changed the trajectory of the country. The legacy of people owning other human beings in this country, with the complicity of the government, affects our past, our present, and our future.

On August 20, 1619, between 20-30 enslaved Africans believed to be from the Kingdom of Ndongo in West Central Africa landed at Point Comfort, Virginia aboard the ship *White Lion*, which was joined by a second ship called *Treasurer*. At Luanda, Angola, the slave ship *San Juan Bautista* departed with 350 enslaved captives from Ndongo. The ship was bound for Vera Cruz, Mexico, but before it arrived it was attacked by the English privateer ships *White Lion* and *Treasurer*. The English ships stole around 60 of the surviving Africans and sailed for Virginia. The ships reached their destination with approximately 30 of the 60 Africans. It is believed the others perished due to disease, famine, and deplorable living conditions on the ships.[42]

The first slaves arrived in America after spending several months aboard a ship where conditions were appalling. The men were packed together below deck with their legs chained to heavy irons. Women and children were kept in separate quarters that allowed them some freedom of movement around a limited area of the ship but exposed women and girls to being raped repeatedly by the crew in full view of others. They also endured other brutal assaults from the crew.

---

[42] History.com Editors. "First Enslaved Africans Arrive in Jamestown Colony." History.com. A&E Television Networks, August 13, 2019. https://www.history.com/this-day-in-history/first-african-slave-ship-arrives-jamestown-colony.

The Africans, who were forcibly taken from their homeland, were malnourished, and often suffering from disease and unsanitary conditions. The air was thick and foul. Epidemics of smallpox and other deadly diseases were frequent, and one in five enslaved Africans died on board and were thrown into the sea. Captives endured these conditions for several months.

The first Africans were Kimbundu-speaking people who shared a common cultural identity and possessed advanced agricultural and industrial knowledge. Between 1618 and 1620, Portuguese colonizers allied with mercenaries to conquer Ndongo and enslave thousands of the kingdom's inhabitants.[43]

Once in America, the men, women, and children were stripped naked, sold, and became part of a system of chattel slavery that continued for more than 250 years, ending only after a war between states that cost more than 600,000 lives.

The landing of the first Africans in Virginia is one of the most significant events in American history. It was the end of freedom for the roughly 30 people who were stolen from their homeland but the beginning of a multigenerational, legalized system of slavery, and systemic racism that defines the Black experience in America.

The social reality of being a Black person in America began at Point Comfort but the influence and legacy of oppression did not end there. The stories of Black Americans' experiences with overt racism and implicit bias can be found in any city in America today, from the halls of the country's Fortune 500 companies to inner-city classrooms that are still burdened with equity challenges, to encounters with police that end with the names of unarmed Black people becoming hashtags to which we post our comments and condolences after they are killed.

---

[43] History.com Editors. "First Enslaved Africans Arrive in Jamestown Colony." History.com. A&E Television Networks, August 13, 2019. https://www.history.com/this-day-in-history/first-african-slave-ship-arrives-jamestown-colony.

# The ChaRIOT

Since 1619, racism and race-based violence against Blacks have been a central part of American life, particularly in the South, though this disease covers the northern, western, and eastern states. Even now the multiple incidents of the use of deadly force by police on unarmed Black men, women, and even children in the cases of Tamir Rice and Laquan McDonald, are further evidence that America's legacy of racism is very much a part of daily life for Black people.

Racism can and does exist even if the people committing a racist act have no conscientious intention to subordinate or oppress others. Some White people may be unaware that their behavior is racist. This may raise the burning question, "How?" The answer is simple and complex: Racism is an effect and is not necessarily what a person intended or did not intend to do in the way of causing harm to someone because of the color of their skin.

Racism is carried out in thousands of ways every day in America, but most of these acts are not obvious to the naked eye as most do not involve name-calling or acts of violence. For example, when a White manager attributes a White employee's success to his or her single-handed hard work or expertise but believes a Black employee's success is only possible due to additional factors such as team members, this is a racist attitude. When that supervisor refuses to advance the Black employee, despite him or her earning the promotion, that is a racist act.

Racial prejudice has shaped America's and Americans' respective histories. They threaten democracy and the country becoming a nation for all will never come to fruition as long as there is systemic racism.

Throughout Black people's 400-year history in America, blatant racism has been a central part of American life. Thousands of racist laws, inferior living conditions, impoverished communities, educational and social institutions, political structure, patterns, norms, and hegemonic and cultural perspectives have resulted in Black Americans being thrust into positions of subordination. Many Whites wrongly believe that explicit racism no longer exists or at least only occurs infrequently or sporadically. The reality is that because racism is systemic and pervasive, Black people experience implicit and explicit forms of it every day: in the workplace, pay and income inequity, educational injustice, schools, housing, loans, political opportunities, and exclusion.

As recently as the 2020 global pandemic, we witnessed instances of blatant racism when the federal government systemically excluded Black businesses from receiving needed funds through the Paycheck Protection Program, which gave loans to small businesses to keep them afloat. Black-owned businesses received 2% of the loan monies compared to 83% provided to White-owned businesses and 15% to other races.[44] More than 50% of Black businesses closed during the pandemic and are not expected to reopen.

From the day the first ship arrived on America's shores carrying African people who had been stolen from their homeland, Black people have experienced grave inequities, despite being central figures in building our country. Native Americans have indeed and without question experienced a deep travesty to their community. Whereas the Native American was exploited, manipulated, and without question murdered to obtain a particular territory, once that territory was secured, then the murderous, villainous practices overall, were not as paramount as they had been in past years.

Without question, people from Latin countries have their own story of being misused and exploited and seen as second-rate persons. Certainly, we all agree that the sights and sounds of wails, cries, and tears by distraught Hispanic and Latino parents and children as they were being separated at our borders during the Trump years, were gut-wrenching to watch. The aim was to disrupt any oppressive social environment with civil disobedience. This included presidential decisions and Trump's political constituents that supported the

---

[44] Gregory Ugwi. "Black-Owned Businesses Received Less than 2% of PPP Loans While White-Owned Businesses Received 83%." The Business of Business. Thinknum, July 7, 2020.
https://www.businessofbusiness.com/articles/black-owned-businesses-received-less-than-2-of-ppp-loans-while-whites-received-83/.

legitimacy of ripping children (of any ethnicity or culture) from their parents and the act of criminalizing the birth of their children.

However, Black Americans have a unique story shaped by more than two centuries of brutal enslavement and being the mechanism for the economic growth of this country. No other race of people in the United States can lay claim to being at the complex intersection of slavery, racism, and not knowing true freedom. Yes, people of other races have most certainly been the victims of racial violence and hatred in our country because of the color of their skin but they have not been oppressed for over 400 years. And the stories of people in other races are not embedded in the fabric of a nation that took pride in destroying, beating, abusing, manipulating, and sometimes murdering a particular race of people to drive the country's economic system.

Studies still indicate that the most segregated hour of the week remains Sunday morning worship, representing how racially polarized our country remains, decades after the civil rights movement and legislation outlawing segregation were passed. Those stats need conversion, as do the racial makeup of our pews, if we are to make a difference in the church and the world.

If ChaRIOTS are to be change agents, and forward-thinking people, those numbers need to transform. Here's what I am saying. This *right now* moment is not about assimilation or accommodation. It is about our social conscience. It is about acceptance and tolerance. It is about people belonging. I do not have to worship with you to recognize when you are being treated unfairly. Different does not mean divisive. Different does not mean deficient. Different does not mean inferior.

ChaRIOT means, as the Apostle Paul said, "Contest the patterns and prescriptions of injustice everywhere with civil disobedience." Within eight months between May 26, 2020, and Jan. 6, 2021, we witnessed two very different forms of protest. First, we saw millions of people of all races and ethnicities stand up and take to the streets against racial injustice. On January 6, we watched a scene of that other protest, the one that happened in Washington, D.C., at the Capitol. I invite you to consider the harm and wide-reaching implications of the poison that was spewed.

I watched what appeared to be sovereign claims of power only to discover I was correct: what I heard had the resonance and reach to usher in that old Antebellum spirit. The cries of "Take Back Our Country," by Whites causes one to recall Billie Holiday's immortal song about "strange fruit" hanging from Southern trees. Then there was this: "Make America Great Again," but for whom? I knew the phrase did not include me, the darker brother, or anyone kissed by nature's sun. Those exclamations were not indicative of an enlarging tent and a shifting attitude. Their words harkened a harsher spirit that continues to divide our country along lines of race, class, and political parties.

Our actions speak for us. What we do makes a difference, how we show up, and where we show up in times of importance and opportunity, like the right now moment at this particular hour. What we do to ensure the ChaRIOT comes matters. ChaRIOTS will tip the balance, change metrics, drive new cultural conversations, and drive change. This shift will place us within the margin of victory, altering scales and changing the future of generations of lives and the social reality that keeps Black Americans from achieving equity and justice.

## Chapter 4

## The Social Reality of Living Black in

## White America

Dr. Martin Luther King Jr., one of the world's greatest architects of what constitutes justice and equity, used to recite a painful story about having to explain to his young children why they could not go to Funtown. He said his children used to plead with him to go to the segregated amusement park the family frequently drove by as they went about their comings and goings. Dr. King said many of those times he told his inquisitive children that they are not able to go now, but he was working on making it possible for them and other Black children to visit the park.

When talking about Funtown years later, Martin Luther King III said he recognizes that his father was trying to protect him and his older sister Yolanda from the realities of living as Black people in a segregated America. After the Jim Crow law that barred Blacks from Funtown was abolished, King said his father and mother took him and Yolanda to the amusement park where the elder King rode every ride and thoroughly enjoyed the experience. But the memory of his father's determination to protect him from the indignities thrust upon Black people by a system of racism is still vivid.[45]

### The Past is the Present

The past and present are always linked and share a symbiotic relationship, which is why Black parents have been taxed with

---

[45] Karen Grigsby Bates. "Amusement Parks and Jim Crow: MLK's Son Remembers." NPR. NPR, August 11, 2013. https://www.npr.org/sections/codeswitch/2013/08/14/209877767/what-happened-to-the-children-of-civil-rights-martyrs.

explaining the social realities of race in America to their children since the days of enslavement. It is an intergenerational ritual that was not easy then and is just as difficult now. When Trayvon Martin was killed by George Zimmerman, it opened dialogue once again about how Black parents must have "The Talk" with their children about how to behave when they are stopped by police as a measure to ensure their safety. At the time, former U.S. Attorney General Eric Holder described having "The Talk" with his 15-year-old son. He lamented that 40 years after his father had that conversation with him, it was still necessary for parents to engage in the ritual, as Black people still must be extra cautious during police interactions.

I often think about what Dr. King and Eric Holder shared from their experiences in talking with their children about being Black in America, and I was reminded of their stories once again during a Saturday morning when I was driving my youngest son to a barbershop appointment. At age 7, he was buckled in the backseat, and we were talking about what we were going to do that day. Suddenly, my eyes were drawn to flashing lights I saw appear in the rearview mirror. I was being stopped by the police. I was not speeding, my tags were current, and I had not committed any moving violations.

I pulled over and had a benign exchange with the officer. I remained calm for my and my son's sake, and after a few minutes, the officer, finding everything in order, let us go about our way.

As I drove for a couple of minutes, the conversation began and went like this:

"Daddy, were you scared?"

"No son, I wasn't scared," I replied, "because I knew I hadn't broken the law."

"He didn't give you a ticket, he didn't sound mean," my son continued with precise inquisition.

"No, he didn't give me a ticket." My calm, vague response to his confusion was intentional to his learning moment.

"Well, why do you think he let you go?" He was genuinely trying to understand what had just happened.

In my son's mind, from what he has digested and learned from media portrayals of cop killings, there was something extremely wrong with this traffic stop. He assumed, although he prayed for the total opposite, that there would be at least some level of aggression projected from the White officer upon me, and sadly, possibly us.

The conversation continued when I answered his question.

"I assume it's because he saw us from a different neighborhood. He probably ran my plates and saw where I lived."

"Well, why did he do that?"

At that moment, we had arrived at the social reality of Black America. It pained me to strip him of a layer of oblivious innocence. But for the sake of his safety and my peace, I had to tell him the truth.

"Because it probably was something in his mind, without knowing what, that led him to think I looked out of place. We are in a certain neighborhood riding in a certain type of car. But all we have to do is make sure we follow the law. Notice, I had my license and my insurance card ready. I had my hands where he could see them, and I didn't make any sudden moves."

Bittersweet joy; we made it through the traffic stop without incident. But there was weighted silence in the car as we continued to our destination. I know at that moment my son realized that simply not breaking any law can still subject his dad, a Black man, to scrutiny through the lens of the dominant perspective. It is problematic that I had to share that narrative with my son, but it was necessary to help him learn how to survive a traffic stop. I did what so many other parents of Black children must do to help keep them safe. I was also very intentional to demonstrate a sense of calm for him so that my reaction would help manage my son's response, should he have an encounter with law enforcement when he begins driving. As a Black male, it is very important that he is prepared to interact with law enforcement safely.

In a society where being White means living a life with all the benefits of a privileged identity, regardless of socioeconomic standing, class, or background, my children and their White friends would view my traffic stop and the racial profiling that prompted it, very differently. Black people share an intimate connection that they do not and cannot share with White friends and co-workers. They are bound to one another by having the same or similar experiences around race in their interactions with Whites no matter who they are or where they live. Black men who are well-educated and successful are as likely to be racially profiled as their Black brothers of lower socioeconomic standing because society tends to criminalize them. Senator Tim Scott (R-South Carolina) has been very open about how many times police have stopped him for driving while Black. Other high-profile Black men and Black women have been similarly candid about their experiences. They also talk about the apprehension, even fear, when they see those flashing lights in their rearview mirror. Blacks have seen far too often how a routine traffic stop can escalate quickly and turn fatal for the motorist.

In my field, we would call what happened to me and my son and many other Black people who are stopped by White police officers and told they were acting suspiciously a word that means *subjectivity*: that is interpellation.[46] This is a process in which an idea or attitude is presented to a person for him or her to accept, and that idea is often presented by someone of another culture, through the sender's lens.[47]That idea is then internalized by the receiver of the idea.

For Blacks, this is often described as "double consciousness," a concept introduced by W.E.B. Du Bois, a Black educator, author, scholar, sociologist, and activist. Young people today call it "code switching," different words but there are ways that we cope, ways that we connect, ways that we must come to grips with what happens on a day-to-day basis. This is the social reality of Black America.

---

[46] "Ideology and Ideological State Apparatuses." Wikipedia. Wikimedia Foundation, March 11, 2022.
https://en.wikipedia.org/wiki/Ideology_and_Ideological_State_Appa ratuses.

[47] "Notes On Interpellation." Notes on Interpellation. Longwood.edu. Accessed December 2021.
http://www.longwood.edu/staff/mcgeecw/notesoninterpellation.htm.

## Black Justice, White Justice

During the formation of the Antebellum South, color was used as a form of weaponry to scare White people when Africans arrived. The color black, and therefore Black people, was presented as being symbolic of all things evil, demonic, and vile. Deeply rooted and ingrained, the concept of black being inferior is something that is generationally conferred from one family lineage to the next, which is why racism today has its roots in the past. The past is the present.

The perception is so deep that unless a White person has an intimate knowledge of or connection to a BIPOC person, he or she is more inclined to be open to the false narratives society tells them about people of a different race. Over time, those teachings contributed to forming the dominant perspective, the lens through which history is told, and perceptions about non-Whites are formed, based on the perspectives of the dominant culture; in America's case, the dominant culture is the White race. Again, the past and the present are intertwined and are most often, cause and effect.

Black persons have, in some ways, fully acculturated to the way the dominant culture exists as well as their social death. In his 1982 book *Slavery and Social Death: A Comparative Study*, Harvard University cultural sociologist Orlando Patterson Ph.D. discusses social death as the condition of a group or race of people not being accepted as fully human by wider society, thus Blacks' exclusion from the U.S. Constitution but labeled "three-fifths" of a person because they were not free but enslaved. [48]

Dr. Patterson submitted that social death likely began at the time captors took captives, as the act of enslavement itself began the process of destroying the person's identity.[49] Loss of heritage,

---

[48] "Slavery and the Making of America. the Slave Experience: Legal Rights & Gov't: PBS." Slavery and the Making of America. The Slave Experience: Legal Rights & Gov't | PBS, 2004.
https://www.thirteen.org/wnet/slavery/experience/legal/docs2.html.

[49] Orlando Patterson. *Slavery and Social Death: A Comparative Study*. Cambridge, Mass: Harvard University Press, 2018.

imposed dress codes, and stripping away the symbols of one's unique identity such as names and physical appearance were also part of enslaved people's social death.

Social death also involves acculturation, the assimilation of a minority group's culture into the dominant culture. Residing right below the subconscious mind, sovereign power still exists; the patterns, the prescription, the way White people have been conditioned to think and be, are all still there.

Justice has always eluded Blacks in America, but injustice more often is a constant in nearly every major aspect of their lives: health, education, environment, economic, and the criminal justice system are the tentacles that help shape the quality of life for most people, and Blacks have experienced injustices in all these areas since they arrived in this country. I will explore the injustices in each of those five aspects later in this chapter.

Injustice is a suppressed story of systemic racism easiest to illustrate juxtaposed with progress. While we can point to many positive signs of Black people's progress—the election of a Black president, Black billionaires Oprah Winfrey, Robert Smith, Tyler Perry, Rihanna, Lebron James, and Jay-Z, and major strides of Black professionals in sectors such as business, entrepreneurism, entertainment management, medicine, law, and science—the race is still woefully struggling for equality and equity.

Blacks still lag Whites in nearly every measure that determines favorable long-term outcomes for individuals and families: wealth, career ladder, homeownership, life expectancy, health, educational attainment, and criminal justice. In 1991, *The Economist* magazine reported the problem of race as one of "shattered dreams." One year later, the first Black U.S. Supreme Court Associate Justice, Thurgood Marshall, observed that he wished he could say racism and prejudice were over but that when he looks around, both Whites and Blacks have lost hope for equality being a reality for all in the United States.[50]

---

[50] Abigail Thernstrom and Stephan Thernstrom. "Black Progress: How Far We've Come, and How Far We Have to Go." Brookings. Brookings, March

Thirty years after Justice Marshall's observation, not much has changed, as evidenced by a Pew Research Center survey taken in September 2020, following the height of the Black Lives Matter protests. I am sure that what struck Pew surveyors was that many Americans were still skeptical that this inflection point would lead to major policy changes in terms of race relations. Specifically, the public was evenly split on whether the increased focus on racial issues and inequities will lead to major policy changes to address racial inequality (48% say it will and 51% say it will not). Also, a notable percentage of Black and White people surveyed (46%) said an increased focus on racial issues would not lead to changes that will improve the lives of Black people.[51]

The COVID-19 pandemic peeled back the layers to reveal a myriad of inequities and examples of how lingering injustices have blocked progress and thwarted a change in the social reality of Blacks. Among the most concerning disparities are those that existed between students from Black families and those from White families, pre-pandemic. It comes as no surprise that the poverty rate is still highest for Black students with nearly one-third of them living in poverty compared with only 10% of White students in families living in poverty.[52]

---

1, 1998. https://www.brookings.edu/articles/black-progress-how-far-weve-come-and-how-far-we-have-to-go/.

[51] Juliana Menasce Horowitz, Kim Parker, Anna Brown, and Kiana Cox. "Amid National Reckoning, Americans Divided on Whether Increased Focus on Race Will Lead to Major Policy Change." Pew Research Center's Social & Demographic Trends Project. Pew Research Center, October 6, 2020. https://www.pewresearch.org/social-trends/2020/10/06/amid-national-reckoning-americans-divided-on-whether-increased-focus-on-race-will-lead-to-major-policy-change/.

[52] Jinghong Cai. "Black Students in the Condition of Education 2020." National School Boards Association. NSBA, June 23, 2020. https://www.nsba.org/Perspectives/2020/black-students-condition-education.

In 2018, 90% of Black students had home internet access compared to 98% of Asian students and 96% of White students.[53]

These disparities show up most often as educational inequity and injustice. Another case in point is the digital divide and how it continues to be a barrier for Black students' academic achievement. A lack of internet access at home became an even greater barrier for Black students to learn as schools shuttered their doors in March 2020 and remained closed well into fall 2021 in response to the pandemic. Students living in households below the poverty line were most impacted by the lack of technology in their homes. Exclusive of the pandemic, the achievement gap between Black and White students has never closed, and the chasm between the two groups continues to result in higher dropout rates among Blacks and lower college attendance rates.

However, there are numerous examples of race-based inequities and injustices that are part of the daily lives of people of color in our country—part of their social reality. I chose to highlight educational disparities to illustrate how injustice continues to contribute to a lack of progress for the Black race because as our children go, so goes the future of America.

I see injustice as whatever philosophical or legal idea, or ideology a person holds and believes it permits them to mistreat people in the BIPOC community simply because their skin is black or brown or tan. Some Whites claim to be colorblind when it comes to race, mistakenly believing this exonerates them from holding racial prejudice or bias. Over time, this view builds a false sense of security that one is not racist or that one is not privileged over others because of their racial identity. It also contributes to the arc of justice bending in the wrong direction. Colorblindness suggests that one does not participate explicitly or implicitly in what the tentacles of race look

---

[53] Cai. "Black Students in the Condition of Education 2020." National School Boards Association. NSBA, June 23, 2020. https://www.nsba.org/Perspectives/2020/black-students-condition-education.

like, or the components of an unjust society. It is a passive seat. Instead of becoming an advocate for colorblindness, a better option is to teach people how to manage and appreciate diversity.

Colorblindness is not the answer. In fact, colorblindness is counter to the principles of the ChaRIOT, as recognition of each other's differences is a key tenet of the movement. The ChaRIOT says, "Awaken and see color. It recognizes the existence of members of the BIPOC community and affirms their racial and ethnic identity."

It takes an awakening to be able to look around and see that there are two types of justice: justice that promises fairness and equity to Whites, and one that often doles out injustice to Blacks and other people of color. The system understands why I, as a Black person, am offered "customer service" in the form of hyper-surveillance at the self-checkout line in the supermarket, while White shoppers are allowed to carry on with their shopping experience without this special service. It is the same system that taught and conditioned a White woman to grip her purse as a Black man approaches or in the case of Amy Cooper, call the police and lie about being threatened by a Black man because she knows her Whiteness would give her a pass no matter how ridiculous or untrue her claims.

Justice in the place where the ChaRIOT resides involves making people aware of their biases and behaviors and how they contribute to or even strengthen wrongness. People may not accept that viewpoint of justice or more so the impact that it might have on them. Nonetheless, the ChaRIOT is concerned with making people aware that disparities in types and levels of justice do exist. The ChaRIOT as a movement aims to unravel the components of the solidarity between injustice and justice to reveal the fibers of unfairness and bias at their core.

## Inequity and Injustice

Throughout this country's history, the benefits, advantages, and opportunities of living in the United States offers have been largely reserved for White people through exclusion, and systemic racism against members of BIPOC communities; of these, Blacks bear the brunt of racial oppression. Blacks, with their unique history in this country, still experience the greatest disparities and inequities of any racial or ethnic group, historically and currently.

What Black people and other people of color need is cultural equity and justice, neither of which has been possible because the racism and implicit bias that created White supremacy and domination have been part of America since 1619.

What the ChaRIOT proposes as justice for Black people in America is tantamount to equity. This includes ensuring they have an adequate and reliable food source, making food insecurity no longer part of daily life. Food is justice.

Justice is making sure Black children have access to educational opportunities beyond their neighborhoods and that a zip code does not determine a child's success or limit that child's opportunities or options.

Justice is ensuring that drugs will no longer be used as a weapon to assault and exterminate the Black community, as crack cocaine has been running rampant, destroying lives and entire families and communities for 40 years. Justice is ensuring that the air Black people breathe in their neighborhoods is as safe as the EPA requires for White neighborhoods. Justice is ensuring that the water supply in which Black communities need to sustain their families is not poisoned by chemicals from a company that values making money more than doing what is morally right. Many people were shocked by the decision to pump tainted water through the pipes that ran into Black and low-income households in Flint, Michigan.

Many more people may be surprised to learn not all people without access to clean water live in third-world countries. More than two million people living in the United States of America lack access to running water, indoor plumbing, or wastewater services[54] jeopardizing their health, wellbeing, and futures. No just or equitable system can exclude any segment of the population from access to basic human needs.

---

[54] George McGraw and Radhika Fox. "Closing the Water Access Gap in the United States: A National Action Plan." U.S. Water Alliance, 2019.

Though inequities exist in every stratum of Black lives, there are five categories having a major impact on their ability to access opportunities, close disparity gaps, and truly achieve the freedom that has not been provided to them. I want to give a closer look at the areas that make it especially difficult for Blacks and other people of color to achieve parity and justice: Health, Education, Environmental Justice, Wealth and Economics, and the Criminal Justice System.

## Health Disparities and Injustice

Imagine enrolling in college and the dean took it upon him or herself to predetermine your grades for each course before you even elect to take any of the courses; going so far as to predetermine your GPA before you graduate. This is the reality of healthcare in America for the Black community. Even when adjusted for income, Black people on average, do not receive healthcare on par with Whites.

Some White doctors, due to their dominant perspective of the Black community, are more likely to address Black patients with a templated approach, assuming that all Black persons engage in the same eating, diet, and exercise habits and are predisposed to the same environments that ultimately contribute to their health status.

There is medical racism that results in negligence towards the Black community justified by what doctors often attribute to heredity. This neglect manifests in the form of gross health gaps and disparities compared to other races in America. In America, health insurance is a matter of life and death, and the lack of it decreases the chances of the Blacks in the lower-income strata reaching their optimal level of health. Even with medical and technological advances, the overall state of health for Black people in America has not improved. They disproportionately develop cancer, asthma, diabetes, heart disease, and high blood pressure, and Blacks' mortality rate from these diseases is higher, even when adjusted for income and access to health care.

Disparities for pregnant Black women are dismal. Even in 2021, the Centers for Disease Control reports that Black women are three times more likely to die from a pregnancy-related cause than

White women due to factors such as variation in quality healthcare, underlying chronic conditions, structural racism, and implicit bias.[55]

Black people see the impact of social and racial injustice in ways more intimate and personal than people of other races because health inequities strike members of their family, friends, church members, and communities. With each health disparity statistic negatively impacting Blacks, whether it is a chronic disease or an acute health matter, structural racism places them at a severe disadvantage.

Affirmation that the past is linked to the present is evident when we examine the bleak history of Black people and the medical profession in our country. Horrible experiences like the infamous Tuskegee study and other experimentation performed on the Blacks have been part of the culture of American medicine for centuries and is at the root of why Black people today are still wary of the medical community. A strong sense of mistrust accompanies Black men and women when interacting with White medical professionals, especially.

Since the COVID-19 pandemic began in 2020 and throughout 2021, BIPOC people were four times likely to be hospitalized and three times more likely to die than Whites. Yet, when a vaccine became widely available in 2021, Black people were trending as the least vaccinated segment of the population. Many cited their mistrust of the government and the Tuskegee Experiment as reasons for vaccine hesitancy and perhaps with good reason.

Hypotheses are sometimes created by medical professionals and then the effort is made to validate them through experiments. Such was the case in 1932 when the United States Public Health Service (PHS) recruited 600 men to be enrolled in a study to monitor bad

---

[55] "Working Together to Reduce Black Maternal Mortality." Centers for Disease Control and Prevention. Centers for Disease Control and Prevention, April 9, 2021.
https://www.cdc.gov/healthequity/features/maternal-mortality/index.html.

blood, as they were told. It was a lie. In reality, White researchers knew 399 of those men had syphilis.[56]

Doctors at the Tuskegee Institute intentionally withheld medical treatment from those infected individuals to study the effects of the disease's progression, although penicillin became available and was a recommended form of treatment for the sexually transmitted disease at the time. After being made aware of the unethical practices going on at Tuskegee Institute, the PHS formed a committee for review and ultimately decided to continue with the research and monitor patients even as many lost their eyesight, went insane, developed major health problems, or died. This inhumane, 40-year experiment on Black men resulted in many men needlessly suffering or dying.

Another case of gross medical injustice was that of young homemaker, wife, and mother Henrietta Lacks. In 1951, while undergoing treatment for cervical cancer, medical doctors at John Hopkins University discovered that Lacks' cancer cells were the source of the first immortalized cell line. Before their discovery, cancer cells harvested from patients would die quickly, leaving little opportunity for in-depth research. But during a biopsy, lab tests revealed that Lacks was the source of immortalized cells; rather than dying off, Lacks' cells were the first cells to live outside the body in a glass tube. Immortalized cells were and still are groundbreaking in medical research and are the foundation of medical discovery.[57]

Without her knowledge or permission or that of her family, scientists and doctors continued harvesting Lacks' cells, building an arsenal of foundational research that would be used as a catalyst for

---

[56] Elizabeth Nix. "Tuskegee Experiment: The Infamous Syphilis Study." History.com. A&E Television Networks, May 16, 2017. https://www.history.com/news/the-infamous-40-year-tuskegee-study.

[57] Benjamin Butunis. "The Importance of Hela Cells." Johns Hopkins Medicine, November 8, 2021. https://www.hopkinsmedicine.org/henriettalacks/importance-of-hela-cells.html.

vaccines, in vitro fertilization, cancer treatments, and much more. Although nicknamed in her honor as the HeLa cells, neither Lacks nor her family were ever notified of the discovery or how her extraordinary cells contributed to breakthroughs in medical research. Lacks died on Oct. 4, 1951, at age 31. She nor her family were ever consulted before her cells were harvested. It was not until 1975, 24 years Lacks' death, that the Lacks family was made aware that the HeLa cell exist. In the meantime, the research and medical discoveries from her cells generated billions of dollars. Her children and grandchildren have yet to benefit monetarily.

Incidents like the Tuskegee experiment and the HeLa Cells have caused deep mistrust of the medical profession by Black people, and even today, tremendous measures had to been expended to convince them to seek the life-saving vaccination for COVID-19, contributing significantly to a pandemic of the unvaccinated.

Even with medical ethics boards in place designed to prevent atrocities such as Tuskegee experiment, healthcare discrimination is still very much prevalent in the American medical system. The gruesome practices invoked upon the men in the Tuskegee experiment, Henrietta Lacks, and so many others throughout history still happen even today. They appear discreetly as disparities or health inequities in the Black community. Why are Black women more likely to die from breast cancer than White women? Why are Black men more likely to die of a stroke than White men? Why are Black people more likely to die under the care of a physician than White people? One reason is the racial discrimination that begins in the doctor's office, even for those with access to medical care.

We have no clearer example of the disparities that still exists as we see Black people dying from the coronavirus a triple the rate of White people due to a myriad of conditions, not the least of which include various forms of systematic racism within the medical system.

We must also acknowledge that racism within the medical community begins outside of it and stretches into the day-to-day lives of many Black people as they grapple with impoverished communities, poor or no preventative care, unsafe neighborhoods, environmental injustice, and pre-existing conditions.

These are the realities of healthcare for a disproportionate number of Black Americans. The system must embrace policies that support healthy outcomes for our vulnerable populations. The ChaRIOT Movement will lead efforts to dismantle the racism that exists outside of the healthcare system so that healthcare is viewed through a lens of equity.

## Education

The U.S. educational system is among the most inequitable systems in the world, resulting in students having remarkably different learning experiences and outcomes, largely based on their socioeconomic standing. The fact that the United States is among the wealthiest nations in the industrialized world makes this inequity even more profound and all the more shameful.

Educational inequity has been part of life in America since before slavery. Native Americans were never educated at parity with White settlers. After Nat Turner led a slave revolt in which many Whites were killed in 1831, all slave holding states except Tennessee, Maryland, and Kentucky, passed a law making it illegal for slaves to learn to read and write and illegal for anyone to teach them to do so.[58] A violation resulted in harsh punishment for the slave and the person teaching him or her. We must also remember that through the 1960s most students of color were educated in segregated schools based on the falsehood of separate but equal facilities, which meant schools serving predominantly students of color were supposed to be on par with schools whose students were primarily White. Even today, more than 65 years after *Brown v. Board of Education of Topeka*, inequality persists and so does separate and unequal. Schools that serve Black, Native American, and Latino students continue to be underfunded, in some cases, grossly so. As a result, those students experience subpar

---

[58] Art Museum, Smithsonian American. "Literacy as Freedom - American Experience."

https://americanexperience.si.edu/wp-content/uploads/2014/09/Literacy-as-Freedom.pdf. Accessed December 31, 2021.

resources, fewer qualified teachers, and dramatically different learning opportunities and outcomes than students in more affluent school districts. This was particularly true of schools in the Southern states and rural areas.

Few people know that after the U. S. Supreme Court's landmark decision outlawed segregation in schools in the *Brown v. Board of Education* case, the High Court partially reversed itself by approving the Pupil Placement Law, which permitted states to determine where school children might be placed. The law allowed states to take into consideration highly subjective criteria that included family background and special abilities of a student. The law had the potential to greatly limit the integration of schools, thereby, almost returning the country to pre-desegregation status.[59]

Although it took more than 30 years after the 1954 U.S. Supreme Court ruling to fully desegregate public schools in America, the assault on Black education is still prevalent today. Only a few decades after desegregation, legislation allowed what was called "zoning" to place children in appropriate schools. School zones were set up according to neighborhoods. On the surface, what that means is children were zoned to schools that were near their neighborhoods. What that meant for students from low-income families living in nearby neighborhoods with poor housing conditions is that they were all zoned to the same underfunded, failing schools.

Often, schools in these areas receive Title I funding, which is provided to schools with high numbers or percentages of children living in poverty. This money is often allocated to make up for the deficit in basic school supplies. Rarely are these schools able to update technology or offer exploratory learning opportunities beyond shared, outdated textbooks, yet those children are still held to the same standards and required to pass the same standardized test as students from well-funded schools in affluent neighborhoods.

At the root of those inequities is a lack of wealth, both household wealth and the wealth of the schools' host community.

---

[59] King and Reverend Jesse L. Jackson. *Why We Can't Wait* (New York, New York: New American Library, 2006).

According to EdBuild, annually, majority-minority school districts receive $23 billion less nationally than affluent, mostly White school districts.[60]

In 2022, the number of multi-racial students in public schools is expected to grow 44 percent while the percentage of White students continues to trend downward, which means we will have an education system not serving the majority of school-age children, creating an even larger achievement gap.[61] Disparities in developmental skills in Black and White children are evident as early as kindergarten due to a number of factors that include low-income households, parents who are not well educated, low-quality daycare centers, and lack of enrollment in Head Start programs.

Black students are less likely to graduate high school or attend and graduate from college than their White counterparts, setting them up to earn less and be less likely to create wealth they can use to give their children better opportunities and increased chances of economic success in their own lives.

Education inequity is a social justice issue affecting our society and even with all other social areas being equitable, people of color would still experience disparities and injustice, which is why the equity movement the ChaRIOT would create with a broad, cross section of people cannot wait.

### Environmental Injustice

In the Floral Farms community nine miles outside of downtown Dallas, Marsha Jackson and her family are suffering from

---

[60] Christina A. Samuels. "Who's to Blame for the Black-White Achievement Gap?" Education Week. Education Week, September 15, 2021. https://www.edweek.org/teaching-learning/whos-to-blame-for-the-black-white-achievement-gap/2020/01.

[61] Lindsey Samuels. "U.S. Education: Still Separate and Unequal | Data Mine ..." usnews.com, January 28, 2015. https://www.usnews.com/news/blogs/data-mine/2015/01/28/us-education-still-separate-and-unequal.

breathing problems, headaches, skin rashes, and a constant cough. Trucks have pulled up and dumped asphalt shingles in a vacant lot outside her backyard since January 2018. More than 100,000 tons of tile are piled high enough to be visible from several miles away, giving the heap the nickname "Shingle Mountain." The company dumping the shingles, Blue Star Recycling, had made a verbal commitment to the predominately Black residents that the shingles would not be a problem and that the discarded asphalt tiles would be minimal. Four years later, dust from Shingle Mountain blows into the residents' homes where they breathe in the intrusive debris. Jackson's family says they have been coughing up black phlegm since 2019. Jackson has filed a lawsuit against Dallas, citing its lax zoning laws, but according to her, city officials are not listening. Meanwhile, other Black Floral Farms residents are fighting against another big company that wants to place a concrete crushing plant in their community.[62]

A few years before trucks began hauling in the poisonous shingles right outside Jackson's property, there was a sudden surge of children coming through the pediatric ward at a hospital 1,200 miles away in Flint, Michigan. A nurse alerted medical and municipal officials in 2014. She noticed that all the children had been exposed to extremely high lead levels, which indicated lead poisoning.

Unbeknownst to residents of Flint, city officials decided to switch the city of Flint's water supply from the city's water supply to getting water from the Flint River as a cost-saving measure.

Residents reported the water as having a pungent odor and being discolored. Water for the mostly Black and low-income Flint residents was inadequately treated and tested, resulting in major health issues, which were ignored, dismissed, or discounted by government officials for 18 months. Treatment and testing of the water resulted in a series of major water quality and health issues, including skin rashes and hair loss. The Michigan Civil Rights Commission concluded that

---

[62] Jacob Vaughn. "After Shingle Mountain, Floral Farms Has a Plan. Residents Say the City Isn't Listening." Dallas Observer. Dallas Observer, September 10, 2021. https://www.dallasobserver.com/news/floral-farms-community-has-plans-for-after-shingle-mountain-clean-up-but-they-say-city-isnt-listening-11988618#newsletterSignUp.

the poor governmental response to the Flint crisis was a "result of systemic racism."[63]

Environmental racism in its simplest terms involves people of color experiencing detrimental impacts from environmental hazards caused by several factors that include intentional acts, neglect, low value placed on people in a community, and low value placed on a certain community. People living in low-income communities typically have low or no power to stop or fight the large corporations that are the culprits in environmental racism.

For years, not only did city officials in Flint deny any wrongdoing, but there was a marked time lapse before they acknowledged what was happening to those residents. Those children and residents who showed elevated blood levels now must brace for the harrowing ordeal of not knowing what is to come of their health long term. Day by day, real justice is denied.

Cancer clusters, one of the deadliest assaults, are at the pit of environmental justice. The poisoning of communities, specifically low-income, Black communities, has become an egregious practice seemingly justified by the United States Environmental Protection Agency (EPA). Cancer clusters are communities diagnosed with cancers that result from contaminates in the environment, not just one person or one family. They develop because of corporate greed, racism, and a low value placed on people in certain communities.

For example, the water, soil, or air are not a result of one's biogenetic makeup. Corporations across the nation engage in this knowingly inhumane method of business, but discreetly. In exchange for money, some municipalities award contracts to corporations with known histories of environmental violations. Corporations like Dupont and its subsidiaries find that rural, low-income communities are the best places to dump their waste, partly because these residents are historically marginalized and overlooked by the government. Once

---

[63] Melissa Denchak. "Flint Water Crisis: Everything You Need to Know." NRDC, November 8, 2018. https://www.nrdc.org/stories/flint-water-crisis-everything-you-need-know#sec-summary.

the alarm sounds, the damage is done. Many class-action lawsuits resulting from these corporate actions go unheard or unsettled, both synonymous with injustice.

Meanwhile, Flint city officials keep assuring residents the water is safe, but they still use bottled water to get through a basic day, citing extreme mistrust. The damage is done and giving residents clean water today will not undo the well-earned mistrust city officials are facing.

## Economics

Income is not wealth-building. Earning money is not always enough to push the needle towards economic justice. First, the system must be reconstructed in a way to close the wealth gap that exists between Blacks and Whites. Justice is the right to participate in and pursue the same, if not better, economic opportunities for wealth as White persons in America. We must hold corporations accountable for moving Blacks who are over credentialed in lower-level jobs into spaces where they can lead corporations and build wealth. Complacency with a "good" salary is insufficient in our fight for economic justice. Blacks must fight for wealth, and the ability to build intergenerational wealth has largely been denied to them. Intergenerational wealth is what sustains families and communities in the decades and centuries to come.

The American system of economics was built around the idea anyone can succeed if they work hard and pull themselves up by the bootstraps and make a way for themselves in the Land of the Free and Home of the Brave. But this falsehood must be faced and debunked. The economic reality of Black Americans is that not all people have a level playing field because the framers of the system created an environment in which pulling one's self up is not possible for everyone. For some, the bootstrap is never intended to help them escalate or climb the ladder toward upward mobility. In actuality, the system is stacked against them being able to attain wealth.

One of the most stellar symbols for Black wealth can be traced back to an affluent Black community in Tulsa, Oklahoma. O.W. Gurley, a wealthy African American landowner purchased 40 acres of land west of Tulsa that came to be known as Greenwood. Gurley had a dream to create a community that valued, respected, and promoted Black enterprise. Greenwood was owned by a conglomerate of other Black businessmen that only loaned money to Black businessmen and sold land to Black people; this principle was the core of their sustainability and prosperity and survival during the segregated Jim Crow South. The irony is that Greenwood would not have existed without the enforcement of Jim Crow laws—laws that left Blacks no choice but to build their own community of banks, merchants, schools, and homes because the White system would not allow them to shop in White-owned stores or live where they chose.

Over time, the Greenwood district grew into what became to be known as Black Wall Street. There were neighborhoods, hospitals, banks, stores, candy shops, movie theaters; all the things of a modern-day thriving society. And the community had one more thing that distinguished it from other Black communities and many White ones in that era: wealth.

Every business was Black owned. The community sustained its own existence. However, its demise came on May 31-June 1, 1921, when an angry White mob descended upon the community. They came with guns, ammunition, and riot armor, including bombs. Within hours, more than 300 Black people were killed and many more wounded. Miles of charred smoking building skeletons served as brutal reminders of the community that was self-sufficient, self-sustaining, and self-contained. Greenwood is still held up as a model in Black wealth building because economics for Black communities in America has not seen such economic autonomy since 1921.

Approximately 101 years since Greenwood was destroyed, the Black-White wealth gap is still one of the starkest examples of how centuries of pay inequity and income gaps due to structural racism has impacted multiple generations. In 2018, Black household income was about 58 percent of White households, which is virtually unchanged from 55 years ago, and in 2016, Black households had 10 percent of the wealth of White households, even adjusted for factors such as education and income.[64]

The impacts on intergenerational wealth-building are persistent and profound and can be traced back to centuries of Blacks being enslaved, Black Codes, Jim Crow laws, lack of homeownership, redlining, policy, and our government being complicit in laws and practices that discriminate against Black progress, and many other barriers to wealth generation and accumulation all contribute to social and economic disadvantages for the race as a whole.

## Criminal Justice

Black people's over-representation in the American criminal justice system is well-documented. Black men comprise only 13% of the male population but are 35% of those incarcerated. Even more disheartening is that one in three Black males can expect to be incarcerated in his lifetime compared to White males born today who can expect 1 in 17 to be incarcerated. Though they make up about 13% of the U.S. female population, one in 18 Black women can expect to be incarcerated.

One could conclude that there is a crisis of Black people being part of the criminal justice system, but the disparity in numbers between races does not necessarily mean that Black people, particularly Black males, commit more crimes. Rather, we should consider that multiple factors contribute to the imbalance of percentages, not the least of which is a history of racism, bias, unfair sentencing, and oppression of Black people. Racism in the U.S. is at the root and the criminal justice system is one of the many areas of our nation in which it manifests.

If we look at traffic stops, for example, the figures tell a story when you consider that Black people are 20% more likely to be

---

[64] Kilolo Kijakazi, Jonathan Schwabish, and Margaret Simms. "Racial Inequities Will Grow Unless We Consciously Work to Eliminate Them." Urban Institute, July 1, 2020. https://www.urban.org/urban-wire/racial-inequities-will-grow-unless-we-consciously-work-eliminate-them.

involved in a traffic stop than White drivers and they are 1.5 to 2 times more likely to have their vehicles searched – even though Blacks are found to less likely be carrying illegal contraband than White drivers. Systemic racial inequities also include over-criminalizing Black people as early as the pre-teen years, over-policing of Black communities, impoverished neighborhoods through disinvestment, and historic targeting by criminal laws that discriminate against people of color. Recidivism rates of those who have been released from prison are also disproportionately high for Black men and women.

The number of Black people in the criminal justice system can be traced to systemic problems stemming from discriminatory laws that include Black Codes, Jim Crow, and the over-criminalization of Blacks for nonviolent offenses such as marijuana and jaywalking, which is why Ferguson, Missouri police initially stopped Michael Brown. In the days of Black Codes, which were introduced to control former slaves right after the Civil War, Blacks were convicted of benign "crimes" such as walking alone at night. Two of the many examples of how Black people are treated differently than White people when encountering law enforcement officers are Daunte Wright and Ma'Khia Bryant, a teenage girl.

Wright, a 20-year-old Minnesota resident, shot dead by police after initially being stopped for an air freshener hanging from his rearview mirror (Minnesota law prohibits objects that could obstruct a driver's view but does not specify air fresheners). Bryant, a 16-year-old girl, was killed by a Columbus, Ohio police officer seconds after he arrived at a call about girls engaged in a fight. Both incidents illustrate a national problem at the intersection of policing, civil rights, and race.

We can point to many bodies of research and data gathering that confirm disparities in arrests and sentencing are rooted in this country's history of racial oppression in the criminal justice system dating back to the slave patrols. It was a Georgia law enacted in 1863 giving ordinary citizens the right to track and arrest slaves that Greg and Travis McMichael used to justify hunting and killing Ahmaud Arbery in 2020.

Beyond the police are others involved in the criminal justice system who contribute to Black people being discriminated against, and they include prosecutors, judges, juries, and parole boards, all of whom practice overt and implicit biases. Those biases and prejudices manifest in more arrests, more convictions, and harsher sentencing and plea bargains for Black people. For example, studies have shown that charges, convictions, and sentencing for crack cocaine versus methamphetamine are unevenly skewed, as Blacks are more often charged with crimes related to crack.

Poverty's connection to crime, especially violent crime, chronic unemployment, and children without significant male figures in their lives, are factors in criminal activity, and Black people disproportionately live in those conditions. The formation of poor neighborhoods in which conditions such as those described are most often found can be directly linked to slavery, what happened to Blacks in the decades following slavery, and America's historic discriminatory housing practices, which made homeownership out of reach for most Black Americans. Even today, Blacks lag Whites in homeownership, a critical factor in building wealth for most Americans of any race.

The racist attitudes, behavior patterns, and institutional structures built over some 400 years—or longer if you include Native Americans—are deeply embedded in the fibers of the fabric in our country. They will not be erased overnight or over a few years. Dismantling the system requires the ChaRIOT to lead a focused, sustained battle involving Whites and BIPOC communities who are passionately and irrefutably committed to transformative change. The ChaRIOT is action-based and involves opening a space for belonging and allowing people the space to show and share their differences without shedding their identities. The ChaRIOT creates space for conversation, a New Cultural Conversation that serves as a force for change.

## Chapter 5

### *Rage:* To My White Former Friends

On the clear, warm morning of June 7, 2020, 80-year-old Congressman John Lewis (D-Georgia) stood on part of a two-block stretch of downtown Washington, D.C. that some racial justice activists call, "a place of hope and healing." The bustling area had long been a gathering place for Black activists, particularly given its proximity to the White House. In the days before Congressman Lewis' visit, seven artists had been selected by Mayor Muriel Bowser to paint "Black Lives Matter" in 35-foot-long yellow letters spanning two city blocks so prominently they can be seen from space. Black Lives Matter Plaza had been created amid the thousands of people that gathered daily in Lafayette Square and surrounding streets to protest following the killing of George Floyd.[65]

As he alternated between folding his arms across his chest in a stance that exhibited strength and gripping a cane that he used to support his body weakened by cancer, Congressman Lewis' rage had driven him to give his blood, heart, voice, and 63 years of his life fighting against racism, inequity, and injustice.

He succumbed to pancreatic cancer on July 17, 2020, but that Congressman Lewis, who knew his mortality was imminent, chose to make his last public appearance at Black Lives Matter Plaza was a powerful statement about the importance he placed on protest and constructive rage.

John Robert Lewis was just 17 when his rage gave him the courage to write a letter to Dr. Martin Luther King Jr. expressing his passion for the cause the civil rights leader was spearheading. The teen

---

[65] Cydney Grannan. "What Does D.C.'s Black Lives Matter Plaza Mean to Locals?" WAMU, August 6, 2021. https://wamu.org/story/20/08/27/what-does-d-c-s-black-lives-matter-plaza-mean-to-locals/.

received a round-trip bus ticket so he could join Dr. King in Montgomery, Alabama.[66]

It was the beginning of more than six decades he spent on the frontlines fighting for justice without ceasing. At 23, Congressman Lewis was the youngest speaker at the historic March on Washington in 1965. He was arrested 40 times between 1960 and 1966 while he led demonstrations against the indignities of segregated schools, public facilities, lunch counters, hotels, and restaurants. Along the way, his skull was cracked from a beating by law enforcement on Bloody Sunday, one of many such beatings he suffered at the hands of police. He had lit cigarettes put out in his hair and spit hurled into his face from the mouths of White people who felt Black Americans had no right to rise above second-class citizenship.

While Lewis and other civil rights workers were marching, fighting, speaking out, and peacefully challenging oppression and oppressors, many did not see the effort as noble. The oppressors—those who were active and bystanders—saw the rage that energized Lewis' and other civil rights stalwarts' struggle not as progress but as an attack on America, as something that must be extinguished because it threatened a way of life that worked for White Americans.

Many White persons in America, and possibly some of those who are members of other underrepresented groups, see Black protests as a gross disregard for civil order and an assault on democracy. Black rage is one of the most misunderstood and mislabeled emotions in the history of civil rights efforts in America. White people hear the term "Black rage," and their minds conjure up images of violent mobs burning, looting, shooting, and committing other acts that violate the law.

---

[66] Jada Yuan. "Documenting John Lewis's Last Public Appearance." The Washington Post. WP Company, July 30, 2020. https://www.washingtonpost.com/lifestyle/style/documenting-john-lewiss-last-public-appearance/2020/07/30/0b1d2d04-cab3-11ea-91f1-28aca4d833a0_story.html.

# The ChaRIOT

My view is that rage, exhibited in the various forms of protests against injustice, is a particular type of grammar. Rage translates into actions such as refusing to stand but instead kneeling during the National Anthem to call attention to issues of inequity and police brutality against Black Americans.

One of Dr. King's statements on riots was recited often in the days and weeks of the protests during summer 2020, and it resonated with people more than ever. In fact, with every cycle of protests after the unjust killing of a Black person by White police, just one sentence of an entire passage of his opinion on riots being the voice of the unheard is most quoted. I offer the entire context of what Dr. King stated during a speech at Stanford University in 1967:

> *But it is not enough for me to stand before you tonight and condemn riots. It would be morally irresponsible for me to do that without, at the same time, condemning the contingent, intolerable conditions that exist in our society. These conditions are the things that cause individuals to feel that they have no other alternative than to engage in violent rebellions to get attention. And I must say tonight that a riot is the language of the unheard. And what is it America has failed to hear? It has failed to hear that the plight of the negro poor has worsened over the last twelve or fifteen years. It has failed to hear that the promises of freedom and justice have not been met. And it has failed to hear that large segments of white society are more concerned about tranquility and the status quo than about justice and humanity.* [67]

When I read Dr. King's words, my take on them is that Black people were saying then as they do today, "We have tried to speak to

---

[67] "Martin Luther King, Jr. Visits Stanford (1967) - YouTube." Stanford University Libraries, September 23, 2016. https://www.youtube.com/watch?v=cYK9xGALPrU.

you in other ways. We have tried to have town hall meetings. We have tried to discuss this in public forums to which Whites were invited. We have participated in the State of the Black Community in America and different types of network television shows. But, White Americans, many of you are still not listening. So, we are going to show you something that television, podcasts, and social media networks cannot ignore. We are going to rearticulate how we feel but do it in a way that no one can ignore."

This is what I mean about rage. My intent is to illustrate, in the most positive sense, that rage is the grammar of how we manage a conversation so that people cannot ignore what Blacks are communicating about inequity and injustice. The ChaRIOT seeks to achieve this.

I am not in any way condoning or supporting vandalism and violence, but when people are speaking out because they want their unheard voices to be heard, I think their rage must be expressed constructively. I also think their voices must be respected.

Rage must be a performative act. Feeling the weight of years of assaults and violence by police officers on the Black community, culminating with the murder of George Floyd, celebrity athletes made history when they pushed team owners to use sports arenas for polling centers. That was the language and the actions those athletes used to express rage.

Constructive rage has led to progress in many of our communities and the Black community as a whole. But we cannot detract from progress by committing acts of violence. Burning a neighborhood and looting businesses cannot be the grammar we use to help demonstrate our frustration or get attention; we must rearticulate our rage.

We must find a gap in the community, a gap in society, a gap in the political process, or a gap in corporate America. And we, the ChaRIOTS, must exploit those gaps with a rearticulated rage that cannot be ignored or denied when it is expressed.

## Rearticulated Rage

Rage is often defined as intense, uncontrolled anger or an increased stage of hostile response to a perceived egregious injury or injustice. But rage in the context of Black people protesting is one of the most mischaracterized and misunderstood emotions in our country.

*The New York Times* posthumously published an essay by Congressman Lewis in which he described the people who took to the streets during the 2020 protests as filling him with hope in the final days of his life. What that American saw as hope for the soul of the nation, many other Americans only saw people who sought to destroy the country; they saw people who do not appreciate being in America and all the unique opportunities the country offers. What they fail to see or admit is that while this is a land of opportunity, it has also been a land of inequities for those who are BIPOC since the settlers arrived and began the erasure of Native Americans.

I believe that rage is a cry from the unheard. I believe rage is a necessary form of expression people turn to when they are pushed enough or forgotten enough or ignored enough by people at the top of the cultural hierarchy. Rage seeks to create a conversation with the dominant culture, the privileged, and those who sit in positions of power. Rage is an unspoken language that says to the dominant culture, "You must stop being who you are to stop the cancer of racism and implicit bias that has kept this country from redeeming and becoming a nation of, by, and for the people."

Even if actions in our immediate communities—the marches, shouting, and chanting—are required to get the attention of those who choose to believe systemic racism does not exist, Whites should not misinterpret what Black people are trying to articulate during protests like America's most recent one.

The 2020 Black Lives Matter protests have been singled out as the most diverse in history. People who saw the indefensible act of a White police officer committing what was nothing less than a public lynching were roiled, disgusted, and outraged. White people have been part of the struggle for racial justice and equality since slavery and their involvement in the Underground Railroad, but this time there was widespread divesting of the divisions of race, ethnicity, culture, language, age, education, titles, and zip codes; they were forgotten by the people who screamed for change. The ChaRIOT seeks to build on that energy and create a new community reflective of the tearing down of the divisiveness that keep us from uniting.

White women and men acted as human shields to protect Black protesters from a police officer's baton. Black people and White people hooked arms and formed human chains as they were met by police. White protesters and Black protesters doused one another's faces with containers of milk to take away the sting of tear gas. People snapped photos of a small Black boy holding a sign with the words, "Am I Next?" They posted the image on their social media platforms to drive home the sad reality that in the land of the free, a Black child must be afraid of being the next George Floyd. The posts went viral. White superstar athletes tweeted support and joined Black fellow players on the basketball court as they engaged in acts of protest. Senator Mitt Romney (R-Utah) joined Black Lives Matter protesters in Washington, D.C., against the backdrop of a photo of his father participating in a civil rights-era march. Senator Romney told a reporter he was marching because Americans need to stand up and say black lives matter.[68]

The titans of industry issued a flurry of statements condemning racism, pledging a commitment to diversity, equity, and inclusion, and announcing a collective $50 billion for racial equity initiatives.[69]

Many described what we saw in 2020 as unprecedented in U.S. history and they are right. But to what end? How do we not end

---

[68] McKay Coppins. "Why Romney Marched." The Atlantic. Atlantic Media Company, June 8, 2020.
https://www.theatlantic.com/politics/archive/2020/06/mitt-romney-black-lives-matter/612808/.

[69] Marco Quiroz-Gutierrez. "American Companies Pledged $50 Billion to Black Communities. Most of It Hasn't Materialized." Fortune. Fortune, May 6, 2021. https://fortune.com/2021/05/06/us-companies-black-communities-money-50-billion/.

up here again? How do we ensure these transactional moments are transformational events that create a new reality?

Americans cannot go back again but how do we create "better" from where we are? I believe there is a better way to exist through the New Cultural Conversation and the ChaRIOT.

The chariot has stood as a symbol of mobility and power since the vehicle was introduced in 2000 B.C. For Black Americans, the chariot symbolizes freedom. We watch Hollywood productions of films about slaves and the one anthem they all seem to sing in a tone heavily laced with a curious blend of faith, hopelessness, and hope is "Swing Low, Sweet Chariot."

The song was first popularized by the Fisk University Fisk Jubilee Singers circa 1871, but its roots lie in the pre-Civil War South. As most of the 60,000 Native Americans struggled to walk the miles on the Trail of Tears, others did not. They rode on horseback and owned the Black people who were forced to walk behind them. One of the Indian's slaves, Wallace Willis, is credited with creating the song, but its exact author remains a subject of debate and myths.

What is not in dispute is that "Sweet Low, Sweet Chariot" was a song of great hope for freedom, for equity, and for a country that would look inside its own heart to see Black people as human beings and not something to be feared or despised or owned.

"Swing Low, Sweet Chariot," was the anthem of the slave who longed to be free, but it was also a song of rage. Rage in the context that we examine it in this book is not about violence. Rage is not always about destroying communities, burning property, or taking to the street even in peaceful protest.[70]

Rage led the mother of Emmett Till to open his casket for the world to see how the disease of racism led two White men to beat her child so severely his mother could only identify him by a ring

---

[70] Jon Little. "Behind the Song: 'Swing Low, Sweet Chariot.'" American Songwriter, December 22, 2019.
https://americansongwriter.com/behind-the-song-swing-low-sweet-chariot/.

inscribed with his father's initials that the boy always wore on one of middle his fingers. Rage is Rosa Parks refusing to give her seat on the bus to a White man. Rage was Dr. Martin Luther King Jr. organizing the history-making 1963 March on Washington for civil rights, and rage is also the overflow crowd of 250,000 people who showed up on the National Mall to hear his prophetic "I Have a Dream," speech. Rage is two young White men, Andrew Goodman and Michael Schwerner, and a young Black man, James Chaney, fighting to register Black Americans to vote only to be abducted and executed in 1964 by Mississippi Klansman, with help from local law enforcement. Rage is a young John Lewis and others risking their lives during the march across the Edmund Pettus Bridge and suffering a violent beating by racist police on "Bloody Sunday" in 1965.[71]

To understand the complex roots of Black rage, we must examine the history of how slave owners shaped false narratives about Black people that created an irrational fear and even hatred among many Whites that continue even today. When Black people were brought from Africa into the United States, their skin tones automatically created a systemic way of viewing them as demonic, troubled, savage people that needed to be tamed. Church history studies and scholars found that when Black people were brought to the United States from the continent of Africa, they were demonized by the theology of Whites, including religious leaders who reinterpreted certain Scriptures by associating the color black with a demonic presence.

Those myths and false narratives erased the humanity of Black people in the eyes of White Americans. They also helped form a set of beliefs, unwritten rules, and practices, and prescriptions for how Blacks should be treated that became part of the social reality of

---

[71] History.com Editors. "March on Washington." History.com. A&E Television Networks, October 29, 2009.
https://www.history.com/topics/black-history/march-on-washington#:~:text=The%20March%20on%20Washington%20was,challenges%20and%20inequalities%20faced%20by.

the Black experience in this country from the time slaves stepped foot on American soil.

## Historical Roots of Rearticulated Rage

Portraying Black people as demonic, inferior, and less than human helped to make it easier to justify harsh treatment like beating, torturing, raping, selling, or killing them.

With such harsh treatment being a norm in the life of a slave, uprisings were not uncommon for Black and oppressed communities of color throughout their history of enslavement. We must explore American history's long and controversial myth about slaves' refusal to express any form of rebellion out of docility and contentment. One of the most harmful and persistent untruths about slaves was that they were docile, and exceedingly loyal to their masters through their "childlike" behavior and simple-mindedness.

Mythology belies the truth: By 1934, historians had identified at least 33 slave revolts in which ten or more enslaved Americans coalesced and challenged the system through careful planning, strategy, and execution. The Servants Plot is believed to be the first slave revolt. The indentured servants were composed of Whites and Blacks. The uprising against the exploitive tobacco industry took place in 1663 in Gloucester County, Virginia, and resulted in four men being hanged. The planters became nervous about future rebellions from indentured servants and began buying more Africans from the Dutch and English slavers. [72]

The next two most notable rebellions took place in 1712 and 1739 in New York City and South Carolina, respectively. Nine white slave owners were killed in New York, while approximately 100 slaves participated in the Stono Rebellion, which was the largest slave uprising in British North America. Two White shop owners were

---

[72] Erin Blakemore. "How Two Centuries of Slave Revolts Shaped American History." History. National Geographic, May 3, 2021.
https://www.nationalgeographic.com/history/article/two-centuries-slave-rebellions-shaped-american-history.

beheaded by slaves. Over the next 100 years of revolts, some Whites were killed by slaves but slave owners killing slaves was most often the case due to slave owners having access to more deadly weaponry such as firearms. The exception was Nat Turner's Rebellion in 1831 involving 70 slaves who set off 30 days of uprising by first bludgeoning to death Turner's master and his family. By the time the slave patrol found Turner and the remaining slaves who had been hiding away for nearly a month, they had killed approximately 60 White people to gain their liberty from a life of bondage.[73]

Then there are the Challenged, the individuals who routinely experience unjust practices and feel they are at the bottom of the sociocultural hierarchy. They know the pain of being penalized, and they feel the constant pressure of having to endure inequities. There has not been a pathway for them to be successful or even be aware of anything that looks like success. If we have any hope of redeeming the soul of America, we must rearticulate rage and address those issues.

We must rearticulate rage so we can rethink how rage should be used. Like injustice and justice, rage fuels the solidarity that exists between the Challengers and the Challenged. The Challengers are individuals who either have the legal legislative or lifestyle influence to bring attention to how unjust practices have, without question, disenfranchised others. Challengers use their platforms to bring attention to wrongdoing and injustice, which is no different than how professional athletes and celebrities are speaking out today.

I believe a deeply intertwined relationship exists between the Challenged and those who can challenge, those who have the courage, the platform, the conviction.

When San Francisco 49ers quarterback Colin Kaepernick began rearticulating his rage by kneeling during the national anthem in 2016 to protest racial injustice, police brutality, and systematic oppression, he drew ire and accusations of being unpatriotic, largely

---

[73] Evan Andrews. "7 Famous Slave Revolts." History.com. A&E Television Networks, January 15, 2013.
https://www.history.com/news/7-famous-slave-revolts.

from White Americans. Even as he explained that his and other players' right to peaceful protest was protected by the Constitution, the president of the United States spewed hateful rhetoric that stoked the flames of race-based anger already deeply embedded in White people who are resistant to any effort to advance any form of equity. Kaepernick was booed and vilified, even as other players joined him in kneeling.

Fourteen months after he was first photographed sitting on the bench during the national anthem, Kaepernick filed a grievance against the NFL for not signing him and keeping him out of the game. He was replaced as quarterback of the 49ers and no other team has signed him. Despite the questionable timing of NFL Commissioner Roger Goodell's half-hearted request for a team to sign Kaepernick, the former quarterback has not played an NFL game since 2017. [74] The timing of Goodell's request came at the height of the 2020 racial injustice protests. After six seasons with the NFL, Kaepernick was driven out of the league by racists and racism for expressing his right to peaceful protest, a right guaranteed to all Americans by the U.S. Constitution. Some say that in losing his contract, he took a hit for the team. I say the team he was fighting for is Black Americans and their civil rights.

Kaepernick took a stand and sacrificed his career for the Challenged, and he is one example of why we should think about the rearticulation of rage, and I can point to many others.

We must rethink how we articulate rage when four years before the NBA's historic walkout during the 2020 playoffs, WNBA athletes wore custom emblazoned with the words, "Change Starts With Us: Justice & Accountability." When the WNBA Minnesota Lynx players turned, the backs of their shirts honored Louisiana native Alton Sterling and Minnesotan Philando Castille, who were tragically

---

[74] Cindy Boren. "A Timeline of Colin Kaepernick's Protests against Police Brutality, Four Years after They Began." The Washington Post. WP Company, August 26, 2020.
https://www.washingtonpost.com/sports/2020/06/01/colin-kaepernick-kneeling-history/.

killed by police on July 5, 2016, and July 6, 2016, respectively.[75] Their shirts included the Dallas police force crest to honor five officers who were killed in a shooting a few weeks before Sterling and Castille were shot to death.

LeBron James, whose passionate activism and vocal advocacy for Black communities are almost as legendary as his moves on the court, is an inspiring force urging other athletes in the NBA and NFL to take a stand. In summer 2020, he launched More Than A Vote, a new organization to protect Black citizens' right to vote amid rising efforts to suppress voting in largely Black districts across the country.[76]

One afternoon during the 2020 summer of racial tension and strife, NBA team Milwaukee Bucks did not show up on the court at the start time for Game 5 of the playoffs game against the Orlando Magic. Instead, they announced they were taking the unprecedented step of boycotting given the August 23 police-involved shooting in which a White officer shot a young unarmed Black man seven times in the back. Jacob Blake Jr. was shot in a city 45 miles from Milwaukee and left paralyzed from the waist down. Doctors told the 29-year-old he will never walk again. Sterling Brown, a Bucks player said of the team's decision, "Despite the overwhelming pleas for change, there have been no actions, so our focus cannot be on basketball."

Recognizing that protest without progress does not advance change or justice, Bucks players talked with Wisconsin Attorney General Josh Kaul and Lt. Gov. Mandela Barnes, while also calling

---

[75] David Zirin. "Athletes Speak out for #Blacklivesmatter; New York Liberty Sets Inspiring Example for All Athletes." portside.org, July 11, 2016. https://portside.org/node/12034/printable/print.

[76] Jack Jack. "Lebron James' More than a Vote Launches New Campaign to Defend Voting Rights." CBS News. CBS Interactive, March 5, 2021. https://www.cbsnews.com/news/lebron-james-more-than-a-vote-voting-rights/.

on the Wisconsin legislature to reconvene and consider bills on policing reform.[77]

Within a matter of minutes of the Bucks' announcement, the entire Wednesday slate of playoff games had been postponed. The WNBA, MLB, and MLS announced they were boycotting as well.

LeBron James, Dwyane Wade, and other Black athletes joined in solidarity with the Bucks and took to social media to let their voices be heard. The boycotts were not just about Jacob Blake Jr. Ahmaud Arbery, Breonna Taylor, and George Floyd and other injustices against Blacks were never far from athletes' minds. Many of the players were using their platforms to be Challengers amplifying the cries of the Challenged for racial justice. Players wore league-approved jerseys with social justice phrases like, "Say Her Name" and "Vote" printed on the back.

### Rearticulation of Rage is Action

Voting rights in the United States, which people like Congressman Lewis sacrificed to gain, are once again under threat, especially in areas that are heavily populated with people of color. The day after the walkout, the Houston Rockets announced that their arena would be used as an early in-person voting center. Within days, the NBA and the NBA Players Association union worked out an agreement to use arenas as polling places for people in communities vulnerable to the coronavirus, which are disproportionately BIPOC communities.

These are living examples of how rage was rearticulated and transformed into action as the Challengers amplify the unheard voices of the Challenged. This is what we have seen in the cases of George Floyd and others who were unjustly treated by law enforcement. People at the base of the power structure in American culture and

---

[77] Isha Thorpe. "Milwaukee Bucks Break Silence about Boycotting Playoff Game." REVOLT, September 7, 2021.
https://www.revolt.tv/2020/8/26/21403526/milwaukee-bucks-boycotting-playoff-game-statement.

society often act on their rage by becoming citizen journalists who use cellphones and technology to show the world what injustice looks like. In the case of Floyd, it was a 17-year-old Black teen who saw something unjust and pulled out her phone and began filming the man's murder. Darnella Frazier uploaded the video of a Black man begging for his life, and people began to become aware of it. The streets filled with protesters calling for justice. Her rage was a sparkplug, a call to action. She is a Challenger.

In some ways, challenging wrongs can build hope, but hope must be actualized, or it can be dashed and then, die. What is needed to push the effort forward is people to take the solidarity of the Challenge and the Challengers and create continuity in a way where people hear the collective voices. What has been missing in most cases where momentum wains and the pendulum gets stuck, and no lasting change is created is that like slaves, we are waiting for a chariot to appear.

No chariot is coming. We are the ChaRIOT. What is at stake is our failure to recognize that and act. It is imperative. We must take the deep pain of the families of victims of police violence—more than 200 Black people across the United States in 2021 alone—merge them with the courage of people who have platforms, political or legal or cultural, and fuse them in a way that helps impact legislation.

As ChaRIOTS, we will bring together people who are non-White and those who are non-Black, and people who are Challenged and Challengers. This is how we see us breaking the ties that bind justice and injustice. This is rage being rearticulated and transformed into actionable, transformative change.

The ChaRIOT

# Chapter 6

## Privileged Identities

## The Juxtaposition of the PatRIOT and the ChaRIOT

On January 6, 2021, like millions of people in America and around the world, I watched a stunning act of domestic terrorism as thousands of self-described "patriots" invaded the U.S. Capitol after violently attacking police officers to force their way inside the building. It was a day that rocked America. Our foreign allies and adversaries watched a mob descend on, break into, and severely vandalize the U.S. Capitol building, sending the vice president of the United States and members of Congress running for their lives. The attackers shook our political system and sought to undermine the peaceful transfer of power between a sitting U.S. president and a president-elect.

I wondered whether the insurrection was an aberration or a signal of a new day in American democracy, one where the president of the United States and his supporters could use deadly force to attempt a coup. What I found interesting is how easily so many people were vulnerable to the specific kind of communication former President Trump used to propagate the formation of certain beliefs and acts that supported his agenda. Americans like to believe that propaganda being used by people at the highest level of government does not exist in our country because it is most often associated with dictators. Nazis strategically used lies and censorship—propaganda— to persuade Germans to subscribe to the Third Reich's ideology and develop an internal belief system supporting the regime. We know how the use of propaganda fulfilled its goal of changing how the German people believed, acted, and adopted behaviors desired by propagandists.

# The New Cultural Conversation

For weeks leading up to the insurrection, Trump had been relentless in denouncing the 2020 presidential election results, floating lies about voter fraud, and claiming the election was "stolen" from him. He also propagated the idea that America has been stolen from White people by people of color, which he knew would instill fear and then action by Whites who believe America becoming a majority-minority country is a threat to their survival.

In the days preceding the January 6 melee, which was the day Mike Pence was to approve the certification of Joseph R. Biden's victory in the 2020 presidential race, we saw an escalation of Trump supporters vowing to avenge the wrong they were told Democrats and far-left groups like Antifa had visited on Trump. At the same time, Trump had managed to paint a picture of Pence as a traitor for his intent to certify the election, an act he was legally bound to fulfill in his role as vice president.

The propaganda being pushed by Trump, years of rising White supremacy, an increase in hate crimes against Black Americans, 2020 racial inequity protests, calls to defund the police, and a pandemic that had upended life in America, all contributed to a climate that created the perfect storm for an insurrection fueled by racism, nationalism, and fear of changing demographics in America.

Eight months before the attempted coup and the conspiracy theories purported by Trump peaked on January 6, the murder of George Floyd prompted the longest, largest, and most racially diverse protest for social justice and civil rights in U.S. history with approximately 15-26 million people participating for several months. Many White people claimed that until they saw a Black man die under the knee of a White policeman, they did not think overt racism or racism still existed in any real form because they do not consider themselves or their family members, friends, neighbors, or co-workers, to be racist. Too often, Whites claim they "did not know." No one ever told them. They did not know what they said was racist. They did not know what they voted for would uphold the values of a racist agenda. They did not know they were allowing a racist work environment to exclude employees of color equal opportunity for advancement. To deny racism exists, to ignore it, or to not be conscious of it, is a privilege in which only White people can participate.

For more than 400 years, overt racism and biases have been part of American life, particularly in the South. Throughout the centuries, thousands of overtly racist events, laws, social institutions, academic institutions, health care systems, living conditions, political power, police brutality, dominant culture viewpoints and habits, and racist acts and crimes have oppressed an entire stratum of American society. Perhaps the greatest of these institutions used to force Black Americans into positions of inferiority and subordination is the legal system. Denial of voting rights. Segregated schools. Laws prohibiting interracial marriage, restrictive covenants that forbade Blacks from living or buying property in certain neighborhoods, and racial separation of public facilities such as retail establishments, busing, and restaurants, are symbolic of the historical dominance of racism in our country.

Since laws supporting these types of overt racism have been struck down and most Americans consider them to be wrong, significant progress has been made. But as a result, many White Americans mistakenly believe overt racism—which is the only form they recognize—no longer exists. Yet, thousands of forms of racism and inequity remain in areas critical to Black people's lives and futures, including education, healthcare, housing, career opportunities, generational wealth, and lack of investment in Black-owned businesses.

For instance, education was meant to be the great equalizer, and it can be, but America's public school system is not just falling apart; it is failing. Even after the unanimous ruling by U.S. Supreme Court justices in the 1954 landmark case *Brown v Board of Education of Topeka* stated that racial segregation of children in public schools was unconstitutional, Black children and children from low-income families continue to experience educational injustice.[78]

---

[78] History.com Editors. "Brown v. Board of Education." History.com. A&E Television Networks, October 27, 2009.

Despite years of court battles, obstacles remain in the path towards equitable education for minority students and students from low-income families. A child's social location should not be a determinant of their station in life but in our country, it does. To whom a child is born should have little to do with what a child can become, or the opportunities extended to them or denied them, but this is the reality for a disproportionate number of BIPOC children and children from low-income families.

When our country experienced a public health crisis in 2020, the obstacles BIPOC and low-income children face grew exponentially. In early 2020, COVID-19 arrived on America's shores, ravaging Black, Latino, and Indigenous communities. At the height of the health crisis, BIPOC people died at a rate nearly three times higher than Whites and were hospitalized at a rate nearly five times higher due to a set of factors that included: serving as essential workers, living in multigenerational households, pre-existing health conditions, health disparities, shortage of COVID-19 testing sites, and a delay seeking treatment due to mistrust of the medical community by Black and Latino people.[79]

America has a centuries-long history of health systems mistreating Black people through diabolical practices such as the Tuskegee experiment, forced sterilization of women, and crude medical experimentations dating back to slavery. Undocumented people in America also hesitate to seek medical help but for reasons that differ from Blacks and include fear of immigration authorities.

Systemic barriers have produced educational inequities for BIPOC children for hundreds of years, but they have fallen further behind due to persistent and now an intensifying effect of the digital divide. About one in five Black children ages 3-18 and families

---

https://www.history.com/topics/black-history/brown-v-board-of-education-of-topeka.

[79] Rashawn Ray. "Why Are Blacks Dying at Higher Rates from Covid-19?" Brookings. Brookings, April 19, 2020. https://www.brookings.edu/blog/fixgov/2020/04/09/why-are-blacks-dying-at-higher-rates-from-covid-19/.

earning less than $40,000 per year have no access to the internet at home.[80] In the United States, 34% of Black adults do not have home broadband,[81] and 30.6% of Black households with one or more children age 17 or younger lack high-speed home internet (over 3.25 million Black children live in these households). For years, the realities of living in homes without technologies or inadequate technologies have meant children standing in long lines at neighborhood libraries to access high-speed internet services just to do their homework or sitting outside a building or home with broadband so they can tap into the internet to complete schoolwork. This is life as families without means know it.

The sudden pivot to online education prompted by pandemic-related school closings across the country created additional stress for students and parents without internet service or computers at home. As school closures grew across the country in response to COVID-19, the nation's most vulnerable students lost ground they may not recover.

If Black children do not close the learning gap caused by the pandemic, they are projected to earn nearly $90,000 less over the course of their lifetimes compared to a $54,000 loss for White students.[82]

---

[80] Emma Dorn, Bryan Hancock, Jimmy Sarakatsannis, and Ellen Viruleg. "Covid-19 and Student Learning in the United States: The Hurt Could Last A Lifetime." McKinsey & Company. McKinsey & Company, November 11, 2021. https://www.mckinsey.com/industries/public-and-social-sector/our-insights/covid-19-and-student-learning-in-the-united-states-the-hurt-could-last-a-lifetime#;

[81] National Center for Education Statistics. (2019). *Figure 4. Percentage of children ages 3 to 18 with no internet access at home, by selected child and family characteristics: 2010 and 2017.* https://nces.ed.gov/programs/coe/indicator_cch.asp

[82] Cortez Phelton Moss. "Black Children Are Underserved and Undermined in School, It's Time to Change That Reality." Southern Education Foundation, October 8, 2020. https://www.southerneducation.org/resources/blog/featured/underserved-undermined/#:~:text=A%20recent%20study%20found%20that,%2454%2C000%20loss%20by%20White%20students.

White students have the technology tools for learning in greater numbers than BIPOC students, and they have other necessities within their reach such as living in food-secure homes, access to tutors, and other supplemental learning tools. At the height of the pandemic, many affluent parents brought privately funded teachers into their homes, creating "pandemic pods" of students receiving instruction for several hours each day. In most cases, pandemic pods developed in disproportionately White communities. This trend is yet another way inequities are perpetuated and one more example of how White privilege contributes to ensuring systemic disparities and race-based injustices persist.

### Privileged by Whiteness

White privilege is a set of inherent societal advantages that White people have over non-white people and they are  sustained through acts carried out in everyday life in what feminist, activist, and scholar Peggy McIntosh calls, "unearned entitlements" and "conferred entitlements."[83]

First, let's establish what White privilege is *not*. No wealth, riches, or educational attainment is required to be bestowed the advantages and benefits that being White in America affords Caucasians. This privilege is not earned through deeds or acts nor is it necessary to be earned. It is not about having wealth, riches, or any of the trappings associated with being elitist. It is not about in what zip code a person resides or his or her socioeconomic status. White privilege is not a law, but rather it is a taken-for-granted assumption, an entitlement that is actualized through a system that advantages one group of people over another as a matter of practice.

---

[83] Peggy McIntosh. "White Privilege: Unpacking The Invisible Knapsack ." *Peace and Freedom Magazine*, July/August 1989. https://psychology.umbc.edu/files/2016/10/White-Privilege_McIntosh1989.pdf

This specific benefit is based on people who have an embedded privilege to be treated better than someone else by members of society even though they may not be better.

In 1989, McIntosh expressed awareness of her inherited White Privilege in an essay titled: *White Privilege: Unpacking the Invisible Knapsack.*

"I was taught to see racism only in individual acts of meanness, not in invisible systems conferring dominance on my group," McIntosh admitted. Throughout the essay, she would go on to list several privileges she felt that she [could] enjoy primarily due to her race. What was so riveting about this piece was that by the end of McIntosh's compilation, it shaped out to be a list of simple everyday tasks. She referenced things like being able to find Band-Aids in her skin tone, being confident that her race would not work against her in the pursuit of legal or medical help, and when asking for the "person in charge," assurance that person would more than likely be a person of her race.[84]

Privilege gave CrossFit CEO Greg Glassman such a high level of comfort in his White skin that in June 2020—while the country was in a moment of social unrest following George Floyd's murder—the executive brazenly stated in a Zoom meeting with gym owners that his company would not mourn Floyd. In that same meeting, Glassman followed up that declaration with a question, "Can you tell me why I should mourn for him? Other than it's the 'white' thing to do?" Emboldened by his own outspokenness, he dug in his heels and went a step further by taking to Twitter to give a dismissive reply to a tweet calling racism and discrimination "critical public health issues." Glassman's tweeted response to that observation: "It's FLOYD-19," a play on the words "COVID-19." Within hours, his tweet had gone viral and the outrage was beyond his ability to contain or control. A few days later, nearly 1,200 gyms had decided to disaffiliate from

---

[84] McIntosh. "White Privilege: Unpacking The Invisible Knapsack ." *Peace and Freedom Magazine*, July/August 1989. https://psychology.umbc.edu/files/2016/10/White-Privilege_McIntosh-1989.pdf

CrossFit, and Reebok announced it was ending a 10-year exclusive deal as title sponsor of the CrossFit Games and the sole licensee of CrossFit apparel and shoes. Other brands followed Reebok's lead. Glassman was left little choice but to announce his resignation from the company he founded. Before he left the company, Glassman released a statement in which he claimed what he said about Floyd was "not racist but a mistake." Like so many Whites who make racist statements or commit racist acts, Glassman immediately claimed to not be a racist and to be ignorant of the privilege that his Whiteness gave him to speak his racist thoughts so freely.[85]

The term "ignorant" is defined by Oxford Languages as "lacking knowledge or awareness in general; uneducated or unsophisticated." For the edification of those White people who choose to ignore or deny they enjoy the benefit of Whiteness, the ChaRIOT allows no pass but instead extends an invitation to abandon that White way of thinking to learn and grow as change agents and influencers.

Some White people have Black friends or acquaintances or co-workers but choose to preserve their White superiority over the Black person's so-called "inferiority." I have also seen some Whites who are aware of the problem of racism but unintentionally preserve their privilege. They may march in the streets alongside BIPOC protesters, but at the same time they are supporting them in the street, they do not see the need to divest themselves of the same type of privilege that allows the people they are supporting to be injured or violently killed by law enforcement officers. In those cases, Whites that choose to be allies are sympathetic, but the irony is that they are unable to extract themselves from the very privilege they are contesting. It is not easy for them to recognize that the same privilege

---

[85] Alyx Gorman and Josh Taylor. "CrossFit CEO Greg Glassman Resigns after Offensive George Floyd and Coronavirus Tweets." The Guardian. Guardian News and Media, June 10, 2020. http://www.theguardian.com/us-news/2020/jun/10/greg-glassman-crossfit-ceo-resigns-george-floyd-protest-coronavirus-tweets-conspiracy-theories.

embedded in their own life is causing, in some ways, the challenges Black people are experiencing.

White people have the *privilege* of choosing to be ignorant of the social realities of life in America for Black people and how their lives can be made easier for them if Whites took the lead as ChaRIOTS. Black people cannot afford ignorance that White privilege exists at every level in our country because it can have severe consequences for them; sometimes, dire consequences. The fact is if a White woman like Amy Cooper calls the police and tells the operator she and her dog are in Central Park being threatened by a Black man or if a White voice of any gender calls the police to report that a Black person looks "suspicious," their narrative—no matter how baseless, ridiculous, or untrue—prevails. *That* is White privilege, and no Black person can afford not to recognize it.

After George Floyd was placed on a gurney and transported to a Minneapolis hospital to his fate, several bystanders that witnessed his murder stayed at the scene as they struggled to process what they had just seen. Among those witnesses was a White woman who said she stuck around because she feared for the lives of the other Black people on the scene. This witness was aware that she had the privilege of knowing she was more likely to be safe in the presence of the police than the Blacks were, and at that moment, chose to use that privilege for the greater good.

More than 400 years after the transatlantic slave trade began, White people are not completely ignorant or uninformed about their privilege but instead *choose* to ignore their own and Whites' racist views, lifestyle, and privilege. When I hear White people claiming to be ignorant of their racism or privilege, it is often more a case of ignoring the proverbial elephant in the room.

A great number of White people may claim they are not aware of White privilege, but it is a concept taught very early in school children's education; in some cases explicitly and in others, implicitly. The curriculum taught in American schools reinforces the value of Whiteness and White privilege. White people have the privilege of seeing their history and heritage represented in the core curriculum throughout their entire academic matriculation. White history is at the heart of the American educational experience.

On the other hand, Black history is largely absent from K-12 education and is offered only as an elective at most higher education institutions. K-12 curricula about Black history and culture are often grossly inaccurate and inadequate. Other races are often depicted as opposing forces that seek to infringe upon the pursuit of life, liberty, and justice by White Americans. Forcing one group to educate themselves on the other while not extending the same requirement to the second group is especially problematic when one considers that education is so fundamental to shaping children's perceptions and beliefs. This can lead to bias and racist views. This lopsided educational system privileges one group over another and attempts to force BIPOC people to culturally assimilate into the world of the dominant culture.

The ChaRIOT creates a climate that forcefully calls for White people to check their privilege at the door. This phrase has come to be controversial, but only among those who possess White privilege. You will commonly hear them ask, "What does that even mean?" Checking your privilege entails one who is privileged to reflect upon their unearned advantage or advantages and how it can affect those with unearned disadvantages. Many Whites feel that because they have encountered hardships, similar to those experienced by people of color, or grew up in similar disadvantaged conditions, that they do not have White privilege. This is not the case. Those individuals must understand that even while in disadvantaged environments, they will always have more opportunities to prevail much faster than their fellow Americans of color because of the hue of their skin.

### The Insurrection of 2021

We witnessed White privilege at its extreme on Jan. 6, 2021, when a violent mob of riotous Donald Trump supporters invaded the Capitol grounds and proceeded to attack the nation's most tangible symbol of democracy. Fueled by a president who, for weeks, had been floating the preposterous and false narrative that Democrats had stolen the election from him *and* his supporters, thousands of White rioters armed with an array of weaponry made history by staging an insurrection against the American government. Trump supporters, White supremacists, Neo-Nazis, and para-military extremists converged as like-minded individuals of the same ilk and melded into one rampaging power that executed a planned attack on democracy.

Trump, the highest authority figure in the United States, had managed to tap into the unfounded fears of those White Americans who felt like they were losing ground and losing their country to people of color, particularly Blacks. Trump had been spewing racialized rhetoric and comments for months leading up to the 2020 election. For example, Trump toured part of Kenosha, Wisconsin after the city erupted in protests following the police shooting of a 29-year-old Black man who was left paralyzed. The president then declared that the Black Lives Matter protest was "domestic terrorism" and then went on to defend Kyle Rittenhouse, the 17-year-old White boy who shot three White Kenosha protesters, killing two of them. [86] In the days leading up to the insurrection, the president strongly intimated that America had been stolen by people of color and his supporters needed to come to Washington and take it back by any means necessary. They had arrived at the Capitol grounds from all over the country and represented all walks of life, from schoolteachers to veterans to blue-collar workers to men and women who held positions in some of the country's top companies.

Some of the insurrectionists were draped in American flags, some were wielding homemade signs with crudely scrawled falsities about election fraud, and others carried "Trump 2020 – Keep America Great" flags. All of them were yelling and snarling at the television cameras about the election being stolen from Trump and their intention to take back their country.

---

[86] Joel Rose. "Americans Increasingly Polarized When It Comes to Racial Justice Protests, Poll Finds." NPR. NPR, September 3, 2020.
https://www.npr.org/2020/09/03/908878610/americans-increasingly-polarized-when-it-comes-to-racial-justice-protests-poll-f.

# The New Cultural Conversation

Those of us who watched the spectacle unfold live on our televisions or streaming devices were stunned. Violence against the U.S. Capitol has happened before but, on that day, the building and grounds were overrun by throngs of people claiming to be exercising their patriotic duty to ensure the peaceful transfer of power—a hallmark of American democracy—would be disrupted. January 6 was the day Vice President Mike Pence was to certify the election results that Joe Biden was to be the 46th president, as required by law, and the people who attacked the citadel of democracy converged to ensure Pence did not have the opportunity to carry out his duty.

Before arriving on Capitol grounds, the rioters were stoked and whipped into a violent frenzy by Trump's early morning speech at the National Mall in which he used inflammatory language like, "We fight like hell. And if you don't fight like hell, you're not going to have a country anymore." Powered by violent imagery painted in Trump's speech, the overwhelmingly White rioters breached Capitol barricades, smashed windows, and scaled the building's balconies as police were overrun and outnumbered. Some carried nooses and, once inside the building, began chanting, "Hang Mike Pence, Hang Mike Pence," which prompted Secret Service agents to hurry the vice president to a secure location and order the Senate floor to be vacated. Lawmakers had moved from the Senate floor and barricaded themselves in various secure rooms.

Members of the right-wing extremist group the Proud Boys stood shoulder to shoulder and yelled obscenities as they formed the "OK" sign that symbolizes White power. They chanted "U-S-A" and told the media they were standing up for *their* country.

Fighting against chemical weapons and explosives, police officers could be heard screaming for help as they were soaked with pepper spray and bear spray, beaten bloody, dragged, crushed, chased, trampled, and spat on by the mob. Black U.S. Capitol police officer Harry Dunn, who became one of the four officers to give televised testimony about that day to Congress, later spoke emotionally about how he was confronted by a mob who called him "nigger" when he tried to hold them back from entering the building.

# The ChaRIOT

One officer, Brian Sicknick, died from two strokes one day after being doused with bear spray. Five people in all died on January 6, and four police officers later took their own lives. At the center of it all was Donald Trump feeding the rioters with words that stoked the flames of hatred and brutality and bloodshed.

On the day of the attack and in the days that followed, I heard people asking the right questions: How does a mob of insurrectionists forcibly enter the building that symbolizes world power and vandalize and trash it without being stopped by police? How do they chase a police officer up several flights of stairs in the Capitol threatening to do him harm? How do they casually stroll into offices of congressional representatives and sit behind their desks and trash their offices? How do they get away with calling out the vice president of the United States so they can lynch him and harm his family? Who gets to break into the Capitol and be free to leave and sleep in their own bed at night? How, people asked, could what we witnessed on Jan. 6, 2021, happen in the United States of America?

I have a simple but complex answer to those questions: White privilege and White supremacy. It is undeniable, undebatable, and unmistakable. The very next day, contrasted against the images of White insurrectionists, were photos of Black and Asian Capitol facilities workers, scrubbing feces from walls, and mopping away urine left by those claiming to love this country.

While some, like President-elect Biden, stated that "America is better than this," I would submit that the fact the Capitol was desecrated at all affirms that America is most definitely not better than this because *this is America.*

If thousands of violent, angry Black people armed with weapons had invaded the Capitol, we would have seen a very different scene—one that would have undoubtedly involved the rioters being hauled off to jail *en masse* at the very least. At the other end of the spectrum and in the more likely scenario, many of the Black insurrectionists would have been shot at the scene by law enforcement officers; some may have lost their lives. Only with the pass White privilege provides could such violent and patently reprehensible and criminal behavior go forward unchecked and unchallenged. It is the fact of the matter in a country that has never faced its racist history. Also, the response of some Republicans to the invasion illustrates this observation.

Instead of condemning the actions of the president and the overwhelmingly White rioters, some Republican congressional members drew comparisons between the insurrection and the Black Lives Matter protests that took place in summer 2020. The parallels some Republicans and others tried to draw between the two are nonexistent and nonsense. In a candid radio interview, Trump supporter Senator Ron Johnson (R-Wisconsin) stated he did not at all feel threatened by the rioters' violence but went on to say he might have been afraid if the participants were Black Lives Matter or Antifa supporters. Senator Johnson also said he knew the insurrectionists would never break the law because they love America and respect law enforcement.[87] His comments were criticized as having racist sentiment, as the idea that armed insurrectionists did not frighten him but people peacefully protesting brutality against Black people is a stark dichotomy.

First, some looting and property damage occurred in a few cities during the early days of the social unrest in summer 2020 but most of the protests and protesters were peaceful. Nothing similar could even remotely be said about the people that invaded the Capitol. Capitol rioters staged an insurrection by every definition of the word. Armed with chemical weapons, hand grenades, guns, and flagpoles, they attacked police and stormed the Capitol grounds and building with impunity.

The building and grounds were severely vandalized and so were the offices of lawmakers, including that of House Speaker Nancy Pelosi (D-California). An angry crowd of mostly men marched

---

[87] Allison Pecorin. "GOP Sen. Ron Johnson Says He Didn't Feel 'Threatened' by Capitol Marchers but May Have If BLM or Antifa Were Involved." ABC News. ABC News Network, March 13, 2021. https://abcnews.go.com/Politics/gop-sen-ron-johnson-feel-threatened-capitol-marchers/story?id=76437425.

through the Capitol's halls ominously shouting for the Speaker to come to them. Bombs, guns, and other weapons were seized as the mob covered the grounds and smashed their way into the building.

Second, Black Lives Matter protesters and the insurrectionists had starkly different missions. The former was demanding racial equity, social justice, and police accountability for a race of people who have been brutalized by rogue law enforcement officers since the slave patrols. The insurrectionists, stirred up by "the big lie" of a stolen presidential election, were at the Capitol to stage a coup, and actions showed their intention to meet their goal by any possible means, including violence against law enforcement officers.

Third, the mob that overran the Capitol building was a curious mix of White supremacists, qanon conspiracists, radicalized Trump supporters, anti-government militias, White nationalists, far-right extremist groups, right-wing populists, and misguided men and women who claimed to be avenging a president who told them the 2020 election results were fraudulent. On the other hand, Black Lives Matter protesters were racially, ethnically, and culturally diverse. They took to the streets for peaceful protest in the spirit of Dr. Martin Luther King Jr.'s marches for freedom, racial equality, and civil rights legislation.

One other foremost difference that cannot be overlooked is how government and law enforcement responded to the two groups. By accurate accounts, Black Lives Matter protesters were largely peaceful but were still met with brute force by law enforcement officers in communities across the country. This over-militarization of the protesters was taken to the extreme in Washington, D.C., on the early evening of June 1, 2020. A plaza filled with Black Lives Matter supporters nonviolently protesting when U.S. Park Police and National Guard troops used tear gas to force them to disburse to clear the way for President Trump to walk from the White House to a nearby Episcopal church where he held a bible upside down in front of television cameras in a flagrant publicity stunt. The scenario was reminiscent of what happens to peaceful assemblies in a police state.

As the number of demonstrations in American cities across the country swelled in the days following the viral video of George

Floyd's killing, outraged people marched in the sweltering heat against systemic racism and a broken law enforcement system tainted by pervasive racist policing. Like the immortal chants that gave momentum and energy to civil rights movement, "No justice, no peace," and "I can't breathe," have become the modern-day rallying cries of the Black Lives Matter movement.

On the other hand, the common theme verbalized by many of the insurrectionists was their claim to be patriots acting in the name of American patriotism. Being a patriot has long evoked a sense of pride in White Americans. Described by Oxford Languages as "a person who loves, supports, and defends his or her country and its interests with devotion," being called a patriot is considered among the highest compliments by many White Americans. For many Americans, being a patriot is synonymous with being White. In 1995, an NBC poll showed that only 2% of Whites view a "prototypical patriot" being Black and a similar poll in 2016 revealed this view to have changed unremarkably.[88]

**Who is the American Patriot?**

Throughout American history, "patriot" has taken on different connotations for different people, some positive and some negative. The NBC poll was taken at the height of the first so-called "Patriot Movement" and the same year as the 1995 Oklahoma City bombing. Since the early 1990s, anti-government sentiment by a growing number of militia groups gave robust energy to the Patriot Movement. By the late 1990s, the movement was waning but, in the days and weeks after the 9/11 attack, a different type of patriotism suddenly appeared as America unified in the wake of the tragedy. This translated into a lucrative "consumer economy" in which brands hurriedly produced merchandise with an American-flag theme, and consumer companies created slogans with "Keep America Strong"

---

[88] Michael Tesler. "Analysis | to Many Americans, Being Patriotic Means Being White." The Washington Post. WP Company, February 14, 2018. https://www.washingtonpost.com/news/monkey-cage/wp/2017/10/13/is-white-resentment-about-the-nfl-protests-about-race-or-patriotism-or-both/.

themes. That display of patriotism gave the country the sense of comfort, unity, and connectedness needed in the difficult days following the tragedy.[89]

During the Trump years, there was a resurgence of White people identifying themselves as patriots, but it meant something very different than it did after the 9/11 attacks; a patriot in the Trump era supported "Trump Values" around White nationalism and alignment with the "Make America Great Again" sentiment.[90]

At the height of the NFL players protesting systemic racism and police brutality by taking a knee during the national anthem, many Whites accused the athletes of not being patriotic and even went so far as to accuse them of hating America. Trump used his bully pulpit to lead the effort to paint the athletes as being unpatriotic. It ignited a social media storm of people sounding off about patriotism versus racism. Let us be clear that patriotism has always been racialized in our country. In 2017, *The Washington Post* ran a story about how being patriotic in America is synonymous with being White. The article also stated that social psychologists' research revealed that Whites who feel a strong sense of being patriots have a long history of being attracted to tangible symbols of patriotism such as the American flag and political party affiliations. Whiteness and patriotism are deeply linked and historically, a high value is placed on being a person who exhibits patriotism.[91]

---

[89] "The World of 'Patriots'." Southern Poverty Law Center, January 1, 1999. https://www.splcenter.org/fighting-hate/intelligence-report/1999/world-patriots.

[90] Jennifer Graham. "Could 'Patriot' Become a 4-Letter Word after the Capitol Riot and National Unrest?" Deseret News. Deseret News, January 13, 2021. https://www.deseret.com/indepth/2021/1/13/22225243/patriot-american-flag-capitol-riot-new-england-patriots-bill-belichick-donald-trump-medal-of-freedom.

[91] Tesler. "Analysis | to Many Americans, Being Patriotic Means Being White." The Washington Post. WP Company, February 14, 2018. https://www.washingtonpost.com/news/monkey-cage/wp/2017/10/13/is-white-resentment-about-the-nfl-protests-about-race-or-patriotism-or-both/.

When the United States declared war against Germany in early 1917 and America's involvement in World War I was in full swing, Black males across the country, volunteered to join the armed forces. Historians say they were motivated by many reasons such as the opportunity to show loyalty to America and help America in a war conflict, but above all, those men wanted to prove their patriotism. They believed it would help White Americans to see them as worthy of equality when they returned home. Though they were considered heroes by their family, friends, and community, Black soldiers were segregated into regimens by race. Very few of them were allowed to serve in combat units but were relegated to menial roles in labor battalions. Those who fought on the front lines of World War I did so with honor and bravery and dedication to serving their country.[92]

Even when an officer training camp for Blacks was created and more than 600 men received their commissions, they were not allowed to command White soldiers. White men refused to salute Black officers and Black officers were denied entry to officers' quarters. Not all but many Black soldiers were forced to go without proper food, clothing, housing, and equipment. Despite these failings, 350,000 Black troops served until World War I ended in 1918.[93]

Whether in combat or labor battalions, Black men served their country with honor but came home to another fight in their own country—the battle for equal treatment and civil rights were still very much part of life as Black Americans. Black soldiers returning to the United States from the war found they were subjected to the same racism and racialized violence they had left behind before the war. Returning Black soldiers from WWI and WWII were no more viewed

---

[92] Jami L. Bryan. "Fighting for Respect: African-American Soldiers in WWI." The Campaign for the National Museum of the United States Army. https://armyhistory.org/fighting-for-respect-african-american-soldiers-in-wwi/.

[93] Alexis Clark. "Returning from War, Returning to Racism." The New York Times. The New York Times, July 30, 2020. https://www.nytimes.com/2020/07/30/magazine/black-soldiers-wwii-racism.html.

as patriots than they were before joining the armed forces and were targeted for ridicule and brutal treatment, especially when in uniform. Black veterans struggled to gain employment, and when hired, were forced to take menial jobs with low wages to take care of themselves and their families. Despite being in foreign countries where they intermingled rather freely with Whites, segregation was still very much a part of life at home in the United States. Black veterans quickly had to face an irrefutable reality: equality was a dream that would not be fulfilled in their lifetime.

Nearly 30 years later, Black veterans returning home from World War II encountered the same racism and violence as returning WWI veterans.

In fact, between 1877 and 1950, Black veterans experienced violence and racial terror at alarming numbers in America, according to the report, "Lynching in America: Targeting Black Veterans."[94] They were brutally victimized by White citizens and police officers, and in some cases, murdered. One notable case in the report was that of a Bardstown, Kentucky mob chasing, stripping, and beating a Black ex-soldier before cutting off his genitals and shooting him to death. These highly- visible atrocities were committed to send the message to Black veterans that in no way did their service earn them equality in America and that fighting for America in a war, no matter how valiantly and honorably, would not earn them patriot status in the eyes of many Whites.[95]

---

[94] Peter C. Baker, Jeffrey Toobin, and Sarah Stillman. "The Tragic, Forgotten History of Black Military Veterans." The New Yorker, November 27, 2016. https://www.newyorker.com/news/news-desk/the-tragic-forgotten-history-of-black-military-veterans.

[95] Clark. "Returning from War, Returning to Racism." The New York Times. The New York Times, July 30, 2020. https://www.nytimes.com/2020/07/30/magazine/black-soldiers-wwii-racism.html.

## The Patriot and the ChaRIOT

It should not be lost on any of us that the patriot and the ChaRIOT share the root word "riot," which in most situations involves people using violence to reject an idea, ideology, law, policy, event, or current state of affairs. The patriot may use violence to communicate, while the ChaRIOT wants to deploy the radical idea of a collective movement of diverse people who recognize that no one is coming to save America from the institutionalized racism that has plagued the country like a deadly disease for centuries. No chariot is coming to save us from us. We have to be that ChaRIOT.

The self-described "patriots" who invaded the Capitol subscribe to the dominant perspective, a norm by which Whites interpret the world as well as nonwhite people through the lens of White culture. People who hold the dominant perspective resist attitudes that are supportive of diversity and environments where diverse people are considered equals. A key assumption of the dominant perspective is that there is a natural superior-inferior place for people in the social structure of society, based on race, ethnicity, and class.

The "patriots" we saw on January 6 do not want change but to maintain a society in which racial inequity and inequality remain embedded in the fabric of our country. These patriots cannot exist in a state of equity. Even at a time when we are bearing witness to more egregious race-based injustices than we have since the civil rights movement, people who subscribe to that way of thinking have a self-interest in maintaining the current stasis to protect their positions on America's socioeconomic hierarchy. People and patriots who subscribe to the dominant perspective believe these injustices and inequities are self-contained, and they are not affected or impacted by them. But they are wrong. If patriots became ChaRIOTS, they would know Dr. King's assertion that injustice to one group of Americans is indeed an injustice visited upon us all.

As a ChaRIOT, I recognize that America's infinite failure to reconcile racism made it possible for January 6 to happen because a climate had developed where hate groups and extremists have multiplied and intensified, including White nationalism, radical-right terrorists, the neo-Nazi movement, and anti-government militias. Failing to remove a White supremacist commander-in-chief who used his position, power, and platform to radicalize his supporters and give new energy to White supremacist culture in the United States, led not only to the Capitol siege but to a rise in crimes against people of color. Three years after Trump's election to president, the Southern Poverty Law Center had identified 900 incidents of harassment motivated by bias against race, ethnicity, or ancestry, a significant increase over the previous few years.

Therefore, to the patriots, America needs you to join the ChaRIOTS in a place of zero degrees belonging where there is no room for titles, privilege, hegemony, power positions, dominant culture, racialized perspectives, prejudice, implicit or overt bias, exclusion, or hatred.

An authentic space must exist that allows different types of persons to make contributions, even when that contribution is presented as a courageous act to flee violence and abuse.

The ChaRIOT will create a place where the privileged use their advantages and power to dismantle systemic racism and create a country where Americans are one and all of the opportunities every system can offer belong to the people no matter the color of their skin.

My vision is for the Patriot Movement to join the ChaRIOT Movement and the rise of a new movement will emerge in which non-dominant culture groups and those people with privileged identities work collaboratively toward equity and justice. The ChaRIOT Movement will be and must be powered by the people who see the urgency of *now* to lead this change. I have concluded that in this *right now* "moment," one needs a cadence of calm but also the courage of confrontation. This *now* "moment" requires a shift led not by the Patriot Movement but by a new movement: The ChaRIOT Movement.

This movement will create a unique space where people freely participate, without legally or socially imposed identity, as they disrupt and dismantle systemic racism, inequality, and inequity. In this space of the zero degrees of belonging for everyone, the ChaRIOT will transport us to a place that lives up to the perpetual personification of America's promise.

# The New Cultural Conversation

## Chapter 7

## Injustice: White Collars, Black Jellybeans, and the

## Crucible of the Cubicle

"Celebrating diversity" is a phrase coined circa the mid-1990s as the number of professionals of color were increasingly being hired and the change winds in corporate offices were ushering in a new day in the employee composition of companies in terms of race, ethnicity, and culture. Managers were pushing forward the idea that diversity should be celebrated and not feared or resented. Businesses with global operations began talking about the competitive edge of a diverse workforce. Diversity training firms were popping up overnight claiming to have the right program to transform White people into color-blind co-workers eager to be part of this new thing called "Celebrating Diversity." Diversity was trending.

But nothing transformative happened. Through my consultancy work, I know of some companies that walk the talk in their stated commitment to be equitable in their hiring and promotions practices, but most organizations have been alternately hot and lukewarm about their commitment to diversity. America is in the middle of a reckoning on race, unlike we have seen since the height of the civil rights movement. CEOs began pledging solidarity with Black people and a renewed focus on diversity in the weeks after George Floyd's murder. In 2020, the corporate social responsibility playbook was reframed as corporate social justice, a focus on social change initiatives or programs that aspire to address societal inequity and injustice. But it remains to be seen if companies will be as conscientious about extending corporate social justice to the extent that the reality Black people experience inside the walls of corporate America every day shifts to become more equitable.

Rosalind "Roz" Brewer made corporate America history three times during her career: She became chief executive officer of Walmart's Sam's Club in 2012, the first Black and female chief operating officer of Starbucks in 2017, and in January 2021, she was named the first Black and first female chief executive officer of Walgreens Boots Alliance. Brewer was listed No. 48 on Forbes 2020 Power Women list. By any measure, she is a trailblazer and the epitome of a corporate success story. The White way of thinking would point to Brewer as evidence that Black professionals are at parity with White professionals relative to hiring and advancement without being leveled down or facing barriers to opportunities for advancement, mentoring, salary, or salary increases.

White people who think that way would have been stunned to hear what she told young Black women during a speech at her alma mater Spelman College in 2018.[96] She said, "When you're a Black woman, you get mistaken a lot. You get mistaken as someone who could have that top job. Sometimes you're mistaken for kitchen help. Sometimes people assume you're in the wrong place, and all I can think in the back of my head is, 'No, *you're* in the wrong place.'"[97]

Brewer went on to tell young women who look like her about the time she was a keynote speaker for a CEO roundtable event, and a White male whom she did not know queried her intensely about what kind of job she held with Sam's Club. He was genuinely perplexed as to how this Black woman managed to get an invitation to an event for the White Boys. Brewer said he was relentless in his curiosity about what kind of job she could have that would earn her a spot in the room with White CEOs, but she kept her identity close to the vest, giving him what she described as a "side-eye." Brewer told the Spelman student that when her bio was read to the attendees, and she rose to

---

[96] Courtney Connley. "Walgreens' New CEO Roz Brewer on Bias in the C-Suite: 'When You're a Black Woman, You Get Mistaken a Lot'." CNBC. CNBC, January 27, 2021. https://www.cnbc.com/2021/01/27/walgreens-new-ceo-roz-brewer-on-dealing-with-bias-in-the-c-suite.html.

[97] Connley. "Walgreens' New CEO Roz Brewer on Bias in the C-Suite: 'When You're a Black Woman, You Get Mistaken a Lot'." CNBC. CNBC, January 27, 2021. https://www.cnbc.com/2021/01/27/walgreens-new-ceo-roz-brewer-on-dealing-with-bias-in-the-c-suite.html.

take her place at the podium, she enjoyed the look on the fellow CEO's face. Brewer described it as a "good day."[98]

## Corporate America: The New Blackface?

Since the United States has never fully reckoned with its legacy of racism, corporate America reflects the country's lingering struggle with race. Having conversations about race is even more tenuous in the specialized environment of the corporate workplace. Exploring race in an open, honest, and frank way is largely still not possible because White people do not want the discomfort of the conversation, and many Black people do not know how to make them comfortable enough to engage in dialogue. And is it their responsibility to do so?

2020 was a flashpoint exposing deep racial and cultural division that prompted yet another national conversation about race and inequity that has already begun to wane. Every time a racial incident captures the national spotlight, it sets off a flurry of commentators, news organizations, and opinion leaders going on the record about the need for honest dialogue on race. What these "conversations" reveal is how vast the differences are between Black and White people in their views on race, racism, discrimination, injustice, and barriers to Black progress. They also differ on just what is needed to stop denials about the existence of systemic racism and how to arrive at all people achieving social, political, and economic equity.

Since Black professionals began entering the corporate workforce, many described their efforts for advancement as beating their heads against the glass walls. Through my work, I know firsthand that many Blacks are repeatedly passed over or denied opportunities for advancement despite being highly competent and meeting or

---

[98] Jennifer Warnick. "Glass Ceiling Slayer Roz Brewer Dubs Grads 'Generation Quest.'" Starbucks Stories and News, May 21, 2018. https://stories.starbucks.com/stories/2018/glass-ceiling-slayer-roz-brewer-dubs-grads/.

exceeding the qualifications. These experiences are not anomalies but rather a matter of being a norm in the workplace. Corporate America's attempts to increase diversity are failing.

As a corporate diversity consultant, I advise employers that they must examine the culture and practices inside their companies for change to happen. Black professionals have been in corporations for decades, but they are still not moving into senior-level positions or executive positions in any remarkable numbers. Blacks make up 13 percent of the U.S. population, but only 8 percent of employees in professional roles are Black. They also only hold 3.2 percent of all executive or senior leadership roles. Even more dismal, less than 1 percent of all *Fortune* 500 CEO positions are held by a Black person, according to Coqual (formerly the Center for Talent Innovation).[99]

Companies have been willing to risk losing talented employees and are losing diverse talent in significant numbers because once inside those walls, Black professionals face daunting barriers to advancement due to the dominant perspective being such a major part of the corporate culture.

Though fewer Black college graduates are opting to go to work for a company, many still see it as the best route to ensuring a steady stream of revenue and benefits. They may enter corporate America with hopes of advancing and building intergenerational wealth for themselves and their family but too often they find that the diversity, equity, and inclusion promises organizations state on their websites and in recruiting materials do not translate into the realities of the day-to-day experience for Black professionals. All too apparent to them and expectations to minimize their differences, blend in and assimilate, and accommodate the views of those holding the dominant perspective.

Many bump up against glass ceiling as well as glass walls and are left feeling like they were hired to fill a quota rather than for the knowledge, skills, abilities, and experience they bring with them.

---

[99] "Diversity, Equity & Inclusion: Formerly Center for Talent Innovation." Coqual, November 16, 2021. https://coqual.org/.

Hiring Black people who have invested in themselves through higher education and experience simply to fill a diversity goal and provide a type of window dressing for their HR numbers reminds us of another ugly chapter in our country: blackface.

The origins of blackface date back to the days of slavery in America. Blackface was a form of racist American entertainment used to amuse Whites by depicting Black people as lazy, dumb, and overall inferior. Groups of White entertainers painted their skin hues of brown and sometimes, black, and mockingly performed the Black experience in America. They claimed to represent Black people and their behavior. These shows came to be known as Blackface Minstrels, and they gained a largesse of fans and followers.

Described by Black abolitionist and writer Frederick Douglass as "...the filthy scum of white society, who have stolen from us a complexion denied them by nature, in which to make money, and pander to the corrupt taste of their white fellow citizens," blackface minstrel groups toured and made money from the cultural mockery of a race of people.[100] The practice was so common that Blackface photos would often appear in school yearbooks, was performed at school plays, and welcomed in some churches. It served as Whites' "education" on Black people and Black culture.

Blackface did not lose its prominent place in American culture until the civil rights movement of the 1950s and 1960s took hold.[101]

Today, blackface is considered an egregious act of racism, and several prominent people who participated in the acts such as former Virginia Governor Ralph Shearer Northam (D-Virginia) have been shamed, criticized, and forced to apologize. Amid calls for his resignation in January 2019, Northam was forced to admit he appeared

---

[100] Fredrick Douglas. "The Hutchinson Family.—Hunkerism." Douglass on minstrelsy. The North Star, September 27, 1848. http://utc.iath.virginia.edu/minstrel/miar03bt.html.

[101] Alexis Clark. "How the History of Blackface Is Rooted in Racism." History.com. A&E Television Networks, February 13, 2019. https://www.history.com/news/blackface-history-racism-origins.

in a racist photo in 1984. He stood with two young men: one was dressed in a Ku Klux Klan robe and the other was in blackface.[102]

At the same time Northam was facing his public crisis, the luxury brand Gucci was forced to remove a sweater from store shelves after complaints about its resemblance to blackface went nationwide. Other people and brands have been scrutinized for appearing to pay homage to the racist symbol.

Corporate America practices a form of blackface today when companies hire well-qualified, and in some cases, over credentialed Black professionals to satisfy diversity goals but then does little to ensure they are afforded opportunities for advancement and pay increases. The new blackface is more about the numbers—window dressing—than a substantive solution that results in notable increases in advancement, let alone senior management positions or C-suite opportunities. In many cases, people of color are not hired to come into an organization and effect change; the agency of the new blackface seeks to assimilate Blacks into the existing culture, preferably as seamlessly as possible. It is very common for vocal persons of color to be chastised when they seek to educate their White peers about the realities they face as Black employees, including having to work harder to advance their careers and facing barriers promotions and salary increases.

This is undoubtedly a form of denial and an attempt to invalidate what their Black co-workers are experiencing inside the same workplace. These micro invalidations from White people can be statements about being colorblind or having a Black friend or Black neighbor. A Black colleague told me that a White manager approached

---

[102] Laura Vozzella, Jim Morrison, and Gregory S. Schneider. "Gov. Ralph Northam Admits He Was in 1984 Yearbook Photo Showing Figures in Blackface, KKK Hood." The Washington Post. WP Company, February 4, 2019. https://www.washingtonpost.com/local/virginia-politics/va-gov-northams-medical-school-yearbook-page-shows-men-in-blackface-kkk-robe/2019/02/01/517a43ee-265f-11e9-90cd-dedb0c92dc17_story.html.

her in the employee cafeteria calling her "Stephanie," another Black woman who looked nothing at all like her.

Microaggressions and microinsults include Whites asking Black co-workers questions about what they eat, whether they can touch their hair, where they live, and even the origins of ethnic-sounding first names. Harvard Business School published an article on a study that revealed companies are more than twice as likely to invite applicants for interviews if they remove or scrub references in their resumes that identify them as being a minority, including ethnic-sounding first names. The article also mentioned bias against Blacks based on information in their resumes as a major factor in those applicants not being interviewed or hired. Twenty-five percent of Black candidates in the study received invitations for interviews when they left details off résumés that identify them as Black, while only 10 percent received an invitation when they left ethnic details in the documents. It should not come as a surprise that companies identifying as "valuing diversity" were found to be just as guilty of these discrimination practices as those that do not claim to be pro-diversity, equity, and inclusion organizations.[103]

All of these acts of racism and bias add up to one thing: Resistance.

## Inside the Walls, Met with Resistance

In my experience working with corporations, I find that not having conversations about race, ethnicity, and culture allows the systems of privilege that White people benefit from to remain untouched. Not talking about race allows Whites to stay in their comfort zone and affords them the privilege of claiming unawareness of the realities their Black colleagues face at work and in their daily lives.

---

[103] Daniel Bortz. "Can Blind Hiring Improve Workplace Diversity?" SHRM. SHRM, August 16, 2019. https://www.shrm.org/hr-today/news/hr-magazine/0418/pages/can-blind-hiring-improve-workplace-diversity.aspx.

# The ChaRIOT

When we follow the ChaRIOT way, Blacks and Whites will engage in a new cultural conversation that breaks the mold of traditional dialogue in which one group of people deny racism and racial bias exists, and the other group expends time and energy trying to address the denial, only to feel devalued and unheard. In the end, these conversations solve nothing and leave both feeling frustrated, angry, and demeaned.

What is it like to be Black in corporate America? Ask Black professionals and most will tell you that it is an everyday battle against resistance.

During the 1970s, following the civil rights movement, companies that had a nearly 100% White employee body began to become more diverse as Blacks and women entered the corporate workforce. Organizations responded by trying to minimize the impact of these new and different, and often unwelcome people through three strategies: denying Black professionals and "others" a place in those spaces, marginalization, or forcing them into homogenization.

I interact with Black professionals who say they experience resistance from White managers and colleagues that may or may not be intentional and who may or may not be conscious of their implicit bias. No matter how it shows up, racism and bias can create an environment where Black people overwhelmingly feel they are being held down in a position for which they are over credentialed. They might experience being excluded from key job-related information that Whites are privy to, as well as exclusion from projects that could lead to greater responsibility, visibility, or power.

Denying Black people a place of legitimacy in the organization also includes viewing them through racial stereotypes. For example, a Black professional woman (I will call her Michelle) who worked at a global company talked about how Whites stared uncomfortably when three or more Black people stood together and engaged in conversation. She said they assumed the Black employees were goofing off or "plotting something," even when their discussions were about work. Supervisors would walk by frequently to show a presence. Michelle said the Whites acted like Black employees were planning a "slave uprising." She said mostly, Blacks felt like they could not be themselves at the office or engage with each other or had to act inauthentically to be accepted and ensure White people did not feel threatened. Her story is not unique or new.

One practice that people who hold the dominant perspective use is to ensure marginalization. Whether denial or marginalization is unintentional or an act of unconscious bias, the outcome is the same: Black people in corporate America, regardless of their educational attainment and professional credentials, are stuck disproportionately in low to mid-level positions often throughout their entire careers—an all too familiar circumstance some Black professionals call the "Black Jellybean Syndrome."

The term was first heard publicly during an ugly chapter in American corporate history when Texaco was sued by Black employees after they were consistently denied opportunities for advancement, high-impact projects, and overseas assignments. Racism inside corporate giants is not new, and it did not begin in the mid-1990s, although that is when one of the most highly visible cases of workplace racial discrimination was brought forward, proving that Black people did not always have to be powerless to stop it. In 1994, long-suffering Black employees at Texaco were handed a smoking gun when a recording of a meeting of high-ranking White executives was leaked. In that meeting at the company's pristine New York headquarters, the company treasurer told a flippant joke that "all of the black jellybeans seem to be glued to the bottom of the bag," a reference to how Blacks were relegated to lower ranks at the company with little opportunity for advancement. He followed up that statement by complaining that all those "niggers" were causing difficulties for Texaco leadership.[104]

Employee after employee came forward with similar stories of a pattern in which less-qualified White employees moved up the ladder—in some cases, becoming their bosses—while Black employees' movement was stationary, held back by White people

---

[104] Charles R. Conrad and Marshall Scott Poole. Essay. In *Strategic Organizational Communication in a Global Economy*, 7th ed., 458. Chichester, West Sussex: Wiley-Blackwell, 2012.

whose dominant perspective on Black people is as much of part of them as an arm or a leg. Ingrained, implicit, undeniable.

After the recording was leaked and the lawsuit was filed, civil rights groups threatened a national boycott of Texaco as well as stock divestiture, but the company continued to deny wrongdoing or that a culture of racism existed at the company. In November 1996, more than two years after the lawsuit was filed, Texaco settled for $176 million, which was then a historic amount of money for a racial discrimination lawsuit.[105]

Peter Bijur, who was CEO at the time, pledged that Texaco would become "a model of workplace opportunity for all men and women." Three years later, minorities accounted for 44% of new hires and 22% of promotions, but White men still accounted for nearly 80% of company executives.

Exactly four years later, one of America's corporate crown jewels, the Coca-Cola Company, settled a racial discrimination lawsuit by its employees for a record $192.5 million. Black salaried employees had come forward with incredible stories of being subjected to racist remarks by supervisors, routinely being passed over for promotions and pay increases, and receiving subpar evaluations, despite meeting or exceeding performance objectives. Their stories were ignored by management and Human Resources.

Those four employees refused to be ignored and filed a lawsuit in 1999. When 45 current and former employees participated in a "bus ride for justice" from the Coca-Cola Company's Atlanta headquarters to Washington, D.C., and the Rev. Jesse Jackson called for a boycott of Coke products, the lawsuit picked up momentum.[106]

---

[105] Thomas S. Mulligan and Chris Kraul. "Texaco Settles Race Bias Suit for $176 Million." Los Angeles Times. Los Angeles Times, November 16, 1996. https://www.latimes.com/archives/la-xpm-1996-11-16-mn-65290-story.html.

[106] Greg Winter. "Coca-Cola Settles Racial Bias Case." The New York Times. The New York Times, November 17, 2000. https://www.nytimes.com/2000/11/17/business/coca-cola-settles-racialbias-case.html.

The company admitted no wrongdoing but agreed to pay $113 million to thousands of Black employees and spend $43.5 million to adjust salaries in November 2000.[107] The company also agreed to create a fund for programs to monitor its employment practices and organize a watchdog group to review the company's diversity efforts and order changes in its employment policies and practices. At the time of the settlement, one plaintiff stated how unfortunate it was that Black people were still fighting racial discrimination on the job, which at the time of the case, was more than 35 years after the Civil Rights Act of 1964 was signed into law.

Those costly and high-profile cases should have given corporate America a clue to get their houses in order and that these cases were not anomalies but represented a systemic problem around race and the workplace. But nothing significant changed for Black people, even after those huge settlements, and 20 years later, it still has not.

In the wake of the social unrest following the killing of George Floyd, C-suite leaders issued a flurry of well-crafted public statements claiming to not know racism still existed to the extent that it does, which if not hard to believe, is certainly one of the privileges of being a White American.

Many CEOs publicly expressed anguish at the image of a Black man being killed by a White cop while he futilely begged for mercy. Apple, Estée Lauder, Facebook, Nike, Ben & Jerry's, Twitter, Target, General Motors, Amazon, and the NFL were among the brands expressing outrage and pledging monies and commitment to achieving racial equity in America. Morgan Stanley Chairman and CEO James Gorman added Diversity as a fifth core value for the company and promoted two Black female executives: Carol Greene-Vincent, Head of Global Internal Audit, to Morgan Stanley's Operating Committee and Susan Reid, Global Head of Diversity and Inclusion, to Morgan

---

[107] Sarah Schafer. "Coke to Pay $193 Million in Bias Suit." The Washington Post. WP Company, November 17, 2000. https://www.washingtonpost.com/archive/politics/2000/11/17/coke-to-pay-193-million-in-bias-suit/6a43c0c7-dcde-4d8c-a95f-3fe57c508c85/.

Stanley's Management Committee. Gorman, like so many others in the C-suite, also pledged to ensure Black employees are extended more opportunities to advance in the company. Businesses have also pledged a historic $50 billion to fight racial injustice and advance racial equity.[108]

For the first time, some businesses like banks closed early on Juneteenth 2020. Juneteenth, the oldest national commemoration of the ending of slavery in America, is celebrated in the Black community on June 19th every year but has never been widely observed by Whites. Many White people have never even heard of the holiday, but in this racial equity moment in America, White companies seemed to be stepping up. But it took the death of a Black man, a public lynching, to get us here. What does that say about America?

Resistance often comes in the form of marginalization to positions of a lower level than one is qualified to hold or the Black Jellybean Syndrome. According to the National Black MBA Association, most of its 21,000 members hold lower-ranked positions in companies, and despite professional programs the organization offers to increase the pipeline of Black executives, they have been unsuccessful in moving the needle in any substantial way.

Lower to midlevel positions offer little power to employees or visibility, and these two things are critical to upward mobility and achieving career goals. This can partly be attributed to how Black professionals are recruited and placed in roles for which they are over credentialed or those offering few opportunities for advancement, such as staff positions with limited or no oversight of other employees.

Corporations require employees to have experience and a track record in mission-impact functions where they can prove their work affects the bottom line. Like the Black Jellybean Syndrome,

---

[108] Jena McGregor and Tracy Jan. "Big Business Pledged Nearly $50 Billion for Racial Justice after George Floyd's Death. Where Did the Money Go?" The Washington Post. WP Company, August 23, 2021. https://www.washingtonpost.com/business/interactive/2021/george-floyd corporate-america-racial-justice/.

staff positions offer little access to or face time with senior leaders, which means few or no opportunities to build relationships with key decision-makers. And that translates into few opportunities for Blacks to demonstrate their managerial skills. I see Black professionals who are mid-career or even late-career and still have not moved up even after many years of service and superior annual evaluations. Black professionals are not reaching the C-suite or senior levels due to a lack of hard work, qualifications, or motivation.

Most of those people, despite doing all the right things, will likely never shatter the glass ceiling because they cannot break out of the glass walls that surround them, creating a barrier to upward mobility that is impenetrable.

I am often asked how institutional racism and marginalization can still exist in companies when collectively, they are spending billions of dollars per year on diversity programs, even before 2020's social unrest.

First, one of the most daunting challenges Black people face is that diversity, equity, and inclusion programs are often a misleading representation of reality, as evidenced by how much corporations spend on diversity initiatives. I have done the research and was interested to find that collectively corporations spend $8 billion on these programs annually, which incidentally do not result in more companies being able to retain top Black talent and do not result in Black professionals advancing in the company.[109] Instead, retention of top Black talent is a problem for corporations and has been since human resources departments began indexing employees by race and gender. Regardless of race, few professionals polled by Coqual more than two years ago felt their employers' DEI efforts were effective. Even Whites felt these programs were ineffectual.

This is not Black people's problem to solve; it is a longstanding issue to which Whites in corporate America are

---

[109] Pamela Newkirk. "The Diversity Business Is Booming, but What Are the Results?" Time.
Time, October 10, 2019.https://time.com/5696943/diversity-business/.

responsible for creating solutions that change outcomes. How can Blacks be expected to provide solutions in spaces where Whites do not recognize, believe, or even care that racial issues exist?

Second, many DEI executives are just as frustrated by the lack of real commitment to change as the people experiencing racism. My firsthand experience working as a consultant to Fortune 500 companies shows me how often business leaders speak about supporting diversity, but internally these programs do not effect change in any meaningful way. Opportunities for Black professionals to move up the ladder to senior executive and C-suite positions are far and few between, and to be real about it, benefit White females more than the groups DEI was created to help.

*Forbes* recently published an article about how White women are now the "face of diversity" and where that leaves Black women. The article explored how Goldman Sachs announced the company would only approve an IPO if a woman held a board seat and how some Black women felt it was yet another backdoor for White women to benefit from diversity programs. They had good reason for concern. According to the article, between 2016 and 2018 there was a total of 230 new board seats within Fortune 500 firms. Black women only obtained 32 compared to 124 gained by White women. It was an open secret that despite all the noise about the unfair advantage Affirmative Action laws gave to Black people, those who benefited most from them were White women.[110]

Black women with advanced degrees, even those from top business schools, face even more barriers to advancement than Black men. I found an intriguing statistic in my research that supports this observation. Harvard Business School, arguably the leading graduate business school program in the country, published a study that only 13 percent of Black female Harvard MBAs over the past 40 years have reached the senior-most executive ranks compared with 40 percent of

---

[110] Maryann Reid. "What Happens When White Women Become the Face of Diversity." Forbes. Forbes Magazine, February 21, 2020. https://www.forbes.com/sites/maryannreid/2020/02/18/what-happens-when-white-women-become-the-face-of-diversity/?sh=5e62cb8b287d.

non-Black Harvard MBA graduates who reach those top ranks of leadership.[111]

The analysis examined the career paths of Harvard Business School's Black female alumnae and found that 532 Black women graduated from the program between 1977 and 2015. Of that number, only 67% of them or 12.6 percent reached chair, CEO, or other C-level executive status, while 19% of Black male Harvard graduates attained similar positions.[112] Both statistics are dismal but Black men fared better than Black women.

The third reason why we are still dealing with institutional racism within companies is that while there is the expression of support for DEI, no substantive commitment to the execution of it really exists. On the one hand, the fact that corporations are investing in DEI appears to signal the human consciousness around it has awakened, but on the other hand, the effort cannot remain at the stage of awakening. Corporate leaders must be committed to walking the walk instead of just talking the talk for large-scale progress to come to fruition and for Black people to have a real shot at advancement.

Finally, Black people experience the duality of the "invisibility factor" inside organizations and both feed the marginalization beast. One side of invisibility involves companies lumping Black people in with "people of color" when the approaches needed to work progressively toward closing disparities in the workplace for them are significantly different than those needed to support Asian-Americans, Latin Americans, White females, and

---

[111] Jena McGregor. "Even among Harvard MBAs, Few Black Women Ever Reach Corporate America's Top Rungs." The Washington Post. WP Company, February 20, 2018. https://www.washingtonpost.com/news/on-leadership/wp/2018/02/20/even-among-harvard-mbas-few-black-women-ever-reach-corporate-americas-top-rungs/.

[112] McGregor. "Even among Harvard MBAs, Few Black Women Ever Reach Corporate America's Top Rungs." The Washington Post. WP Company, February 20, 2018. https://www.washingtonpost.com/news/on-leadership/wp/2018/02/20/even-among-harvard-mbas-few-black-women-ever-reach-corporate-americas-top-rungs/.

people that identify with the Greater Middle Eastern culture or the LGBTQIA+ community. Whereas these groups encounter workplace bias as well, programs targeted to Black people need to be developed to address their unique history in America, which began with four centuries of enslavement.

The other side of the invisibility factor is Whites choosing to close their eyes to how racism is embedded in every aspect of a Black person's life in America, including Blacks who are well-educated and earn good salaries; in other words, people they work alongside every day. They choose not to see it at their workplaces and refuse to see their own biases and how they contribute to racist culture. Black professionals are screaming, "See me," while many of their White colleagues overlook or ignore Blacks' talents or the barriers standing in the way of them moving up when they have earned it.

Treating someone as though they are invisible means not acknowledging what is important to them, refusing to be an accomplice or choosing not to support Blacks from a place of authenticity. Something as simple as not avoiding cultural conversations or difficult conversations about race helps to remove the invisibility factor and put a stop to the psychological distancing that occurs along racial lines.

If I were to add a third element of the invisibility factor, it would be the lack of Black representation at senior levels, particularly the C-suite. Going back to Rosalind Brewer's experience at the roundtable for chief executives, part of the reason why that White male executive was so surprised that a Black woman would be a CEO undoubtedly can be attributed to his implicit bias and dominant perspective, but it is just as likely he reacted as he did with good reason: The *Fortune 500 List* was established in 1955, and there have only been 19 Black CEOs in the publication's 67-year history.[113] Brewer's new CEO position is certainly noteworthy, but of the 40 women running a Fortune 500 company, she and Thasundra Brown

---

[113] Phil Wahba. "Only 19: The Lack of Black CEOS in the History of the Fortune 500." Fortune. Fortune, February 26, 2021. https://fortune.com/longform/fortune-500-black-ceos-business-history/.

Duckett are the only two Black women. I can point to an even more profound indication of the dire state of Black professionals in corporate America. The total number of Black *Fortune* 500 CEOs is just four: Brewer, Duckett, Marvin Ellison at Lowe's Home Improvement, and René Jones at M&T.[114]

Years of institutional racism, bias, and down-leveling means that the pipeline of Black executives being groomed for the C-suite is barren of candidates due to decades of Blacks being excluded from executive track programs. Black people who did reach senior management describe how they felt increasingly isolated as they moved up the ladder and saw fewer and fewer people who look like them.

Through the lens of the dominant perspective, the four Black CEOs are "others," which is why Brewer describes her experiences with some Whites as interacting with people who cannot imagine her as a chief executive officer. Others—people of color, women, members of the LGBTQIA+ community, people of a certain socioeconomic or sociocultural class—work in U.S. corporations that are disproportionately White, even today. Most middle-class and upper-class White people have few meaningful experiences interacting with Black people and often feel awkward or uncomfortable when conversations move beyond surface subjects or safe subjects like work, weather, or weekend plans.

In my work in the faith sector and as a consultant, Black people share their experiences with me of entering the American corporate workforce and feeling the need to assimilate by minimizing their cultural differences and accommodating the cultural norms of the dominant group, which is White people. What this means is checking your cultural authenticity at the door every morning and making sure

---

[114] David Gura. "You Can Still Count the Number of Black CEOS on One Hand." NPR. NPR, May 27, 2021.
https://www.npr.org/2021/05/27/1000814249/a-year-after-floyds-death-you-can-still-count-the-number-of-black-ceos-on-one-ha.

White people feel comfortable. This unspoken message from Whites to Blacks is "act like us."

It is a dual role Black Americans must play, the weight of "double consciousness," a term W.E.B. DuBois first introduced in his 1897 published work, *The Soul of Black Folks.* In it, he proposed the idea that Black people are forced to look at themselves through the eyes of an oppressive and racist White society. Moreover, DuBois proposed that double consciousness meant Blacks must measure themselves and their worth through the lens of a country of colonizers that viewed them with contempt and pity. He also warned of the inner turmoil double consciousness creates in Black men, women, and children.[115]

Double consciousness has survived multiple generations of Whites and Blacks in America since the idea was first introduced by DuBois more than 120 years ago. Black professionals may not describe what they experience in their workplaces using DuBois term, but they certainly can identify with the concept. They know how it feels to be viewed or assessed through the lens of White managers and co-workers who are racially biased.[116]

BIPOC professionals must come to grips with what happens on a day-to-day basis in societal America and corporate America, and how they must take care not to call too much attention to their otherness through actions like verbal and nonverbal communication. Neutralizing otherness is an important strategy in navigating one's way through organizational settings when you are a person of color. This is a particular necessity when you are a Black person. Black people are made to feel like it is their responsibility to minimize the unique aspects of their culture to help White people feel comfortable,

---

[115] W. E. Burghardt Du Bois. "Strivings of the Negro People." The Atlantic. Atlantic Media Company, June 24, 2020. https://www.theatlantic.com/magazine/archive/1897/08/strivings-of-the-negro-people/305446/.

[116] Vincent Wimbush. *Theorizing Scriptures: New Critical Orientations to a Cultural Phenomenon (Signifying on Scriptures)* (New Brunswick, New Jersey, London: Rutgers Press, 2008), s.v., "Jim Todd."

including speech patterns, language, and expression. How Blacks must accommodate some Whites who feel uncomfortable with cultural communications is also another form of duality symbolic of the Black experience in corporate America. The practice used most often is what young Black people like my sons refer to as "code switching."

Code switching is a strategy Black people use to fight negative interracial stereotypes in settings where there are Whites and in interactions with White people. Code switching can take many forms that include modifying, speech, speaking patterns, mannerisms, behavior, and nonverbal communication. One of the most common ways Blacks do this is to switch the code between how they talk at home (using African-American Vernacular English) and how they talk at work (using standard English).[117]

Code switching does not mean Black people act or speak in ways unlike an educated person but some have become subsumed by the dominant culture's way of talking and belonging because they seem to accomplish more or go further in their careers. They are seemingly able to achieve more at a faster pace. They can scale more quickly. I see some Black persons acclimate more to the White way of thinking or behaving because it seems to expedite or even escalate what they are aiming to achieve or where they are trying to go.

When Black people assimilate into a corporate culture, it requires them to behave in a way that cancels out stereotypes about Black people no matter how ridiculous the misbeliefs Whites are holding.

For example, a stereotype about Black people is that they are highly emotional and are quick to anger or violence. So, a Black person who has every right to express anger without being disrespectful or rude or violent must manage how he or she appears

---

[117] Courtney L. McCluney, Kathrina Robotham, Serenity Lee, Myles Durkee, and Richard Smith. "The Costs of Code-Switching." Harvard Business Review, November 15, 2019. https://hbr.org/2019/11/the-costs-of-codeswitching.

and remain emotionless or overly poker-faced no matter what is happening around them or to them. Black people describe feeling an enormous weight to represent not only themselves but their entire race, as Whites tend to lump all Black people together and judge them as a group rather than as individuals.

## Corporate America's Link to the
## Persistent Black-White Wealth Gap

Corporate America directly or indirectly reinforces a variety of racial inequities, from environmental injustice to housing but the greatest of these is the Black-White wealth gap.

I first learned about the energy of money when I was a young man working in a boutique corporate hotel. When I was 18, I became a desk clerk to offset the cost of college. By the time I was 21 or 22, I had earned the trust of the owner, who made me the general manager of all his hotels—even though he had two able-bodied sons. Both sons worked for the hotel. One was quite a bit older than me and one was slightly older than me.

When the owner promoted me to general manager instead of his younger son, which shocked me, I'll never forget the reason why he gave me. Mr. Hussey said, "I bet you want to know why I chose you over Jason." I said, "Well, yeah, I actually do." He said, "Well, it's really simple. Yes, Jason is my son, but I trust *you* with my money."

I was not only surprised that he chose me for the role instead of his son; it was something I would have never expected because George Hussey and I could not have been more different. He was an older White man raised in the middle of the civil rights era, and I was just coming into my own identity as a young man—a young Black man.

Mr. Hussey not only gave me that opportunity but made sure I was equipped to do well. He had his accountants and CPAs teach me how to read the financial statements and balance sheets. They taught me how to find employees who were trying to steal money from the counter or use other means to embezzle from the business.

Eventually, I learned the process, and even now, I can look at a balance sheet and quickly determine if something is wrong and how to address it.

When I began to work with the church, I was able to provide the ministry with my skill set, as there was so much relevant experience that I was bringing from that corporate space to help drive how the church managed its monies or resources or programs. I was able to do more than I had ever imagined was possible. I was able to achieve and maintain in ways that I could not have gotten without George Hussey being a part of it.

My experience taught me something powerful about money: the economic aspects of race have many more touchpoints than the cultural and communal aspects of the race. Managing the hotel's business taught me about the rules of wealth and finance and income and that race determines how people see you or allow you to be in certain spaces.

The economic aspects of race have implications for nearly every part of one's life. Money or the lack of it determines where we live, how we live, and in many cases, how long we live. A person's financial status is linked to a string of inequities and injustices—health, educational, environmental, social, housing—among many others.

The inability to build wealth can have multigenerational impacts in areas such as how/where we can buy a home, send our children to college, financial planning, retirement, and what we can leave behind for our children and grandchildren.

I have a friend who is a culturalist and futurist who often says that a child's zip code should not determine his or her opportunities or educational attainment and nor should a zip code determine a person's lifespan. But they do. Studies have shown people who live in a middle-class or above community have a life expectancy of as much as 15 years more than those who live in impoverished communities where there is disinvestment, food deserts, liquor stores, and where there is little access to health care. The Urban Institute released research findings showing that the relationship between income and the quality of a person's life as well as longevity are connected step-by-step at every level of the economic ladder, regardless of race.[118]

Black Americans have low levels of homeownership, which is key to building wealth for most Americans. Lack of access to affordable housing keeps Blacks from building intergenerational wealth, as less than half of black households are homeowners, compared to nearly three-quarters of Whites.

Some experts point out that one of the roots of wealth inequity is housing discrimination. In the 1950s, millions of White families pursued home ownership as the path to giving their children a better shot at the American dream. Blacks were excluded from participating in that boom time in the country's economy through egregious acts of discrimination. Mortgage denial was a matter of policy and practice by the government.

The federal government was complicit in the exclusion by determining which areas of a city or town were eligible for government mortgage loans. If an area was disproportionately Black, the people who lived there did so without necessities such as adequate sewer systems and utilities and inferior housing. These areas were also "red lined" on a physical map as being considered a poor financial risk, and therefore, ineligible for government-back loans. Whites who were afforded the benefit of homeownership were able to pass wealth down to family members over generations but Black families who were denied home loans could not build wealth. More than 60 years since the home buying boom, Blacks are still experiencing the ramifications of systemic exclusion from home ownership by discrimination practices of mortgage lenders, banking institutions, and our federal government.

---

[118] Steven H. Woolf, Laudan Y. Aron, Lisa Dubay, Sarah M Simon, Emily Zimmerman, and Kim Luk. "How Are Income and Wealth Linked to Health and Longevity?" Urban Institute, May 4, 2020. https://www.urban.org/research/publication/how-are-income-and-wealth-linked-health-and-longevity.

This also means Blacks tend to live in neighborhoods with a higher incidence of injustice around education and access to health care.

It is a given that Black professionals are unlikely to live in a community where there is disinvestment but on average they are paid less and promoted less than their White colleagues. In this way, corporate America contributes to the Black-White wealth gap and economic inequity. During the height of the 2020 protests, *Fortune* magazine issued a call for Black professionals working in corporate America to share their stories of experiencing systemic racism in the workplace.[119] One story stood out to me. A middle-aged Black man, who felt he had no choice but to resign after learning he was being paid less than half of what his White colleagues earned, confronted HR and his manager about it, but they lied by denying what he uncovered was true. The fact is that his story is not uncommon; Black people's salaries are often disproportionately lower than their White counterparts, even when they have more education and experience. Why does this matter? Besides the obvious, that this sort of thing is wrong and unfair, wage discrepancies directly feed the Black-White wealth gap.

There is a difference between a wage or a salary and the ability to build wealth. Wealth provides a safety net to households during crises like the 2008 recession and more recently, the COVID-19 economic downturns. Wealth has several advantages when compared to wages. A person can be working every day and still be unable to build wealth due to the wages being paid to him or her being so low.

Wealth inequity for Black people has its roots in slavery. A few slaves received small payments, but most slave labor was unpaid. For example, the only enslaved person at Thomas Jefferson's plantation who received something approximating a wage was George Granger, Sr. Working as an overseer at the slave owner's Monticello

---

[119] Karen Yuan. "Working While Black: Stories from Black Corporate America." Fortune. Fortune, June 16, 2020. https://fortune.com/longform/working-while-black-in-corporate-america-racism-microaggressions-stories.

plantation, Granger earned $65 a year, which was approximately half the wage of a white overseer.[120]

The Black-White wealth gap today is a continuation of a centuries-long history of wealth inequity. Over the past 30 years, the median wealth of White households has consistently outpaced Black households. In 2019, the average Black household held approximately $142,330 in wealth, as reported by The Center for American Progress. The Black-White wealth gap comes into perspective when we compare that figure to the average White household in 2019, holding an average of about $980,549 in wealth.[121]

But recall, we are *seeing* more and more Blacks with managerial positions. What I want to get across is that the deficit of the Black-White wealth gap exists within the culture of corporate America; a culture born from systemic racism. The dominant perspective has long sought to curb the ability of Blacks to gain wealth in critical mass to overcome cultural oppression. This perspective, which is part of life in corporate America for Black people, strangely co-exists in the same space as the collective $8 billion companies spend annually on diversity programs. The Black-White wealth gap, created in part by corporate America, does not present an opportunity to access better healthcare coverage. The Black-White wealth gap does not offer the opportunity for Black children from low-income families to further their education, thus, making them less competitive in the global workforce and the least likely to build intergenerational wealth. This disparity has been part of Black Americans' lived experience since 1619.

But the starkest difference in income exists between Black working women and White males, experiencing both a racial wealth

[120] "Slavery at Monticello FAQs- Work." Monticello. Accessed December 6, 2021. https://www.monticello.org/slavery/slaveryfaqs/work/#:~:text=The%20vast%20majority%20of%20labor,he%20served%20as%20Monticell.

[121] Christian E. Weller and Lily Roberts. "Eliminating the Black-White Wealth Gap Is a Generational Challenge." Center for American Progress, March 19, 2021. https://americanprogress.org/article/eliminating-black-white-wealth-gap-generational-challenge/.

gap and a gender wealth gap. Black women are paid 39% less than white men and 21% less than white women. Black women on average are at the bottom of the pay scale even when adjusted for educational attainment and management positions at corporations. By middle age, single White men hold more than 8.1 times more wealth than single Black women.[122]

Without the opportunity to generate wealth at parity with Whites, Black people will continue to lag Whites in wealth building, despite educational attainment and professional accomplishments. And the new blackface will continue to serve as window dressing in building companies' diversity, equity, and inclusion credibility but without any real substantive change, unless or until attitudes of decision-makers change and corporate DEI policies are enforced. When I read stories like the one a Black female diversity and inclusion executive told to *Fortune,* it does not bode confidence that the large-scale change needed to address this lingering disparity will come to fruition. The executive talked to *Fortune* about being privy to derogatory comments about hiring diverse talent from of all people, her DEI colleagues.

What stood out most to me about her story is the dichotomy: a team of people who are being paid to ensure the company meets its diversity goals are actively working to shut people of color out of the hiring process.

## The ChaRIOT in Corporate America

At the time of the lawsuit against the Coca-Cola Company, a brand that is a symbol of Americana, the news that such a company would engage in racist practices was shocking. However, the reality is that Black people experience these kinds of incidents inside the

---

[122] Emily Moss, Kriston McIntosh, Wendy Edelberg, and Kristen E. Broady. "The Black-White Wealth Gap Left Black Households More Vulnerable." Brookings. Brookings, December 8, 2020. https://www.brookings.edu/blog/up-front/2020/12/08/the-black-white-wealth-gap-left-black-households-more-vulnerable/.

hallowed halls of corporate America every day, pierced by the doubled-edged sword of the dominant perspective and hegemony.

In the nineteenth and twentieth centuries, most societies were built on a platform of segregation along racial, gender, and class lines, which created a cultural hierarchy in which those at the top were considered to be "thinkers" and those at the bottom were thought to be best suited for "doing." This dominant perspective carried over to corporate America and even today exists in how Black people are viewed and how preconceived assumptions form the structure of an organization that supports the White way of thinking: It is normal and natural for White people to be the thinkers and Black people to be doers supervised by them.

The difference is that Texaco and Coke were held accountable by a group of people—Challengers—who realized that no one was coming to their rescue, and they would have to lead the change against the people denying them a legitimate place in the organization.

This is where the ChaRIOT lives, a place where the Challengers come together to transform situations and circumstances that oppress marginalized people. ChaRIOTS in corporate America will work in solidarity to disrupt power structures and move the workplace community to and through systemic change to build an equity-oriented culture that offers more than a space in which all people are included but also feel they belong. Those members of the company with privileged identities will join people with oppressed identities at the zero degrees for self-examination and to have those critical New Cultural Conversations in a safe space where an evocative and transformational exchange of thoughts move forward. It will be the ChaRIOT's mission to do the hard work of dismantling the structural barriers to equity inside their workplaces.

## Chapter 8

## And Still They Rise

I recently had the honor of delivering the eulogy at the funeral service for a 96-year-old woman who was a long-time member of my church. It was a bittersweet moment. I have always considered eulogies an opportunity to bring words of comfort to the living and capture the essence of the deceased, and the life lived and what the person gave to others while they were here. Jessie Tann was not famous or rich or a celebrity but her impact on the people she touched and the places she passed through was powerful and enduring. Ms. Tann was certainly instrumental in helping me and supporting my spiritual journey as pastor of Mount Pisgah Baptist Church. I will continue to draw on the insight, wisdom, and experiences she imparted to me, which were gleaned from living nearly 100 years as a Black person in America, a Black woman, and a lady of abiding faith.

Jessie Tann undoubtedly played a very important role in my life, but the first Black woman who taught me and nurtured me was my mother. Along with my dad, she had and has a great influence on shaping me from childhood to adulthood. I would not be the man I am today without her and my dad's love and guidance. Over the years my life has been enriched and enhanced by many Black women who play different but very critical roles in helping shape the man I am. I would be remiss if I did not express my deep appreciation of the strength, intellect, and love that my wife and life partner, Dwan, shows our children and me every day. Her partnership in marriage and raising our children, and her unprecedented role as Lady Dwan are irreplaceable.

All my life, I have had the opportunity to be surrounded by Black women who contributed to my success as a human being and faith leader. They are my colleagues, mentors, mentees, critics, and friends. I am surrounded by beautiful, strong, intelligent Black women. My appreciation of them is deepened by the unique

156

challenges and triumphs that come with life as a Black woman in America.

## Black Womanhood and Triple Consciousness

*"It is a peculiar sensation, this double-consciousness, this sense of always looking at one's self through the eyes of others, of measuring one's soul by the tape of a world that looks on in amused contempt and pity. One feels his two-ness,—an American, a Negro; two souls, two thoughts, two unreconciled strivings; two warring ideals in one dark body, whose dogged strength alone keeps it from being torn asunder."[123]*

This is an excerpt from the article, "Strivings of the Negro People," by W.E.B. Du Bois published in the August 1897 issue of *The Atlantic Monthly* more than 120 years ago, but his argument is as valid today as it was at the time he wrote it. When you factor in Black Womanhood, you go from double-consciousness to tripling the weight of being Black in America.

Black women's lives have been marked by trauma since they were forcibly taken from their homeland to become part of the transatlantic slave trade. The complexity of navigating American life in Black Womanhood is something we as Black men can observe but never experience. We bear witness to what our wives, daughters, mothers, grandmothers, granddaughters, sisters, and aunts face living at the intersection of racism, sexism, objectification, and stereotypes—a reality the Black woman in America has experienced ever since she arrived at the 1619 Landing in Point Comfort, Virginia, brutalized and broken.

During her keynote address at a gathering of Black professional women many years ago, former *Essence* magazine editor-

---

[123] Du Bois. "Strivings of the Negro People." The Atlantic. Atlantic Media Company, August 1897. https://www.theatlantic.com/magazine/archive/1897/08/strivings-of-the-negro-people/305446/.

in-chief Susan Taylor, said, "People always want to say Black women are angry. Black women are *not* angry; Black women are tired." Taylor was referring to the wariness from the discrimination, microaggressions, and sexual trauma Black women have historically faced for being both Black and female. To mitigate these daily assaults, Black women have to 'put on armor' any time they go outside the sanctity of their homes; they often must wear the armor inside their homes. That armor is the protective shell called the "Strong Black Woman," and it is armor that supposedly can protect her against any racial or gender-based discrimination that comes her way. The truth is Black women are subjected to daily assaults on their humanness, worthiness, and their very existence.

The American system has never acknowledged the need for justice for the Black woman. Rather it has kicked her down, time and time again. Despite living in a country that for more than 400 years has excluded them, tried to erase them, and treated them like they are less valuable than their White counterparts, Black women are still among the most resilient group of people in the world.

And as in legendary poet Maya Angelou's poem "And Still I Rise," Black women still rise every day.

Black women are unstoppable and unflappable, and they are still standing. They have beaten the odds and accomplished in all aspects of life, career, business, and education. They are the bedrock of the Black church and the Black family. The pulse of America is in the chest of Black women.

They are also a wonder in dichotomies. They over-index as single mothers *and* as college students; they enroll in college at rates higher than other races, including White males. Two Black women broke barriers on Jan. 20, 2009, and Jan. 20, 2021, respectively: Michelle Obama became America's first Black First Lady, and Kamala Harris was sworn in as the first Black vice president of the United States. Black women hold the most degrees. At the same time, Black women are indexed as having the highest unemployment rate in the country. Of the 5.4 million women that became jobless during the first year of the COVID-19 pandemic, women of color bore the brunt of job losses, particularly since they are disproportionately employed in service industry jobs, which were hit hardest. So many women were affected, there is now talk of the need for gender-equity recovery strategies.

In addition to the myriad of dichotomies from their lived experiences, Black women are also subjected to the identity of being the Strong Black Woman, a schema that is part reality, part stereotype, and part unfair expectation.

Let me be clear: I *know* Black women are strong. They are fierce. Even amid traumas and brokenness, they soar, often seeming to defy gravity. We may ask, *'How could she possibly rise with that much weight on her shoulders; the weight of viewing herself through the triple consciousness of being Black, American, and a woman.'* She is undaunted by her path but rather because of it, and has been bold about lifting her mind, body, and voice to meet what life presents her.

I bear witness to it every day as I watch my wife, mother, and daughter navigate life as Black women, and as I have been blessed to be surrounded by Black women who are my colleagues, friends, critics, and cheerleaders. But the cultural trope of the Strong Black Woman being almost superhuman is a heavy lift and can be harmful to women's psyche and health.

Since slavery, the Black woman has had to summon extraordinary strength, beginning with the fight for agency over her own body on the vessel during Middle Passage. She had to accept the heart-shattering reality that the babies she carried in her womb did not belong to her and would never truly belong to her because, at any time, her master could and often did take her children and sell them to another plantation. In those cases, enslaved mothers usually never saw their children again; they had no idea where there were, how they were, what they had become, or even if they were still alive. No other race of mothers has been tasked to overcome such physiological and psychological warfare, yet society is often hasty to criticize and label the Black woman as angry.

While they have had to be strong amid the adversity and trauma life deals them, the societal expectations for Black women to be dominant, self-sacrificing, and emotionally neutral are problematic and burdensome. On the one hand, the armor of the Strong Black

Woman is a shield against the onslaught of racial and gender discrimination Black women experience in their careers and daily lives. On the other hand, it is oppressive when White people, as well as Black people, expect the Strong Black Woman to always show up, no matter what life has handed to her. How many times have we seen the stoic Black mother with a shattered heart on our evening news talking about getting justice or declaring forgiveness after a police officer or a perpetrator has murdered her child? I am reminded of the woman who told Dylann Roof she had already forgiven him just days after he gunned down her elderly mother and eight other Black people during the mass shooting at Emanuel African Methodist Episcopal Church in June 2015. She was lauded by the mainstream media as a marvel for being so strong and merciful. It is likely that few of those people really considered just how torn up that woman was inside and what emotional cost she paid for her "strength."

To add to Black women's pain, society, family, and the Black church often expect them to suppress their vulnerability, fear, or other emotions because they are Strong Black Women who must also keep hidden their alter ego "The Angry Black Woman," which is another cultural trope created and perpetrated by a White-privilege agenda, adding to the weight she carries. Debunking the dominant perspective that essentializes anger in Black women as one of their natural characteristics is exhausting and can cause real harm, particularly in organizational settings, resulting in fewer promotions and lower performance evaluations.

To fully appreciate the state of the Black woman in our country today, we must know and understand her journey.

## Black Womanhood and History

The story of the Black woman in America is a complex medley of experiences unlike those of women of other races. Black women have a unique history and place in America. No other race of women was forcibly removed from their native country in masses, placed on cramped, dirty cargo ships where there was little food, water, or protection from being violated, and then sold into slavery once they reached the shores of the United States. Human trafficking spans thousands of years and crosses multiple cultures, but the ugliest and most egregious chapter in history could be the 400 years that the transatlantic slave trade fed the U.S. economy through the sale of millions of Black people as well as through the labor they were forced to provide with no compensation.

The Middle Passage, the months-long trip from West Central Africa, could also be considered "the journey of erasure" for the captured African men, women, and children, as they headed to a world where they would become part of a legalized system of labor through chattel slavery. African captives had their clothing seized and discarded by their captors. Often, their physical appearance was altered through rituals such as head shaving, symbolizing the social death discussed in Chapter 5. The journey erased all the elements that define one's individual and collective identity: dignity, hope, dreams, security, home, health, family, and sense of belonging. The voyage erased the history and culture of the more than 12 million African people who were captured and taken away from their native homeland and enslaved. In many cases, the forced removal of Africans wiped out the history of entire families, villages, and communities in their homeland.

After they arrived at "the New World," the stripping of their identity, agency, and hope continued with intensity. This was the beginning of the erasure of self, and with it, human dignity. Taking away a human being's given name and personal and cultural identity is equivalent to erasing the very essence of what makes a person who they are. In the epic miniseries "Roots," one of the most remarkable scenes is the unmerciful beating of 17-year-old Kunta Kinte with a whip as he continuously refused to say the new name his master had given him when he arrived in America, which was Toby.[124] His flesh torn open by the strikes of the leather bullwhip, Kinte was determined to hang on to the last shred of the identity that had been ripped from him the moment he was captured from his native land by answering

---

[124] *Roots*. United States: Wolper Productions, 1977.

"Kunta Kinte," every time his master asked him his new name. With his body ravaged from the beating and his will shattered into pieces, Kinte finally surrendered and uttered "Toby," letting go of one of the last vestiges of his identity and the hope that he could one day return to the life he had known for 17 years. Forcing captives to repudiate their personal and cultural identities began the process of how newly enslaved Africans were systemically treated as less than human and indoctrinated into the culture of chattel slavery.

Enslaved men, women, and children were subjected to dehumanizing treatment, along with daily exposure to harsh working conditions, malnourishment, disease, and chronic fatigue. But Black women had a unique experience because from the moment a Black woman was stolen away from her homeland and forced onto a ship and sold into enslavement, she had no agency over her body. Black women and girls had to endure the added trauma of rape and sexual assault by their captors and slave masters. These atrocities began as early as the Middle Passage when women were often kept on the deck rather than the belly of the ship where as many as 700 men were chained to one another using bilboes, which are leg irons with shackles used mostly for prisoners. While on the deck, women were often raped and beaten in full view of children and other women. As stated earlier, many sexual assault victims arrived at the New World pregnant with the babies of their rapists. Their voices muted, they suffered silently, with no autonomy over their own bodies.

That type of abuse did not stop once they were sold to a plantation owner but continued, even when the woman had a partner or husband. Slaves were not legally allowed to marry, but many couples entered marital unions and considered themselves to be spouses, making it even more painful when Black men had no choice but to look the other way when a White slave master or plantation employee violated his wife. The men were no less anguished when their daughter or sister or mother or aunt or female friend was sexually abused. If she became pregnant, the woman was forced to bear and raise the violator's child. Since they were considered to be members of the Black race, having a White father did not protect biracial children from experiencing the same treatment as children with Black fathers. And Black mothers and fathers had to endure the pain of being powerless to stop whatever harm or fate befell their children, including being sold, beaten, or sexually violated.

Though the validity of this part of the slave experience is debated among some historians, there are books and articles with tales about enslaved women using their sexual capital to win favors or better their living conditions, particularly those who had lighter skin tones. True or not, many more enslaved women risked their safety and, in some cases, their lives to resist sexual abuse and reproductive oppression.

## The Challengers

I first introduced the concept of the Challenged and the Challengers in the chapter on Rage. There will always be people who are challenged by circumstances and there must be. Without the Challenged, there can be no Challengers. Without people willing to be fearless, unabashed Challengers, we stand little chance of creating ChaRIOTS. I became a Challenger in ninth grade when I accepted a teacher's daunting request to give the "I Have a Dream" speech to an audience composed of the high school community. I continued to be a Challenger throughout high school, college, and my career. All those experiences prepared me to be the ChaRIOT I am today.

As presented in Chapter 5, enslaved people staged uprisings, insurrections, and other forms of resistance during the transatlantic voyage and while on plantations. Black men such as Gabriel, François-Dominique Toussaint Louverture, and Nat Turner are etched in the history books as famous leaders of revolts. They were Challengers. The names of women—particularly Black women—and the pivotal roles they played in resistance efforts have been ignored or minimized to a large degree by the history books and even by the Black community. However, enslaved Black women and free Black women were among our greatest Challengers fighting for the Challenged. They were active participants and leaders in resistance efforts that included organizing work stoppages and providing food and shelter to slaves who had escaped from their masters. It was women who organized and oversaw the clandestine meetings that fueled the

Black church. They also served as critical pipelines for information that kept the fight for freedom alive. By some historical accounts, women planned and coordinated many of the slave uprisings during the Middle Passage. Nearly all large-scale social changes were built and executed on the backs of Black women, dating back to slavery.

Black women have been at the forefront of momentous movements for centuries. The Honorable Amy Ashwood Garvey and Mittie Maude Lena Gordon gave way to the public outcries of White American hypocrisy from Black women around the world. Ida B. Wells, a journalist who was known for exposing lynching, was a prominent female pioneer in the Women's Suffrage Movement. She began as an investigative journalist who wrote about and exposed lynching practices in the South. After gaining the attention of the masses through the lens of her papers, Wells established The Alpha Suffrage Club in Chicago, as ratification of the Nineteenth Amendment in 1920 gave Black women the vote in name only due to violence, legal restrictions, and literacy tests that set the bar for passing them impossibly high. When Wells founded The Alpha Suffrage Club in 1913, its main mission was to register Black women and men to vote.[125]

Though largely in the shadows and relegated to no real public leadership role in the civil rights movement, we must not minimize Black women's works and impact on social transformation. The problem was not absence from doing the work but the erasure of Black women and their contributions to causes on the front lines of leading social justice and social change movements. The most prolific and best known of those warriors is by far "The Moses of her People," Harriet Tubman. Known for her expertise in engineering daring escape routes, she risked her life to help free hundreds of slaves from bondage as "conductor" of the Underground Railroad.

---

[125] Ashawnta Jackson. "The Alpha Suffrage Club and Black Women's Fight for the Vote." JStor Daily, September 8, 2020. https://daily.jstor.org/the-alpha-suffrage-club-and-black-womens-fight-for-the-vote/.

Born Araminta "Minty" Ross in Dorcester County, Maryland in 1820, Tubman suffered a life-changing injury in her early teens when an overseer was chastising a runaway slave inside a dry goods store.[126]

There are conflicting accounts of exactly what happened. By one account, Tubman was attempting to render aid to a slave that was escaping when the overseer struck her deliberately. By another, the overseer threw a two-pound weight at the man but hit Tubman instead, striking a crushing blow to her skull. Either way, Tubman experienced severe headaches, trance-like blackouts, and narcolepsy until death, but it was the beginning of her lifetime of groundbreaking courage in leading social justice.

Tubman was such an effective railroad conductor that slave owners placed a $40,000 price on her head to be paid to anyone who captured or killed her. Undaunted and focused on her calling, Tubman risked her life by returning to the south 19 times to lead 300 slaves to the north and freedom. Her architecture of escape routes and knowledge of towns and territories made her valuable to Union commanders. A scout, spy, guerrilla soldier, and nurse for the Union Army during the Civil War, Tubman is considered the first Black woman to serve in the military. She was also a respected guerrilla operative.

Tubman was a lifelong social justice and social change activist. After the Civil War, she raised funds to aid freedmen and played an active role in the Women's Suffrage Movement, the White female-led fight to win the right to vote for women in the United States. She was an astute business owner as well as an author, wife, mother, and caregiver to her aging parents.

The movement to free the enslaved had many sheroes. Another social change leader who left an indelible imprint on history was Isabella Baumfree, who changed her name to Sojourner Truth

---

[126] Debra Michals. "Harriet Tubman Biography." National Women's History Museum, 2015. https://www.womenshistory.org/education-resources/biographies/harriet-tubman.

after she felt a call from God to begin a ministry. Born in southern New York in 1797, Truth was bought and sold many times before the Dumont family owned her. Baumfree bore a child that Dumont fathered through raping her but had four more children with her husband before walking away from her master one year before slavery in New York was abolished in 1827.[127]

Baumfree came into her own as an activist when she learned her son Peter had been sold illegally. She took the man to court and won her son's freedom. This case was one of the first in which a black woman challenged a White man in a court and won.

In 1843, when she received what she described as a calling from God, Isabella Baumfree changed her name to Sojourner Truth and began living in her purpose as an abolitionist, social change leader, and preacher of salvation on topics such as women's rights. During the Civil War, Truth worked for the Union Army, recruiting Black troops. Truth left her footprint on history by riding Washington, D.C. streetcars to force desegregation in public transportation, a bold act in the long and arduous journey toward civil rights.

The fact is that Harriet Tubman, Sojourner Truth, and countless other Black female foot soldiers who risked their lives for change were the foremothers to future generations of women who served as the backbone of the civil rights movement and the Black Lives Matter movement. The civil rights movement—the planning, strategy, architecture, organizing, writing, execution, and fighting—could not and would not have happened without Black women. Many of them fought valiantly, were beaten, jailed, and killed alongside Black men. Others help to build the infrastructure of the movement, plan protests, marches, and lunch counter sit-ins. They gave guidance

---

[127] Debra Michals. "Sojourner Truth." History.com. A&E Television Networks, October 29, 2015. https://www.history.com/topics/black-history/sojourner-truth.

and mentoring to young people who sought to participate in the movement. More than 50 years after the Civil Rights Act of 1964 and the Voting Rights Act of 1965 were signed into law by President Lyndon B. Johnson, the names of so many Black women who played vital roles in making these turning points possible remain missing from the annals of history. Even when they were alive, the women of the civil rights movement were largely in the shadows, their voices largely unheard due to the period in which men's voices dominated.

It is irrefutable that Dr. Martin Luther King Jr's iconic 1963 speech, "I Have a Dream," at the historic March on Washington for Jobs and Freedom remains unparalleled and immortal. Congressman John Lewis also gave a pivotal speech on freedom at that event, which drew 250,000 people. One female leader of the movement, Daisy Bates, gave a brief pledge right before a tribute to Black women civil rights workers but was not part of the group of men who gave major speeches at the main event: no woman was part of that elite group.[128] On that day, August 28, 1963, America did not hear the Black woman's dreams, hopes, fears, frustrations, or anguish because only men were given a platform to speak at any length.

Black women of the movement were not deterred by the marginalization they were subjected to intentionally or unintentionally. Nor were they passive participants in their low visibility but actively shaped strategy and created opportunities to shine a light on their contributions to the cause. Ella Baker had pivotal roles in the NAACP as well as the Student Nonviolent Coordinating Committee, co-founded by Diane Nash. Fierce, fearless, and outspoken, Baker blazed a trail for other Black women activists to take a role in the civil rights movement, while Nash helped to organize marches and lunch counter protests. Dorothy Height, an unfettered

---

[128] Alia E. Dastagir. "The Unsung Heroes of the Civil Rights Movement Are Black Women You've Never Heard Of." USA Today. Gannett Satellite Information Network, February 18, 2018.
https://www.usatoday.com/story/news/nation/2018/02/16/unsung-heroes-civil-rights-movement-black-women-youve-never-heard/905157001/.

leader who earned a place on the speaker's platform alongside Dr. King, organized an all-female march that ran concurrently with the men's march as part of the March on Washington events. Another warrior, Fannie Lou Hammer was a leader of the 1964 Freedom Summer Campaign, which drew 700 young people, most of them White college students, to Mississippi for a voter registration drive. This campaign was instrumental in helping lead to the Voting Rights Act of 1965.

The work of the women in the civil rights movement influenced women to work in other social protests such as the Vietnam War, anti-feminism, and discrimination against gay and lesbian people. Black women such as Black Lives Matter founders Alicia Garza, Patrisse Cullors, and Opal Tometi, and Me Too Movement founder Tarana Burke, stand on the shoulders of the mothers of social change movements. Those mothers of the movement and contemporary Black female movement leaders stand on the broad shoulders of women like Harriet Tubman, a seminal social change warrior who literally risked her life fighting for justice more than 100 years before.

Black women have been sexual violence survivors since the transatlantic slave trade began in 1619, and enslaved women were abused by White men as a means of domination and oppression. Before Burke founded the nation's largest survivor justice movement for women who have been sexually violated, little has been written about the role of Black women in the history of sexual assault. However, some survivors who were among the first to speak openly about it were a group of Black women that testified before Congress one year after the Civil War ended. A race riot broke out in Memphis May 1-2, 1866, after a rumor circulated that a group of Black soldiers had killed several White policemen when they tried to arrest a Black soldier. After two days of violent unrest during The Memphis

Massacre, 46 Black people and two White men had been killed and several Black women were raped by White terrorists.[129]

Some of the survivors courageously gave testimony to a congressional committee that investigated the riots, demonstrating that Black women have been leaders in efforts against sexual violence since Reconstruction.[130]

Therefore, it is imperative that Black people be aware of their history and culture: this knowledge opens the door to the future. Knowing this piece of history about Black women's historic leadership against sexual assault, we should not be surprised that Burke founded a movement against sexual harassment and assault that reverberated around the country and the world. Her first job after college brought her in touch with many young Black women who told her their stories of experiences with sexual assault, sexual violence, and abuse. It was like looking in a mirror: Burke was also a survivor of sexual abuse. Her activism, advocacy, and passion for justice fueled her determination to do something transformative. Burke created a way for young women of color to share their stories. When she coined the phrase "me too" in 2006, she wanted it to be a way to empower Black women, help them foster empathy for one another, and shed the silence about their experience with rape and sexual abuse.[131]

In fall 2017, the phrase went viral, igniting an international conversation and setting off a movement to disrupt rape culture, sexual harassment, and victim shaming. Though it became a storytelling platform largely for White women, #MeToo was founded by a Black woman. From the workplace to the streets, men were put on notice

---

[129] Mackenzie Lanum. "Memphis Riot, 1866." Black Past, November 20, 2011. https://www.blackpast.org/african-american-history/memphis-riot-1866/.

[130] Gillian Greensite. "History of the Rape Crisis Movement." VALOR, November 1, 2009. https://www.valor.us/2009/11/01/history-of-the-rape-crisis-movement/.

[131] Tarana J. Burke. "Me Too Movement." Me Too, October 15, 2017. https://metoomvmt.org/.

and the tens of millions #Me Too tweets helped carry the message. Soon, a global cultural shift emerged in how people see and treat sexual abuse survivors and the men that assault them, and it began with a visionary Black woman's fierce commitment to social justice.

Before #Me Too became a global movement, three powerful but otherwise conventional Black women saw a grave injustice that reminded Black people that they were still in the civil rights struggle. When George Zimmerman was acquitted for the murder of Trayvon Martin on July 13, 2013, Cullors, Garza, and Tometi knew they had to do something momentous to unify people in a collective cry for justice. Their response to the Trayvon Martin case was visual and visceral and would tell the world that Black people are human beings whose lives have value. The same day the verdict was handed down by an all-female jury composed of five Whites and one biracial woman, Cullors, Garza, and Tometi posted #blacklivesmatter. What began as a hashtag grew into a movement-building project to address a burgeoning epidemic of state-sanctioned violence against Black men, women, and children by police officers.

Despite the ridicule, rejection, and attempts to counter Black Lives Matter with Blue Lives Matter or All Lives Matter by some White people, the movement grew into a global community working towards Black liberation and freedom. Black Lives Matter was at the forefront of the protests in the summer of 2020 following the killing of George Floyd. *The New York Times* reported that Black Lives Matter protests peaked on June 6, when half a million people turned out in nearly 550 places across the United States, the largest protest movement in our country's history.[132]

In Chapter 1, I wrote that protest without progress is not optimal for achieving transformative change. Dr. King knew that ultimately that must come through legislation. Under the guidance of

---

[132] Buchanan, Bui, and Patel. "Black Lives Matter May Be the Largest Movement in U.S. History." The New York Times. The New York Times, July 3, 2020. https://www.nytimes.com/interactive/2020/07/03/us/george-floyd-protests-crowd-size.html.

the founders and support from corporations, organizations, and individuals, Black Lives Matter has developed BLM PAC to elect officials who create Black-affirming policies. The organization also cultivated the Black Lives Matter Global Network Foundation, a philanthropic arm that invests in the work to heal and strengthen Black people across the diaspora.

I cannot leave the subject of Black female Challengers without lauding a woman who rose like a Phoenix when many people counted her out after her narrow loss of Georgia's gubernatorial race in 2018. Stacy Abrams made history as the first Black woman to become the gubernatorial nominee for a major party in the United States, and the first black woman and first Georgian to deliver a Response to the State of the Union Address. [133] When she and others around the country witnessed the mismanagement of Georgia's gubernatorial race during her campaign, she did not sit on the sidelines and groan. She not only challenged the system that made it possible for her opponent to oversee the voting system in a race in which he was running, Abrams created an organization that turned the red state blue during the 2020 presidential election. Abrams and her organization, Fair Fight Action, is credited with launching a voter registration drive that registered a record number of Black Georgians. President-elect Joe Biden singled Abrams out and credited her hard work and strategy for delivering Georgia's votes, which helped him win the presidency in 2020.

I must concur with musical artist and entrepreneur Rihanna's powerful message to America about Black women. She said, "We are impeccable. We are just impeccable, and the world is going to have to deal with that."[134]

---

[133] Action, Fair Fight. "About Stacey Abrams." Fair Fight, May 13, 2021. https://fairfight.com/about-stacey-abrams/.

[134] ESSENCE. "Rihanna Has a Message for Black Women | Essence News | Essence." YouTube. YouTube, September 13, 2019. https://www.youtube.com/watch?v=F3R4ypAQMIo.

**Black Womanhood and the Workplace**

No matter how impeccable, how accomplished, how educated, or how brilliant, being a woman in the American workplace comes with a set of challenges men can only imagine. Besides the crucible of the cubicle, women often face gender discrimination, labeling, stereotyping, implicit bias, and in some cases, misogyny. But, if you are a Black woman, or woman of color, these gender-based challenges are often accompanied by racism, microaggressions, underestimates of capabilities, marginalization, subpar compensation regardless of educational attainment, and many other race-based inequities that make it harder to move up or even navigate the corporate environment. The White way of thinking has encroached so far into the Black culture, even some Black men exhibit a few of the same behaviors toward Black women at home and work. This includes the workplace where Black women often find few male mentors and champions of any race willing to advocate or intervene on their behalf.

Black women account for 7% of the population of the total U.S. workforce but makeup 12% of minimum wage earners, according to data from Lean In. Women make up 21% of C-suite leaders and just 1% are Black women.[135]

Rosalind Brewer and Thasundra Brown Duckett are the only Black women in the country occupying a seat in the C-suite and they just became CEOs in 2021.[136]

Women have always had a harder time than men in the workplace, but Black women have historically had the most difficult experiences of any race or gender. Being subjected to race and gender-driven microaggressions—small and subtle insults or comments—is

---

[135] "The State of Black Women in Corporate America." Lean In, 2020. https://leanin.org/research/state-of-black-women-in-corporate america/introduction.

[136] Emma Hinchliffe. "The Female CEOS on This Year's Fortune 500 Just Broke Three All-Time Records." Fortune. Fortune, June 2, 2021. https://fortune.com/2021/06/02/female-ceos-fortune-500-2021-women-ceo-list-roz-brewer-walgreens-karen-lynch-cvs-thasunda-brown-duckett-tiaa/.

the tax Black women pay whether in academia, the halls of corporate America, or blue-collar work. Black professional women in my circle tell me that across the country there seems to be an assault on them in the workplace, and the race and gender-based microaggressions they are experiencing are not just being doled out by White males and White females but Black men and other Black women as well.

A case in point is complaints about mistreatment from current and former employees of Essence Communications, publisher of the iconic *Essence* magazine brand. In June 2020, #BlackFemaleAnonymous began trending after publishing "The Truth About Essence," a scathing open letter demanding the resignations of key executives at the venerable magazine for a litany of maltreatments of Black female employees. The letter also described a toxic environment in which abuse of power is part of the corporate culture. According to the letter's author, Essence Communications, publisher of the 52-year-old magazine that is synonymous with Black female culture, is a toxic place to work due to employees being "systematically suppressed by pay inequity, sexual harassment, workplace bullying, intimidation, colorism, and classism." The letter's author also claimed that the media company is failing Black America and thwarting efforts to create a more equitable workplace for Black women.

Though two law firms that had no prior relationship with Essence Communications or its leadership investigated the allegations in the essay and determined them to be unfounded, the possibility of what the anonymous writer described is not implausible.[137]

Black professional women tell me that kind of toxicity is happening in sectors such as private industry, academic institutions, health care organizations, and entertainment, to name a few. Those

---

[137] Adenike Olanrewaju. "Investigations at Essence Find No Evidence of Abusive Work Culture." The New York Times. The New York Times, September 8, 2020. https://www.nytimes.com/2020/09/08/business/media/essence-magazine-harassment-investigations.html.

who are inflicting the pain and trauma on Black women often look like them, harkening back to the days of "drivers," enslaved men whose slave owners gave the "job" of managing other slaves, often by treating them harshly.

Black women are also more likely to experience the affinity bias, which involves the majority of the decision-makers in the workplace being White males who are more likely to be attracted to people who look like them or have shared experiences with them. Often, this means they do not reach out to support or mentor women or people of other races and ethnicities – even in companies that prioritize diversity initiatives, as many of those efforts are failing or falling short of their intent.

Fearless and always rising to meet the moment, research shows Black women being just as likely as White men to say they are interested in top executive jobs, which is substantially more than any other racial or ethnic group of women. More than half of those Black women expressed that part of what drives them is how an executive role would position them to influence the levers that weaponize their Whiteness against women of color.

Toxic environments are fueled by racism, colorism, and gender bias. Pay gaps of as much as 38% between White and Black professionals, microaggressions, implicit bias, stereotypes, and a persistent inability to penetrate the dominant perspective inside corporate America are some of the assaults Blacks deal with daily. When coupled with the toll on their mental health, there is no wonder why Black women are leaving jobs across industries in record numbers and I applaud them. In this moment of reckoning on race in America, Black women are starting businesses faster than any other racial group, according to American Express, but Blacks continue to be shut out of access to capital. The Small Business Administration Office of Advocacy reports that women and minority business owners are denied loans and pay higher interest rates than White counterparts, even factoring in credit scores.

Project Diane released a report in December 2020 that on its face appeared to be good news for Black female business founders. Upon closer examination and context, the state of venture capital for these women is not so bright; in fact, it is disheartening. According to the report, only 34 Black female entrepreneurs had ever raised $1 million in venture capital for their respective companies. By 2020, that number had tripled to 93 women reporting they had raised $1 million from investors. That 93 Black women in the history of this country have raised $1 million is hardly disruptive when we consider women of the Black race have been business owners since Harriet Tubman founded a caregiving home for elderly people.[138] While lack of access to capital is a roadblock, Black women inevitably prevail by figuring out ways to go around the barriers and walk into their respective purposes as entrepreneurs and business owners.

When Joseph R. Biden Jr. was a presidential candidate and announced Kamala Harris as his running mate during election season in 2020, we should have been able to look at her achievement as one of many well-earned recognitions of the exceptional work she and other Black women have done throughout their careers. Her appointment should be lauded but 2020 should not have been the first time a Black woman was tapped for the role. But if we are ever going to make sustainable change, as ChaRIOTS we must ensure that organizations in the public and private sectors make room for more Black women to shatter the institutional barriers keeping them from rising.

For the Black woman, corporate America is an entire system unto itself. There she must prevail and surpass not only the stereotypes that proceeded her arrival, but she carries the plight of every Black woman in pursuit of success despite a work environment that often does not support her or recognize her value.

The same racism Black people experience in their social reality outside their places of employment greets them inside the walls of the workplaces. I do not mean that every Black person faces a daily

---

[138] Emma Hinchliffe. "The Number of Black Female Founders Who Have Raised More than $1 Million Has Nearly Tripled since 2018." Fortune. Fortune, December 2, 2020. https://fortune.com/2020/12/02/black-women-female-founders-venture-capital-funding-vc-2020-project-diane/.

racialized assault; many Black professionals report having good experiences in their workplaces, which is encouraging and inspiring. However, these cases are often exceptions, as many more Black people, especially Black women, share stories of marginalization, barriers to leveling up, and bumping up against the proverbial glass ceiling.

Many Black women are choosing to leave these types of challenges in corporate life behind to forge a path they control by becoming entrepreneurs. Following in the footsteps of the legendary Madam C.J. Walker, America's first Black female self-made millionaire, and currently, Janice Bryant Howroyd, the first black woman to own a billion-dollar company, the staffing agency ACT-1, Black professional women are leaving nonprofit and corporate jobs in record numbers because they are unable to attain the same level of success as their White counterparts or non-Black women of color. Black women are now the fastest-growing group of entrepreneurs among women, having grown by more than 600% between 1997 and 2017.[139] Their reasons for exiting corporate positions and nonprofit organizations include affinity bias, racism, and gender bias. While they hold the most degrees, they are still grossly underrepresented at the highest ranks of leadership in private industry, academia, nonprofit organizations, and board seats. Yet, through their ever-present resiliency, tenacity, and Black Girl Magic, Black women have always thrived in times of adversity and they have always risen to meet challenges life deals them. They have stood with so many others in their fight for rights and justice, from White women during the Women's Suffrage Movement to Black men during the civil rights movement to playing pivotal roles in Black Lives Matter and LGBTQIA+ equal rights movement. America owes a debt of gratitude to Black women for their contributions, courage, and unbreakable

---

[139] Pamela Nonga Ngue, Raena Saddler, Jordan Miller-Surratt, Nikki Tucker, Madison Long, Rachel E. Cooke, and Darion McCoy. "What Black Women Are up Against." Lean In, 2020. https://leanin.org/black-women-racism-discrimination-at-work.

spirits. They are natural Challengers, making them ideal for helping to lead the ChaRIOT Movement we will build.

## Black Women as ChaRIOTS

Ava DuVernay has built her career as a groundbreaking filmmaker and activist by unapologetically and purposefully living her personal mission as a disrupter of systems that maintain racism, oppression, and privilege. She is vocal and outspoken about what she sees as the road to racial equity. She has said she does not want a seat at the table but that she wants to *make the table.* As a Challenger, DuVernay finds a way or makes a way to push the boundaries and advocate for the Challenged.

Not all Black women have DuVernay's platform, but throughout history, they have refused to be shuttered or silenced, and they are not shy about letting their voices be heard when demanding social change or justice. This is how I know that Black women will be critical to the ChaRIOT and the new equity movement that is rising. Their unique set of experiences and perspectives, shaped by the reality of the world they must move in, make them perfect for the transformative role of the ChaRIOT.

When we examine history, it reveals that Black women were the pillars of the civil rights movement. They were the flesh, bone, blood, and grassroots of the hard work to bring racial justice to Black Americans. Often working in the shadows, their roles and contributions may not have been visible, but their impact was no less powerful. They were the Challengers, the voices, and the strategists of the civil rights movement. They were the conscious of the movement. Despite the realities of dealing with violence, sexual assault, and even death during the movement, Black women persisted and became the critical mass that brought about powerful and sustained action for change.

Though overlooked in conversations about racism and gender bias, Black women will bring a unique perspective to the ChaRIOT Movement through the triple consciousness under which they must navigate the world and the intersectionality of marginalization, racialized sexism, resiliency, and greatness that define their experiences. They will use their unique lens and vibrant voices to help lead the New Cultural Conversation on which the ChaRIOT relies to carry forth its mission.

From the time Black women were forced to leave the safety and familiarity of their homeland and brought to America, they have contributed intellectually, physically, and emotionally to end systemic racism, racial inequity, injustice, and oppression. They persevere through what talk radio executive Sara Lomax-Reese pens as the "triple consciousness" that burdens them, marginalizes them, and seeks to make them invisible.[140] Black women know how to translate triple consciousness into being a triple threat to racism and racists: they are fierce fighters for justice, extraordinary strategists for movement building, and passionate advocates for racial and social equity.

Just as the civil rights movement could not have happened without Black women as architects and advocates, the ChaRIOT will not fulfill its mission without their exceptional leadership and unparalleled contributions.

---

[140] Sara Lomax-Reese. "Essay: The Triple Weight of Being Black, American, and a Woman." WHYY. WHYY, March 22, 2018. https://whyy.org/articles/the-triple-weight-of-being-black-american-and-a-woman/.

## Chapter 9

## The ChaRIOT Will Awaken the Human Conscience

When I was a teenager, my pastor was very influential in framing how I viewed the world. Without telling me what to believe, he shaped and showed me not what to think but *what to think about* and how to engage things critically so that I could shape my way of understanding.

What I learned from him was instrumental to the degree that when I was offered what would be a pivotal opportunity, I was ready. The opportunity came in the form of my ninth-grade algebra teacher; unbeknownst to me I was selected by a minister to give Dr. King's most famous speech, "I Have a Dream," for the entire high school.

By that time, many of my White childhood friends had stopped engaging with me and stuck to socializing with other White students. However, when I gave that speech, it was a turning point in my young life and in what had become race-based ostracizing of me by White kids. Everyone looked at me differently. It was so well received that from that point on, honestly, I did not have one threat of a fight or violence while I was in high school. In fact, I was almost protected, as Black students and White students saw me as "the young preacher."

The response to the speech was even more important to me because some longtime friends had disassociated with me. After all, they saw my Blackness as being so different from their Whiteness, they felt it necessary to stop socializing with me. It could have been them, it could have been their parents; nonetheless, it happened. I was aware of the chosen or forced segregation of White kids from Black kids but I still held a genuine desire and hope to be in partnership, conversation, and community with people who did not look like me as well as people who did. It never went away because even today, I know it takes a community to create change, a new community that I want to build with others to lead a new movement: The ChaRIOT Movement.

I will never forget being on the field at my graduation ceremony a few years after giving the speech when my classmates, particularly those who were White, came to me and said that throughout high school the one thing about me that stood out to them about me was the "I Have a Dream" speech. I think what was still so memorable about that speech three years after I gave it was my delivery: I spoke with conviction about what was possible because I believed the words of the speech, I believed what was possible, and still do.

There is one other thing that stands out to me about giving that speech. At that moment, I became aware of what my third-grade teacher had really done in denying me the opportunity to retake the spelling test I mentioned in Chapter 1. Her actions, consciously or unconsciously, of extending the opportunity to the White children but not me was racially motivated. I understood.

My classmates may not have realized it at the time, and neither did I, but the reason they were so struck when I gave the speech is that they were experiencing a kind of awakening.

An awakening of the human conscience is a moment that people who are outside the Black community acknowledge that things are happening to a race of people that should not.[141] Taking it a step further, an awakening inspires people to become active Challengers of systemic racism and partners in paving the way for new conversations and change.

For example, in 2020 NBA players, WNBA players, and their coaches launched a racial equity initiative to address the traumas Black people are experiencing in our country. They are a new breed of Challengers.

## Wake Up, Challengers

By the time I was 11½, I had taken a deep interest in Jesus and how he dealt with people. I saw that Jesus was someone who welcomed others. He had conversations with people that others did not

---

[141] Luise Schottroff. *Let the Oppressed Go Free: Feminist Perspectives on the New Testament* (Gender and Biblical Tradition), trans, by Annamarie S. Kidder (Louisville, KY: John Knox/Westminster Press, 1991).

want to have and did not have. Uncomfortable conversations but necessary conversations.

If I am looking at one of the pivotal moments in my life, it would be my classmates coming to me wanting to talk about the ideals put forth in the "I Have a Dream," speech because I knew those are the types of conversations I should be having with White people and that people should be having with each other across racial lines.

I wondered then and I ask now, why don't we have cultural conversations on a broad scale? Why is systemic racism still such a problem for a nation that presents itself to countries around the world as the epitome of freedom, democracy, and equality for all? Why can't we close the racial chasm dividing us? More than 400 years after the first slaves were stolen from their homeland and brought to this country to be owned by other human beings, the deep racial and ethnic inequities that existed in 1619 still exist today.

One would think that 620,000 Americans dying in the Civil War would have ended the issue in 1865. The Southern slave-holding states, determined to protect their economic interest by maintaining a system that enslaved approximately 3,950,511 million people in 1860, went to battle with Northern states in 1861.[142]

As we know, the South lost the Civil War and that should have been the final chapter in the country's racist history. But it was not, and for me, there are some clear reasons why.

First, the South was never really rebuked for having slaves. Southern states were not fined, punished, or nailed to the cross of immorality. Instead, White people reframed the war over enslaving human beings as "the War Between Brothers" to avoid dealing with why the war happened in the first place, which was the fact that chattel slavery formed the backbone of the Southern economy. This also made it easy for there to be no attempt to make Southern racists face up to their inhumanity or change their hearts and minds. Since they

---

[142] Jenny Bourne. "Slavery in the United States". EH.Net Encyclopedia, edited by Robert Whaples. March 26, 2008.
URL http://eh.net/encyclopedia/slavery-in-the-united-states/.

could pretend that the Civil War was not about owning slaves, the denial allowed them to live their lives in a state of altered reality.

Second, America looked the other way as Southern states built another form of institutional racism through acts such as creating Black Codes and later, Jim Crow laws and legalized segregation. If the Union remained intact, racists could do whatever they chose and treat the now-free Blacks as they pleased. Southern Whites instituted another form of bondage through sharecropping. They lynched, looted, and stole from Black people. They raped Black women and girls. They murdered Black men and often Black women as well. Whites were allowed to beat, threaten, and intimidate Black people. They could strongarm them and bully them. Whether White Americans acknowledge it or not, apathy and continued unwillingness to be Challengers is how systemic racism was born and has been fostered throughout history.

The failure of most White Americans to allow these events to penetrate their human conscience is why they have not abandoned the privileges of being White to challenge the system of racism. This unwillingness to be a Challenger is a mindset, a choice with roots deeply embedded in many American institutions, including the nation's police forces, which grew out of groups of White men created to catch runaway Blacks slaves. This mindset is how the country can produce a Derek Chauvin and the police officers who aided him in the killing of George Floyd.

A person does not need money, power, or influence to develop an awakened conscience or to be a Challenger. When George Floyd was being murdered, the people who stood on the sidewalk and shouted and dared to intervene when they saw something wrong were Challengers. Darnella Frazier, the courageous 17-year-old girl who kept filming Floyd's murder and then posted it to social media for the world to see, is a Challenger.

The third reason why racism persisted and has survived unchecked for centuries has origins in the Antebellum South and its reliance on slavery to maintain the economy. Not everyone in the South agreed with the legality of slave ownership, but the system was keeping food on the tables of White people, and the unpaid labor was making many of them quite wealthy; therefore, the institution of chattel slavery remained part of life in America, despite creating deep divisions politically, socially, and morally.

After President Abraham Lincoln signed the Emancipation Proclamation ending the legal ownership of slaves, segregation, denial of basic civil and human rights, mistreatment, and oppression of Black people continued to feed the beast called "systemic racism."

I would submit that we must be cognizant of how racism forms and how bias shows up, and where it shows up. It is a mistake to think racism only occurs in a conflict between two people on the street, and one of the persons is Black, and one is White. That is probably the most basic level of it, but so many more layers and forms of racism exist, from unconscious bias to White privilege. In our world many people do not look beyond the color of skin when they are defining it.

Finally, within America, there is a dichotomy of cordoning off the roots of racism by insisting the past is not related to the present and that the injustices inflicted on Black people by Whites of yesterday as having no relevance to events today. Simultaneously, America has allowed a myriad of symbols of racism to be introduced into the sociocultural landscape of this country. The past is very much part of the present.

Here is what I mean. America watched as hundreds of statues and monuments honoring Confederate leaders were erected and re-enactments of famous Civil War battles were held in which members of the Confederacy were lauded as heroes and patriots and not traitors to our country. America stood by and watched as Black people were redlined in the housing market for decades. The country allowed educational injustice to take root and keep Black children from access to educational parity with White children. White Americans, detached from their Black co-workers, neighbors, and fellow countrymen, did not challenge the system as health disparities shortened the life expectancy of Black people. The pandemic reaffirmed that health inequities among Black, Brown, and Indigenous people still exist and still mean lower survival rates during a health crisis like the COVID-19 pandemic.

White America stood by and allowed racists to destroy progressive and prosperous Black communities through several race riots resulting in deaths and destruction. In May 2021, media organizations and television networks ran stories that examined the centennial anniversary of the Tulsa Race Massacre on May 31, 1921. The Greenwood neighborhood in Tulsa, Oklahoma, where about 10,000 Black residents lived, also flourished as home to many thriving Black-owned businesses in the 1900s. Blacks called Greenwood "Black Wall Street," but among Whites, the community was mocked as "Little Africa."[143]

The massacre began with a White female elevator operator claiming a teenage Black boy, Dick Rowland, acted inappropriately. The next day, May 31, the boy was arrested, and then rumors swept through Tulsa that he had sexually assaulted the young woman, Sarah Page.

A group of White men went to the courthouse where he was being held and demanded he be turned over to them for punishment. Twenty-five Black men, aiming to protect Rowland from a fate that had befallen many Black men and boys accused of assaulting White women, went to the courthouse to offer to guard the boy. Soon, that number grew to 75 armed Black men, but they were incredibly outnumbered by 1,500 White men facing off against them. Shots were fired and the fighting broke out. Fearing an insurrection of Black people, thousands of Whites converged on Greenwood and began looting and burning Black homes and businesses to the ground. They destroyed the school, library, hospital, stores, and other buildings vital to any community.[144]

---

[143] History.com Editors. "Tulsa Race Massacre." History.com. A&E Television Networks, March 8, 2018.
https://www.history.com/topics/roaring-twenties/tulsa-race-massacre.

[144] History.com Editors. "Tulsa Race Massacre." History.com. A&E Television Networks, March 8, 2018.
https://www.history.com/topics/roaring-twenties/tulsa-race-massacre.

Within two days of Page's false accusation, the Greenwood community no longer existed. A 2001 state commission examination of events confirmed 36 dead: 26 Black and 10 White, but historians have estimated as many as 300 people—mostly Black—were killed over two days in the bloody racist attack.[145]

Greenwood was not a one-off incident: Racist massacres in Black communities took place in cities that include Atlanta (1906),[146] Elaine Arkansas (1919),[147] and one of the most well-known, Rosewood, Florida (1923).[148]

I have heard many White people say, "Slavery has nothing to do with me. I never owned slaves," or "Let it go. Let the past stay in the past." Black people do not have that luxury because the past is the present and racism is very much a mainstay in the daily lives of Black Americans.

I know this to be true through my observations, my research, and my roles as a faith leader, corporate diversity consultant, and as a Black American. Through it all, hearts and minds may not have liked or agreed with these uncivil and inhumane behaviors, but the human conscience slept. I would argue it is still asleep because we have not reached a critical mass of people being conscientious Challengers. Without Challengers, there can be no ChaRIOT.

---

[145] History.com Editors. "Tulsa Race Massacre." History.com. A&E Television Networks, March 8, 2018. https://www.history.com/topics/roaring-twenties/tulsa-race-massacre.

[146] Clifford Kuhn and Gregory Mixon. "Atlanta Race Riot of 1906 - New Georgia Encyclopedia." New Georgian Encyclopedia , September 23, 2005. https://www.georgiaencyclopedia.org/articles/history-archaeology/atlanta-race-riot-of-1906/.

[147] Grif Stockley. "Elaine Massacre of 1919." Encyclopedia of Arkansas, November 18, 2020. https://encyclopediaofarkansas.net/entries/elaine-massacre-of-1919-1102/.

[148] Carmelita Pickett. "Rosewood Massacre of 1923." Encyclopedia Britannica. Encyclopedia Britannica, inc., January 1, 2021. https://www.britannica.com/topic/Rosewood-riot-of-1923.

# The New Cultural Conversation

I believe it getting to critical mass requires an awakening of the human conscience. It takes an awakening to be able to look around and see how people are being manipulated or harmed and how others are participating in it or supporting it with their silence. It takes a specific kind of awakening for people–White and Black but mostly White–to see that something must be done. We all must become Challengers who reach that zero degrees of belonging I presented about earlier.

The Challengers must be willing to shed or even abandon their executive titles and stations. They must have the courage, vision, and fortitude to accept that being the president or provost of a college or general manager of a high-end hotel chain or the millionaire or billionaire owner of a company does not mean they are above responsibility when it comes to ensuring systemic racism and racial injustice are dismantled. When they can walk into a room, divulge themselves of those identity markers, and be united on the front of what should be done and what is right, that is how people can become Challengers who are on their way to becoming ChaRIOTS.

But first, people must be awakened. They have to be shaken awake. Unfortunately, that often means a tragedy must occur, a tragedy befalling a person living at the margins of life or is positioned at the lower base of the sociocultural hierarchy.

## Awakening the Challengers

I believe some images startle us and strike us so deeply in our inner core they act as spark plugs jarring awake our individual and collective conscience when we see them. When it comes to seeing Black people being mistreated or oppressed by White people, these spark plugs rattled Americans so deeply as they watched them on television or social media or through the lens of a cellphone camera, people were moved to rise, meet the moment, and answer the call to be a Challenger.

Many images have shaken people, but I believe five were so egregious, so shocking that they prompted movements to emerge.

The first of these images appeared in *Jet* magazine in September 1955. The magazine published photos of the horribly disfigured and battered body of 14-year-old Emmett Till lying in a casket as his young mother wailed in unimaginable anguish and grief at the sight of her only child, who was recognizable only by the ring he wore on one of his fingers. The boy had been beaten unmercifully, tortured, shot, and thrown in the Tallahatchie River by two White men who had kidnapped him from his uncle's home in Money, Mississippi after young Till allegedly whistled at the wife of one of his murderers.

In 2016, Lonnie Bunch, founding director of the National Museum of African American History and Culture, described Till's lynching as a boy being nailed to the racial injustice cross.[149]

The sight of a boy whose face was so disfigured from a lynching that his mother had to identify him by a ring on his finger became a symbol that shook Americans to their core. Till's murder and the acquittal of his killers by an all-White jury represented just how deep the disease of racism ran in America. This incident also showed White people the racial terrorism that had long defined Black life in the South, and how so many Black lives—Black men in particular—were taken due to lies told by White people in places like Mississippi. What Americans saw served as a rallying cry that helped ignite the civil rights movement.

The second image that penetrated the American psyche was several days of violent assaults on young Black protesters, engineered by Theophilus Eugene "Bull" Connor, who served as director of public safety in Birmingham, Alabama, for 22 years. A tyrant and ardent segregationist, Bull Connor prided himself on two things: keeping Black people in their place and his willingness to use the police force to attack and even kill Black people who dared to challenge White authority in a quest for civil rights.[150]

---

[149] Katie Nodjimbadem. "Emmett Till's Open Casket Funeral Reignited the Civil Rights Movement." Smithsonian.com. Smithsonian Institution, September 2, 2015. https://www.smithsonianmag.com/smithsonian-institution/emmett-tills-open-casket-funeral-reignited-the-civil-rights-movement-180956483/.

[150] "Connor, Theophilus Eugene 'Bull.'" The Martin Luther King, Jr., Research and Education Institute, August 4, 2020.

Dr. King and Southern Christian Leadership Conference President Fred Shuttlesworth, both determined to end the racist reign of Connor, developed and executed a massive campaign against segregation in Birmingham. In his book *Why We Can't Wait*, Dr. King wrote a vivid recount of how the ambitious plan could "break the back of segregation across the nation." Gripped by Jim Crow laws for decades, Birmingham restaurants refused to serve Blacks at lunch counters, White merchants offered them only limited services, and employers hired Blacks for jobs far below their qualifications and then refused to promote them. The city had long been considered the capital of Jim Crow South.

The Project C campaign was launched by college students having lunch-counter sit-ins during the first few days of April 1963, which resulted in 35 arrests. On April 6, Blacks marched on Birmingham's City Hall. As 42 were arrested, they sang songs of freedom on their way to jail. Soon, days of nonviolent demonstrations by Black people of all ages followed. During the first days of the campaign, protesters were handled without violence or abuse when they were arrested by Connor. On May 2, there were more than 900 campaign participants. By the next day, Connor ordered firemen to use their hoses on protesters and onlookers. As demonstrators tried to escape the skin-searing pain from the firemen's hoses, Connor directed police to chase them down with vicious police department-owned German Shepherds.

People across the country saw images of Black Americans, including teenage girls and boys, being beaten with police batons, hosed down with powerful streams of water from hydrants, and bitten by snarling German Shepherds. As these incidents played out over several days, television reports and newspapers across the country showed these images. White people sitting in the safety of their living rooms, often choosing to be oblivious to the realities of racism in America, were shocked at the sight of the images. Reacting to national outrage and demands from White Americans to do something, President John F. Kennedy sent someone to Birmingham to negotiate an end to the attacks on Black demonstrators. By May 10, an agreement between Black leaders and White merchants was reached and two weeks later, the Alabama Supreme Court ordered Connor and other city commissioners to vacate their offices. Although Connor was elected to the Alabama Public Service Commission a year later, Dr. King and Shuttlesworth scored a major victory for civil rights.

The third moment of awakening took place in the same city just a few months after Dr. King's campaign. The campaign had led to some small changes but nothing major enough to stop racists from violating civil rights or committing murder against Blacks. One of these egregious acts played out as an attack on the bedrock of America's Black community: The Black Church. Black churches were the first institutions built and run by Black people independent of White oversight. They played a vital role in the lives of people who had been dehumanized, disenfranchised, and discriminated against in their own country for centuries. The Black Church was and continues to be a refuge, a place of healing, a place of gathering and spiritual sustenance, and a place of hope. Few pillars in Black communities are held in such esteem as a physical symbol of faith, love, and opportunity for social change.

In the 1950s and 1960s, Black churches were also the headquarters for people to organize and strategize during the civil rights movement. Black church music is distinguished by being euphoric, spiritual, and uplifting; the singing careers of Aretha Franklin, Whitney Houston, and other artists have roots in the Black church. The Black Church has long been a place for family gatherings on Sundays and throughout the week. It serves as the centerpiece of social life in the community through annual events like Women's Day, Men's Day, fish fries, holiday-themed programs, and Youth Day programs.

The 16th Street Baptist Church was a historic and prominent church located in downtown Birmingham. In 1963, the church was more than 52 years old and served as a fixture in the Black community, offering the building as a meeting place, social center, and lecture hall.

The church also served as a vital headquarters for civil rights mass meetings and rallies in the early 1960s.

On September 15, 1963, it was Youth Day at the 16th Street Baptist Church and families were excited about the Sunday service. Five young girls in particular, two of them sisters, gathered in one of the church's restrooms to prepare for their part in the Sunday morning services. Their families said the girls were very happy and excited about their role in the special service that morning.

At eleven o'clock that morning, a bomb exploded from underneath the front steps of the 16th Street Baptist Church and tore through sections of the building. Four girls, Addie Mae Collins, Denise McNair, Carole Robertson, and Cynthia Wesley were killed. Collins' sister Susan was left permanently blind. The inhumane attack and the deaths of the four little girls shocked the nation and shined a light on Blacks' harsh and painful struggle for civil rights in Birmingham. The sight of the decimated church drew outrage from many Whites across the country, who also demanded change and threw greater support behind the civil rights movement. Most of all, they were frightened by the cold fact that they were living in a country where four children had been murdered by racial animus.[151]

As racist people saw the threat of change from the growing number of Challengers, both White and Black, they intensified their efforts to ensure they maintained the status quo. This led to a fourth paramount event in American history, and the human conscience was awakened once more: It became known as "Bloody Sunday."

Selma, a city within a state that some have described as the most segregated in the country at one time, had a long history of segregationist activities, including a very active Ku Klux Klan membership. After the Civil Rights Act of 1964 was signed into law by President Lyndon B. Johnson, nothing of significance changed for Black Americans right away, especially Blacks living in the South.

---

[151] "16th Street Baptist Church Bombing (1963) (U.S. National Park Service)." National Parks Service. U.S. Department of the Interior, November 19, 2020. https://www.nps.gov/articles/16thstreetbaptist.htm.

# The ChaRIOT

The Student Nonviolent Coordinating Committee (SNCC) had been making some progress in registering Black voters in Selma, Alabama, but their efforts were impeded even after Dr. King visited the city and pledged that SCLC would back SNCC. Thousands of peaceful demonstrators, including Dr. King, were arrested and jailed. Tensions escalated when a young, Black man, Jimmie Lee Johnson, was killed by police as he tried to protect his mother from the baton of a White police officer.

This triggered civil rights leaders to plan a march for voting rights that would take them from Selma to Montgomery, the state capital. On Sunday, March 7, 600 voting rights advocates, a young John Lewis among them, set out on a 54-mile march that would take them across a famous bridge.

The Edmund Pettus Bridge, named for a Confederate general and unabashed leader of the Ku Klux Klan in Alabama, was built over the Alabama River, which was a key route for the state's plantation and cotton economy during slavery and Reconstruction.

As the peaceful marchers reached the crest of the bridge, they saw state troopers, county sheriff's deputies, police dogs, and White onlookers waiting ahead. Within a few minutes, they knocked many marchers—some of them White—to the ground and began beating them with nightsticks. The marchers, following the strategy of nonviolence, did not fight back despite taking blows and being stepped on by horses ridden by police. Many of the marchers were seriously hurt, including John Lewis, who suffered a fractured skull.

TV cameras were rolling, and their lenses captured Americans, whose skin happened to be Black, being beaten to the ground by their fellow countrymen—White Americans with badges—for simply demanding the right to vote as citizens of this country. The images penetrated people's conscience; tens of millions of Americans were once again shown life in Black America through the TV sets that beamed the images right into their living rooms, making it impossible to escape the reality of what was happening in the land of the free and the home of the brave.[152]

Black and White Challengers, shaken by what they saw, left their homes to stage sit-ins and demonstrate in solidarity with the voting rights marchers. Some even traveled to Selma from other cities and states. When a federal court order permitted the protest, the number of voting rights marchers swelled to 25,000. This awakening led Congress to pass the Voting Rights Act of 1965, which became law on August 6, 1965.

Two and a half years after the new voting law was enacted, one of the greatest tragedies in American history took place and shock reverberated around the world on April 4, 1968. The Voting Rights Act of 1965, which followed the Civil Rights Act of 1964, symbolized significant strides in the struggle for justice and equity, but they did not eradicate systemic racism in our country. Several years after these pivotal laws were passed, the Rev. Dr. Martin Luther King Jr. was still fighting against racism in cities like Memphis where Black sanitation workers were systematically being denied basic rights relative to their wages and working conditions.

Dr. King was a towering figure in the civil rights movement, having led the massive effort against segregation since the mid-1950s. Born into a family of Baptist ministers, he decided to enter the ministry at age 18 while a student at Morehouse College. By the time he was 25, he had completed a Ph.D. program, theological seminary, and was called to become pastor of the Dexter Avenue Baptist Church in Montgomery, Alabama in 1954. One year later, he answered another calling, one that took him into his destiny as a civil rights luminary. In March 1955, 15-year-old Claudia Colvin refused to give

---

[152] Christopher Klein. "How Selma's 'Bloody Sunday' Became a Turning Point in the Civil Rights Movement." History.com. A&E Television Networks, March 6, 2015. https://www.history.com/news/selma-bloody-sunday-attack-civil-rights-movement.

up her seat to a White person on a city bus in Montgomery, a violation of Jim Crow laws.[153]

In December that same year, Rosa Parks, a Montgomery seamstress refused to give her seat to a White person and was jailed. The two incidents set off a yearlong boycott that was planned and organized by Dr. King and several other civil rights leaders. He was arrested and jailed during the boycott and his house was bombed. During that time, his public profile began growing as national media organizations covered those incidents.

Over the next 13 years, Dr. King organized and led numerous boycotts, sit-ins, campaigns, and mobilized thousands of people across the South to participate in marches for racial justice. He founded the Southern Christian Leadership Conference, was among the few leaders who organized the 1963 March on Washington for Jobs and Freedom, which drew approximately 250,000, the largest gathering of people for civil rights at the time, and the event at which he gave his most famous speech, "I Have a Dream." After that extraordinary address, Dr. King won a Nobel Peace Prize, authored several books, and led several peace movements and campaigns on behalf of poor people. Dr. King's convictions about justice and civil rights were remarkable. So much so that the Black sanitation workers' strike for financial justice drew Dr. King to Memphis, where he was assassinated as he stood on the balcony of the Lorraine Hotel on April 4, 1968. The jarring photo of him lying on the ground mortally wounded set off weeks of shock, grief, and social unrest around the country.

Finally, there have been many images that should have caused an awakening since the civil rights movement. But nothing really galvanized people and brought the country to the inflection point we are currently experiencing in America until we saw that unforgettable

---

[153] Margot Adler. "Before Rosa Parks, There Was Claudette Colvin." NPR. NPR, March 15, 2009. https://www.npr.org/2009/03/15/101719889/before-rosa-parks-there-was-claudette-colvin.

image of a White cop kneeling on the neck of a Black man and choking the life out of him as he pleaded for mercy on May 25, 2020.

### The Challengers and Challenged

In 2020, activism became second nature to many people who never thought of themselves as people who would challenge systemic racism and injustice. More and more people outside the Black community joined the fight against the unjust slayings of Black people by police and advocated for equity, many for the first time. Whether it was because they had a personal connection to the Black community or had, in some way, aligned themselves to the Black Lives Matter movement, non-Black individuals were awakened when George Floyd was killed by three White police officers. It is estimated that between 15 to 26 million Americans participated in marches between May 26 and July 1, 2020, to protest the killing of George Floyd.[154] Polls show that White people marched alongside Blacks more than at any other time in history. Challengers, Black, White, and Brown, answered the call when their conscience shook them and awakened them.

Most of the new participants were not directly impacted by what happened to a Black man who was not a celebrity or a celebrated athlete or wealthy or well-known. I think that is what struck me about the Challengers that the protest drew; they did not know Floyd, but they knew that what happened to him was wrong. Within this awakening, the Challengers also realized they had to bring attention to injustice to advance the movement and achieve justice; the Challengers are fuel for the ChaRIOT. But it takes more than an awakening, more than just acknowledgment. The awakening must move to action through the coupling of the Challenger and the Challenged.

---

[154] Buchanan, Bui and Patel. "Black Lives Matter May Be the Largest Movement in U.S. History." The New York Times. The New York Times, July 3, 2020. https://www.nytimes.com/interactive/2020/07/03/us/george-floyd-protests-crowd-size.html.

# The ChaRIOT

Challengers are individuals who either have the legislative or even lifestyle influence to bring attention to how unjust practices have, without question, disenfranchised others. Challengers use their platforms to bring attention to racism and racist acts just as athletes and celebrities have done.

Challengers would not exist without those who experience injustice, the Challenged. They know the pain of being disenfranchised and left behind. They feel the pressure of having to endure and persist regardless of there not being a pathway for them to be successful or even having a sense of what success could look like for them.

I see the relationship between the Challengers and the Challenged as being deeply intertwined. This is where that partnership exists. Like the solidarity between injustice and justice, solidarity must exist between the Challengers and the Challenged.

My perspective may be problematic for some people but to me, it is clear: I believe that there must be some people who are challenged to give an opportunity for the gifts in others to rise. The Challenged must exist to help make the impacts of unjust practices known to people who have the capacity to change that way of being for them or help redirect the viewpoint of other persons who hold racist beliefs.

It takes disenfranchised people, people who feel like they are at the bottom to see themselves and say, you know what, I am tired of feeling like this. I cannot change it by myself but perhaps if I tell my story, then someone will help change it for me.

I think that is what have been seeing in America around the cases of Ahmaud Arbery, Breonna Taylor, George Floyd, and more recently Jacob Blake Jr., 20-year-old Daunte Wright, and 16-year-old Ma'Khia Bryant—people at the base of the infrastructure of power and at the bottom of cultural and societal hierarchy. Bryant was shot by a police officer moments after he arrived at an incident involving a fight between teen girls. Bryant allegedly lunged at another girl with a knife. The officer did not attempt to de-escalate the scene before using deadly force.[155]

Increasingly, the Challengers are deciding they have had enough. Darnella Frazier became one of them when she stood at 38th & Chicago in Minneapolis and filmed Derek Chauvin killing George Floyd. People like Frazier are pulling out cameras and becoming citizen journalists and social change agents. Soon, they began to circulate videos that go viral. People began to become aware of it. The streets fill with Challengers protesting for the Challenged because just like the gruesome face of Emmett Till, the video images were a spark plug, a call to action, an awakening of the human conscience.

If we take another look at the civil rights movement, we realize that it was not until the brutality of what happened to Black citizens under Bull Connor's orders was publicized on TV that the hearts of people were penetrated and moved to action. We then saw people of diverse races, ethnicities, and backgrounds coming to aid Birmingham Blacks because they had seen people being treated in a way that they believed was unjust.

**Challenger to ChaRIOT**

What is missing is someone to take the relationship between the Challenge and the Challengers to a new level of collaboration. This is the space I want to fill with the ChaRIOT. There is a gap between the collective voice and someone driving a specific action of what should happen, why it should happen, and who can be involved. This is the continuity the ChaRIOT brings. This is where I want the ChaRIOT to live and be able to take the courage of people who have political or legal or cultural platforms—Challengers—and merge them with the cries of the Challenged.

---

[155] Kevin Williams, Jack Healy, and Will Wright. "'A Horrendous Tragedy': The Chaotic Moments before a Police Shooting in Columbus." The New York Times. The New York Times, April 21, 2021. https://www.nytimes.com/2021/04/21/us/columbus-police-shooting-bryant.html.

# The ChaRIOT

I would count my former professor and Ph.D. advisor, L. L. Welborn, among the Challengers. He is someone who has courageously taken a position with the disenfranchised or the lowest slave in the ancient world and has given that slave a positive evaluation in ancient culture. White scholars and theologians say that is just not possible, but we gained the evidence and dared to present the evidence. I think the role of the Challenger is someone who has the courage to dig deep and the courage to see how the Challenged are being exploited, substantiate their stories, and take them public. Challengers point out the components of what racism looks like: structural, systemic, and explicit and implicit biases.

Challengers are diverse: they can be people with legislative power or they can be citizen journalists brave enough to use their social media platform and their following to speak out. They do not necessarily have to be people of high influence or high wealth or high profile. They can be people who are just courageous.

The Challengers are aware of the problem and are willing to confront the problem or injustice. They also have rhetoric or messaging that allows others to connect to the problem without them polarizing people or marginalizing them because of their views and voices. Those are the Challengers.

The ChaRIOT is the continuity that helps the Challengers and the Challenged come together and speak on behalf of the Challenged in a way that helps to impact legislation and helps a lawmaker to understand what needs to be changed and then, champion that cause.

The ChaRIOT has another important role in bringing the Challengers and the Challenged together. I would explain it like this: Galatians 3:28 says, "There is neither Jew nor Greek, there is neither slave nor free, there is neither male nor female; for you are all one in Christ Jesus." Like the bible verse, the ChaRIOT helps people get to the zero degrees of belonging by stripping away the differences that separate them because whether we want to acknowledge it or not, we must use a gathering of people with differences to make a difference. Black people and people of color must create space for people who do not look like them to be part of the cultural conversation and move to advance change.

## The New Challengers

During the 2020 awakening, CEOs of some of the world's most powerful brands were compelled to take a stance beyond making their expected statements against racism. Some companies pledged money and made commitments to increase business with Black suppliers. Others made commitments to increase support of Black-owned businesses, while still leaders of other companies vowed to increase Black representation on their executive boards. There were even companies that took the initiative to go beyond financial partnerships.

Corporations like the Quaker Oats Company and Mars Inc., responsible for Aunt Jemima and Uncle Ben's, respectively, took a reflective approach in 2020 and examined the cultural consciousness of their brands. Aunt Jemima was a fictional character that was based on the Black "Mammy" stereotype stemming from slavery and reinforced in blackface minstrels. She was depicted as joyful and happy. Uncle Ben's face is alleged to be based upon a Black hotel worker who had nothing to do with the Texas rice farm. Due to its insensitive history, The Quaker Oats Company decided to discontinue its use of the fictional Aunt Jemima in its packaging and Mars Inc., long criticized for promoting stereotypes through its Uncle Ben's brand, announced the company's decision to rename the venerable brand to "Ben's Original" and no longer use the image of the Black man in its logo.[156;157]

Big tech companies IBM, Microsoft, and Amazon seemed to answer the call and challenged racism and bias. Advancements in

---

[156] Kelly Tyko. "Aunt Jemima Brand to Be Renamed Pearl Milling Co. with New Syrup, Pancake Boxes Coming in June." USA Today. Gannett Satellite Information Network, February 10, 2021.
https://www.usatoday.com/story/money/food/2021/02/09/aunt-jemima-pancake-mix-renamed-pearl-milling-company/4460628001/.

[157] Alicia Wallace. "Uncle Ben's Has a New Name: Ben's Original." CNN. Cable News Network, September 23, 2020.
https://www.cnn.com/2020/09/23/business/uncle-bens-rice-rebrand-bens-original/index.html.

technology have made facial recognition a valuable resource to police. However, after evaluating the history of police brutality against Black Americans, all three companies terminated their exclusive partnerships with police forces across the nation regarding facial recognition technology. The companies took challenging the dominant culture even further by discontinuing their investments to innovate the software.

The Awakening must affect every aspect of the system, and money is an integral component to addressing systemic inequities. Ice cream giant Ben and Jerry's was among the first companies to set the bar for lasting change in the fight for justice. On Oct. 17, 2019—the year marking the 400th anniversary of the first enslaved Black Americans being brought to this country—Ben and Jerry's spoke directly to the system of racism by posting a bold stance on the company's website with the headline "We Stand in Support of H.R. 40 and Reparations for African Americans."[158] H.R. 40 is a bill that proposes creating a commission to study the effects of slavery and discrimination from 1619 to the present-day and recommend appropriate reparations to Black Americans.

In the statement, the company acknowledged that facing the structural racism created by White people could be difficult or even shameful but that doing so is the only way forward to America facing its brutal history with regards to slavery and racism's lingering presence in the fabric of our society.[159]

Reparations that were promised to Black Americans—a debt that to this day has gone unpaid—have been met with centuries-long resistance and rejection at every stage. The idea of using taxpayer money—which experts say could run into the trillions of dollars—to pay damages to descendants of enslaved people and address the effects

---

[158] "We Stand in Support of H.R. 40 and Reparations for African Americans." https://www.benjerry.com, October 17, 2019. https://www.benjerry.com/about-us/media-center/reparations-statement.

[159] "Silence Is Not an Option." https://www.benjerry.com, June 2020. https://www.benjerry.com/about-us/media-center/dismantle-white-supremacy.

of persistent and pervasive racism, is unappealing to most people polled by Reuters during the height of 2020's demonstrations. Even with Americans becoming more aware of racial inequity, one in five people in the Reuters/Ipsos poll oppose reparations to approximately 40 million Americans. Unsurprisingly, the greatest chasm exists along partisan and racial lines, as only one in 10 Whites polled supported the idea and only half of Black respondents endorsed it.[160]

In 2019, Sen. Mitch McConnell (R-Kentucky), then the Senate Majority leader, stated that no White person living today is responsible for slavery and should not have to pay for reparations. McConnell's views are shared by the majority of White Americans. While a Democratic presidential candidate, Joe Biden voiced support for creating a commission to examine reparations but if he keeps his pledge as president, he will be fighting an uphill battle that he, unfortunately, will likely not win because he would be the lone Challenger against a truth that White America rejects: The truth is that while White people living today did not own slaves, many are the descendants of slave owners, and they hold wealth or are positioned to gain wealth because of America's chattel slavery system and the structural racism that persists. The truth is that America, particularly the South, was largely built through the enslavement of Black bodies who did not have agency over their being. Not even Jesuit priests were above profiting from Black bodies, as we learned in 2016 when the prestigious Georgetown University was forced to publicly own up to the fact that the sale of 272 slaves in 1838—at least one as young as two months old—saved the premier Catholic institution from whence Georgetown evolved from going bankrupt. Those prominent Jesuit priests owned plantations in Maryland and relied on their slaves to work the fields that financed Georgetown University's operations. The

---

[160] Katanga Johnson. "U.S. Public More Aware of Racial Inequality but Still Rejects Reparations: Reuters/Ipsos Polling." Reuters. Thomson Reuters, June 25, 2020. https://www.reuters.com/article/us-usa-economy-reparations-poll-idUSKBN23W1NG.

sale of the slaves paid off a large chunk of debt, as the school was struggling financially in 1838 and faced closing its doors.[161]

A 2016 *New York Times* article on the topic said that the Jesuit priests described the enslaved as panicked grandmothers and grandfathers, pregnant women, mothers, fathers, children, and infants who experienced their families being torn apart by the sale.[162]

Awakened when the story became public in 2016, Challengers made up of Georgetown students organized a protest and created a social media awareness campaign that went viral. Three years after the story became public, bowing to continued pressure and shame, on Oct. 29, 2019, Georgetown president John J. DeGioia announced that the university would commit to raising about $400,000 a year to create a fund to provide reparations to the descendants of the 272 slaves sold by the college in 1838, as researchers had found many of those descendants.[163]

Not everyone was satisfied with the plan. Some people thought more reparations should be given because Georgetown survived and thrived from the sale of those human beings, but others felt that the university owed the descendants nothing.

Many Black people see the opposition against reparations expressed by some Whites as blatant hypocrisy since the American government has paid reparations to several other mistreated

---

[161] Ryan Di Corpo. "Georgetown Reparations Plan for Slaves Sold by University Draws Criticism from Students." America Magazine, November 4, 2019. https://www.americamagazine.org/politics-society/2019/11/04/georgetown-reparations-plan-slaves-sold-university-draws-criticism.

[162] Rachel L. Swarns. "272 Slaves Were Sold to Save Georgetown. What Does It Owe Their Descendants?" The New York Times. The New York Times, April 16, 2016. https://www.nytimes.com/2016/04/17/us/georgetown-university-search-for-slave-descendants.html.

[163] Di Corpo. "Georgetown Reparations Plan for Slaves Sold by University Draws Criticism from Students." America Magazine, November 4, 2019. https://www.americamagazine.org/politicssociety/2019/11/04/georgetown-reparations-plan-slaves-sold-university-draws-criticism.

populations, including $20,000 paid to 100,000 surviving Japanese American victims of internment camps during World War II.[164]

Given the subject of reparations are fraught with controversy and division along racial and political lines, Ben and Jerry's decision to publicly challenge the dominant perspective on reparations for Black Americans shows the company's willingness to be in solidarity with the Challenged. This is an awakening and a shedding of one's titles and statures to reach that zero degrees of belonging required for the ChaRIOT.

But there are levels to the Awakening and becoming a Challenger. The goal of the Awakening is not just to become aware of systemic racism in America. My vision is for the Awakened to become Challengers, and in solidarity with the Challenged, become ChaRIOTS who together, dismantle racism. As ChaRIOTS, we will build a ChaRIOT Community, a ChaRIOT Movement, and ultimately, a ChaRIOT Nation.

The key is that solidarity must exist between the Challengers and the Challenged and nonwhite people and White people. When I think of Challengers, what comes to mind is one of the great philosophers, John Stuart Mill, who developed utilitarianism to guide people in making ethical decisions that can result in the best outcome for the greatest number of people.[165] The true Challengers are willing to sacrifice their position, and sometimes their privilege, for the greater good.

Colin Kaepernick is a Challenger. Despite fans and Internet trolls denouncing him as an American, calling him unpatriotic, calling

---

[164] Bilal Qureshi. "From Wrong to Right: A U.S. Apology for Japanese Internment." NPR. NPR, August 9, 2013. https://www.npr.org/sections/codeswitch/2013/08/09/210138278/japanese-internment-redress.

[165] Julia Driver. "The History of Utilitarianism." Stanford Encyclopedia of Philosophy. Stanford University, September 22, 2014. https://plato.stanford.edu/entries/utilitarianism-history/.

for his firing, and accusing him of hating his own country, Kaepernick was immovable in his convictions.

The NFL was not willing to consider Kaepernick's kneeling as a form of civil protest until the death of George Floyd. It was not until then that NFL commissioner Roger Goddell went public and claimed he did not understand Kaepernick's motive for kneeling in protest during the national anthem. Instead, Goddell did nothing to address people who accused Kaepernick of being unpatriotic, including the president of the United States at the time, Donald Trump. Eventually, Kaepernick lost his NFL contract but stands by his decision to protest.

On the same day in May 2020, two events that went viral epitomized racism and racial polarization in America.

On the morning of May 25, a Black man who was bird watching in Central Park asked a White woman to follow published park rules by leashing her dog. Amy Cooper responded by calling the police and falsely claiming a Black man was threatening her and her pet's lives. The incident went viral and the next day, Cooper was fired from her executive position by her employer Franklin Templeton.

Later that day nearly 1,200 miles away, a Black man's killing by a White police officer kneeling on his neck for more than nine minutes, became the symbol of racial injustice. Amy Cooper's and Derek Chauvin's decisions to use their White privilege as a weapon set off a social justice pandemic that shook America awake to the racism that has been the social reality of Black Americans for hundreds of years.

The reaction to these events by NBA and WNBA athletes was decisive. There were moments that NBA players refused to come out of the locker room during the height of the 2020 protests. The response from coaches was to join the players in allyship with the Obama Foundation, Mothers Against Police Brutality, and the Equal Justice Initiative and form the Coaches for Racial Justice Initiative. During the 2020 elections, it was the Coaches for Racial Justice Initiative that converted arenas into voting sites to increase voter access in Black communities. These Challengers are using the initiative to combat racial injustice, promote truth-telling about America's racial history, and aim to bring change in every NBA market.

# The ChaRIOT

## Chapter 10

## A ChaRIOT'S Letter to America

### To My Fellow Americans:

We saw people march when police refused to arrest George Zimmerman after he killed Trayvon Martin in February 2012, and protests erupted nationwide when Zimmerman was acquitted in July 2013. A year later, the killing of 18-year-old Michael Brown by White police officer Darren Wilson and the grand jury's decision not to indict him set off intense protests and at times violent unrest that went on for weeks in Ferguson, Missouri. I point out these two demonstrations because they gave rise to the global Black Lives Matter movement, which so far has only led to some isolated incidents of shifts in American policing such as self-imposed reforms, body cameras, and limited conversations about race.

Then in 2020, George Floyd's murder pushed throngs of anguished people into the streets in record numbers in the United States and abroad. Moved by the trauma of three Black people slain in high profile killings by White current or former police officers in just three months (Arbery, Taylor, and Floyd), Black protesters were joined by Challengers of all races for massive demonstrations around the United States and other countries. That largest and longest protest on injustice ignited an unprecedented national conversation on race that should have been foundational to a transformational period in our country. Instead, it seems we are settling for another transactional moment in which we watch legislators issue statements condemning the racist act that prompted the national outcry, Whites join Blacks in yet another turnout of vocal protests against racialized police violence against Black people, and business leaders make profound public pledges to help end discrimination through diversity hiring and programs led by their companies. By May 2020, many major American companies had collectively pledged a stunning $50 billion to fight systemic racism and racial injustice, according to a study by Creative Investment Research.[166]

A reckoning on race. An inflection point. A watershed moment. A turning point in systemic racism. An equity movement. Whatever words we use to describe what happened in 2020, it presents an opportunity for us to create a space for an awakening, a shift, an unparalleled event that combats the organization of power and racism authorizing the sentiment that BIPOC people, Black people in particular, have no value.

For a new community to emerge and erase the centuries of attitudes and beliefs that served those Whites who sought to oppress Black people and served those who may not have actively engaged in oppressive acts but nonetheless turned a blind eye or refused to speak out against injustices, this time in our history requires an irrefutable polemical statement on racism by a new community of activists: The ChaRIOT Community.

Every Black person who was part of the forced voyage of enslaved Africans across the Atlantic Ocean to the Americas during the Middle Passage, every slaveowner who held a human being in bondage, every Black man, woman, or child who was dehumanized, brutalized, or murdered because of the color of their skin, brought us to the need for the ChaRIOT.

My sense of identity is inextricably tied to my upbringing in the church. Everything I have experienced, every place I have gone, every book I have read, and every person I have met along my life journey, prepared me for this moment in our nation. They prepared me to not only be a ChaRIOT but to be the spark plug that creates a community of ChaRIOTS—a community of people across America who are fiercely committed to ensuring that this is not a transactional moment on racial injustice but a transformational experience that

---

[166] Marco Quiroz-Gutierrez. "American Companies Pledged $50 Billion to Black Communities. Most of It Hasn't Materialized." Fortune. Fortune, May 6, 2021.

demolishes racism. No ChaRIOT is coming. The ChaRIOT is already here. It is us. We must recognize that and act on it.

I would argue that instead of being overt and advocating for a widespread explosion where you are turning over every system in the country, my vision is of the deconstruction and dismantlement that happens during an implosion—strategically placed conversations, strategically placed contestations, and dialogues that lead to an internal collapse of different types of systemic problems as well as implicit and explicit biases.

As a person of faith, I see myself addressing and answering questions that many other faith leaders have avoided. I envision managing conversations that some of the community leaders who are non-faith-based dare to speak about in smaller circles but not in public transcripts.

I am the ChaRIOT who is not afraid to carry the messaging and the hard truths to the people but who also can manage those conversations and bring people from different walks of life to a point of dialogue that impedes their ability to deny or ignore racism exists. By creating the New Cultural Conversation, we will come to understand the implicit and explicit ways racism is part and parcel rooted in our culture and America's fabric in a toxic way that reinforces a lower societal status on those who are subordinate to the so-called "dominant culture."

As with so many past efforts, our hopes for real dialogue and real change after the extraordinary 2020 protests have been dashed and what remains is a deep and abiding reaffirmation that what is required is *radical action* by ChaRIOTS. We have no more options available to us if we are to ever dismantle systemic racism in the United States of America.

## Why We Need Radical Action for Change Now

We have arrived at a critical and unique juncture in our country. No matter race or ethnicity or faith, I believe most Americans know our country should not be operating like this. But the imperative, irreversible shift away from the current state of race in America requires us to take action in ways we have not before to jumpstart the change process and dismantle systemic racism. We cannot wait. We simply must not let this opportunity dissipate. We must become fanatical. We must be willing to create a movement that means sacrificing more than we thought possible to achieve a goal that seems impossible. We must work harder and differently than we ever have at this because it will take radical action to ensure radical change is achieved and sustained.

Some people reading this may question the position I have taken on radical action being our only option. I say to those people do not allow the word "radical" to make you apprehensive about building a ChaRIOT Movement because of images of extremist behaviors or the violence often associated with radicalized action. However, I do stand by my assertion that extreme measures have to be taken and, in this way, perhaps ChaRIOTS could accurately be considered extremists. Just as Dr. King decided that rejecting the notion of being categorized as an extremist for social change was not optimal for him, I accept the idea that as a ChaRIOT, I must exhibit behaviors that may seem extreme to help lead a movement of movements for justice, freedom, and equity for Black Americans.

Why radical action?

We know the legal permissions—the political platforms that allow people to act as racists—sustain longstanding, long-established, unwritten practices of the social rules around race. We must remember that those unwritten rules and practices are prescriptions for how Blacks should be treated in America without question were systemic from the time enslaved people stepped foot on American soil. Church history studies and scholars tell us that Whites demonized enslaved people through their self-created theology and biased way of interpreting scripture, citing the color black as being associated with a demonic presence. When people were brought to America from Africa, their skin tones automatically prescribed a systemic way of how White people responded to them because they were seen as troubled, seen as demonic, and seen as savages that needed to be tamed through bondage. The systemic racism aspect started there but migrated and morphed until it found its way into how Blacks are treated in all aspects of society, even today.

# The ChaRIOT

Radical action seeks to develop a sense of urgency mandating that systemic racism be confronted and dismantled, and waiting is not an option. We must raise the vibration around the seriousness of this issue to the point that it no longer can be ignored by those who choose to deny its existence. As a ChaRIOT, my vision is that a community of ChaRIOTS will break down the silos that keep people clustered together and bound to one another by the common threads of race-based hatred, bias, lies, myths, and fears. Just as Aristotle's Theory of Persuasion proposed that Logos (presenting a logical argument), Pathos (appealing to one's emotion), and Ethos (credible source of information) are critical to influencing people, ChaRIOTS must leverage this strategy to ignite a push within society to eradicate the "community of the oppressed" formed by racism and prejudice and apathy.

ChaRIOTS will push the envelope, challenge the boundaries, and make people who want to maintain the status quo feel the pressure to join the community of ChaRIOTS or get out of their way. I believe inflicting this pressure is mandatory for some White Americans who have been unwilling and resistant to ensuring racialized inequities and injustices are replaced with equity and justice for every American.

## The ChaRIOT Movement's Radical Action Roadmap

Racism in America is complex and deeply mired in the soul of this nation. As a result, only an equally complex set of actions will begin to penetrate, deconstruct, and dismantle it in any way that is effectual and enduring. Described under five headings, each of the following steps are critical elements in the Radical Action Plan the ChaRIOT Movement will lead to achieving two objectives in the struggle to dismantle systemic racism and injustice: changing the behavior of White people so they will no longer actively or passively support racism and stop engaging in what Dr. King described in his famous "Letter from the Birmingham Jail," as the "do-nothingism" of being content in their complacency.[167] We must draw to the movement as many Whites and nonwhites as possible in becoming Challengers and then ChaRIOTS so that we can overcome the disease of racism and its ensuing effects.

We are standing amid *the urgency of now.*

### Action Step One: Break the Cycle of Denial

Make all Americans—Whites and nonwhites—aware of racism. This includes acknowledging that it exists, its pervasiveness, what it looks like, feels like, and all of its various forms. Help Americans, particularly White Americans, accept their role and contributions in perpetuating racist beliefs and behaviors and the immense costs we all pay for living in a country where this disease is so much a part of every system. Many Whites have not had a meaningful interaction with a Black person. For them, no problems exist.

For them, race is something that should not even be acknowledged or discussed. The lack of meaningful interaction gives to even have a sympathetic or emphatic heart towards someone that does not look like them. There are social, political, economic, and most importantly, human costs of an unjust nation.

### Action Step Two: Confront the People Who Need to be Part of the Movement

Many Whites are unaware or apathetic to all the ways they are part of the problem, support the problem, and give energy to racism and bias. They unintentionally preserve their White privilege even while marching in the streets side by side with Blacks. Radical action must involve Whites seeing themselves. The ChaRIOT challenges them to remove the protection those blinders provide them and find the courage to be uncomfortable while they face the realities of how

---

[167] Martin Luther King Jr. "Letter From Birmingham Jail," August 1963. https://www.csuchico.edu/iege/_assets/documents/susi-letter-from-birmingham-jail.pdf.

their behaviors support the persistence of institutionalized racism and racialized injustice. While some move through life with their implicit or unconscious bias, others are intentional about being racist, maintaining their racist stance, and committing racist acts.

As ChaRIOTS, we must be clear-eyed about this group of people and accept that they will probably never change. It is ingrained in who they are, but for those whom we can reach, we must begin by confronting the individuals whom we need to participate in this equity movement. The ChaRIOT Community members must create a place of zero degrees belonging and invite them to become part of it on a large scale and without our judgment or persecution. We must make room by identifying as many ways as possible to help a Challenger become an ally and accomplice.

## Action Step Three: Building the ChaRIOT Community

We will build a community that has never existed before. Critical to building community is open communication and dialogue. In that zero degrees space, we will build relationships across racial, ethnic, social, cultural, and political lines. We will create a community where members are invited and welcomed to participate in a constructive new cultural conversation. We will set a goal for that dialogue using patience, honesty, and belonging to help people divest themselves of deeply held attitudes and beliefs created by living in a country that has fostered an unbreakable cycle of race-based hegemony and hierarchies. ChaRIOTS will lead the New Cultural Conversation that produces a hierarchy of effects, beginning with relationship building as the foundation. Next on that hierarchy are relationships that cultivate trust and narrative change. Ultimately, narrative change will seek to destroy the barriers that keep us from transformation.

## Action Step Four: Building the ChaRIOT Movement

The ChaRIOT Community will construct the framework—a roadmap—to design, execute, and evaluate the ChaRIOT Movement. The centerpiece of the radical action plan will be effectively engaging people outside the ChaRIOT Community, those people who are White and BIPOC, to bolster the movement by leveraging their influence to impact the economic, political, social, legal, and cultural levers that control the system but can also change the system in unprecedented ways. We need ChaRIOTS and non-ChaRIOTS to join this movement. Everyone who wants this radical action for change is welcome and needed.

We will communicate with one another regularly, check-in, and encourage the ChaRIOT Community and those who support it to stay focused on the goal to dismantle and destroy the intergenerational racism that keeps this country from rising. Realizing transformational change is a marathon, not a race, the ChaRIOT Movement will be constructed as a movement of many movements for systematic change of hearts, minds, and institutions.

### Action Step Five: The ChaRIOT Movement

As a ChaRIOT, I know there is no magical carriage coming forth to rescue this country from itself. There is no chariot of any kind appearing but that which we make through a community of alliances and accomplices composed of people crossing all sectors of society who are pushing to combat racism.

True to the structure of a movement of movements, the ChaRIOT Movement will accept nothing shy of collective effort, collaboration, and coordination of people because we know this breaks down the mistrust, fear, division, and hostility that will weaken the overall effort.

Radical action will be most effective when people in the movement and outside the movement are rocked from their places of comfort to a state of discomfort by a truth that directly challenges colonization, racist beliefs and actions, exclusion, and any form of a racialized hegemonic society. We will take the ChaRIOT Movement to the front line and call on lawmakers and leaders of power structures to use their influence to pass legislation and policy that implode the systems of oppression.

The result of our radical action will be a new social structure of our society that is unrecognizable from what we have today. This new society, built by ChaRIOTS, will be better and superior to the dominant system we have had in the past or have currently. This outcome is remotely possible only through radical action that directly challenges White supremacy and systemic inequities and injustices at this moment in time. But that action must begin with breaking the cycle of denial.

## Waiting is No Longer an Option for America

Few BIPOC people have escaped experiencing racial injustice or at the very least witnessing acts of racial discrimination. They know the indignity of microaggressions and oppression while at work, school, police encounters, shopping, in their neighborhoods or even in the sanctity of their own homes. How many times have we seen news reports about Black people being fatally shot or violated by White police officers while in their own homes? Some cases that come to mind include 92-year-old Kathryn Johnston, Botham Jean, Atatiana Jefferson, Breonna Taylor, and Casey Goodson, all of whom were killed in their own homes by police officers while going about their daily lives (i.e., sleeping, eating ice cream after dinner, playing a board game with family, or returning home from a dental appointment).

Justice for their families may come in the form of monetary settlements, but true justice means those people would have never fallen victim to police violence in the first place simply because they were Black. Incidents like these are extreme pain points for all Black Americans, the pain they have endured throughout 400 years of oppression, denial of God-given rights, and suffering unimaginable human indignities.

For too long, too many White Americans have been silent when they should have spoken up, denied racism still exists, denied they are racist, or that they were participants in racism and racist acts. Too many Whites have chosen not to use their privilege, power, and influence to disrupt oppression and join a community of people doing the hard work of taking radical action to advance the transformative social change that ends systemic inequities and injustices. Too many have told Black people to be patient and wait for change.

Slaves and the people risking their lives to end slavery were told to wait. During the turbulent 12 years of Reconstruction, as the country struggled to reintegrate Confederate states and integrate freed slaves into society, Blacks were asked to cling to the falsity that they would be given equality—even as states passed Black Codes that denied them rights as free human beings. Let me point out that throughout decades of race riots destroying entire communities, Black Codes and Jim Crow laws, Blacks being beaten or murdered as they fought for the civil rights Whites were born into, enduring the pain of indignities, fears, segregation, exclusion, and disenfranchisement, the Black race has been told to wait in this land of two Americas: one White, one Black, one just and one in which injustice frames everyday life.

One of the most significant and visible evidence of the two Americas is race-based injustices. It is worth repeating that there is a solidarity between justice and injustice in that justice will never be achieved without someone suffering an injustice. In August 2020, on the heels of months of Black Lives Matter protests, Jacob Blake Jr., a 29-year-old father, was shot seven times in the back by Kenosha Wisconsin police officer Rusten Sheskey after Blake opened his car door to get inside. The officer detained Blake by holding his shirt while he pumped seven bullets into the young father's body as his children watched from the backseat of the car.

Juxtaposed against that incident was a 17-year-old White boy walking down the street with an AR-15 style rifle in full view of police officers during a night of unrest in Kenosha following Blake's shooting. Kyle Rittenhouse killed two protesters that night and still managed to walk by police with the rifle and travel back to his home in Antioch, Illinois.

To illustrate how divided Americans are when it comes to race and racial issues, many conservatives considered Rittenhouse to be a martyr. More than $2 million was raised for his legal defense.

The two men he killed were White Challengers who had joined Black Lives Matter protesters in the days following Blake's shooting. Fourteen months later, at a pretrial hearing for Rittenhouse, the White judge in the case said the two men he killed should not be called "victims" in his courtroom but could be called "looters" or "rioters" instead. Given the bias shown at trial by the judge and the defense, it should not have been a surprise when Rittenhouse was acquitted of all charges, even after traveling out of state and using a gun he obtained illegally, as he was only 17 at the time of the killings.

Fourteen months after Blake was shot, the Department of Justice issued a decision not to prosecute Officer Sheskey due to insufficient evidence that the officer "willfully used excessive force." Meanwhile, Blake is now partially paralyzed and will likely not walk again. His children will be haunted by that horrific image forever. On the day the Justice Department announced its decision, Blake's father said, "What other roads do we take when the justice system fails us. What are we supposed to do?"

Is it any wonder why our country needs a ChaRIOT Movement?

Systemic racism and injustice live in the same space; they are two sides of the same coin. Justice for all is fundamental to a fully functioning society. So often in recent years, we hear the chant of protesters declaring, "No justice, No peace. Know justice, Know peace." Throughout history, the concept of justice has focused on avoiding harm. I lean more into Aristotle's theory that there must be an indelible link between justice and equality, and that a truly just society requires egalitarianism—all people being treated fairly and equally regardless of race, ethnicity, class, gender, socioeconomic status, or educational attainment.

In dismantling racism, the ChaRIOT Movement would tear down systemic injustice and inequity, but first ChaRIOTS must bring to the light and expose the still-prevalent delusion that this disease does not exist.

When the video of George Floyd's public execution went viral and the country watched the life drain from his body as three White police officers pinned him to the ground, White people poured into the street to protest alongside BIPOC people because there was no denying a racist act had occurred. The exposure of racism was the catalyst for collective action. As I said in an earlier chapter, many Whites claimed they did not believe racism still exists until they saw the Floyd murder.

The ChaRIOT Movement will hold up a mirror for those people in denial to peer into and see that the very act of denying racism exists *is in fact, racist*. And that denial is at the heart of why Black lives continue to be devalued, despite blatant evidence to the contrary being exposed daily through mass media and transmedia. Whether the denial stems from hatred, guilt, or fear, the result is clear: hundreds of generations of people have been affected by more than 400 years of discrimination, oppression, and injustice. This disease harms everyone in America.

Many people said that the 2020 protests felt different from others and that it would be a turning point on race. Like many people, I hoped that would be the case, but that event was not the magic bullet. It was a wake-up call that has proven to be more transactional than transformational. But it does not have to be if we use this special time we have been given. We cannot wait. In Dr. King's famous *Letter from the Birmingham Jail*, he wrote about the importance of how human beings use the time we are granted. He also suggested that human progress is never inevitable but must be an intentional series of works.[168]

Through radical action, ChaRIOTS must make the time—this particular time in our country's history—a central part of its strategy to ensure the United States of America keeps a promise that has eluded fulfillment: "All men are created equal."

I, as a ChaRIOT, believe the time for radical action has not been this opportune since the civil rights movement began more than 65 years ago. The men and women of that era struggled and suffered through beatings, boycotts, and even death because back then they recognized the *urgency of now* to end segregation. We are in such a moment today. We owe a debt to future generations to make this a powerful moment for irrefutable and irreversible change. ChaRIOTS have a role and a responsibility to "disturb the peace" for social change, to quote James Baldwin.

---

[168] King. "Letter from Birmingham Jail." Letter from Birmingham Jail, by Dr. Martin Luther King, Jr., April 16, 1963. https://letterfromjail.com/.

# The ChaRIOT

I am calling on allies and accomplices to use the privilege of their identities to join ChaRIOTS and the Challenged in allyship and accompliship to dismantle oppression while disrupting the status quo that keeps bringing us back to the need for civil rights efforts. Together, we will deploy radical action to directly tear down systems of racism, colonization, left-wing extremist views, racist structures, and the dominant perspective.

Much like the many White people who risked their safety to march alongside civil rights workers, rode buses to sit-ins and social justice protests, gave their lives in the fight for equality, the allies and accomplices of the ChaRIOT Movement will be instrumental in doing the work in support of the mission.

Our radical action plan seeks to make people uncomfortable with the state of things and their role in maintaining it. We need to move people out of their comfort zone and into allyship with the movement, including White faith leaders, most of whom have been mere spectators of racism and racial injustices for decades.

As a faith leader, I have been disappointed and disturbed by the lack of presence of many other faith leaders of all races at this moment, as well as their unwillingness to lead on this issue. Their silence sanctions the very behaviors they should be speaking out against to encourage members of their flock to weaken the grip of racism in our society. I do not judge them but want to highlight the fact that as influencers and faith leaders, they have a responsibility to repudiate the racial oppression inflicted by the dominant culture and help spearhead social change. I challenge leaders in the faith community to join me in becoming a ChaRIOT and urge their congregations to become part of the radical change movement we are building. I am asking the faith community to accept the challenge at this crucial moment.

Should faith leaders continue to maintain their silence and complacency, judging from the allies and accomplices that joined Blacks in the massive national protests in 2020, I am confident that the ChaRIOT Movement will reach its goal with a rainbow community of White, Black, Latino, Jewish, Asian, Native American, LGBTQIA+ and other ChaRIOTS leading the radical action necessary to create the implosion that dismantles a disease permeating every stratum of American society.

## The ChaRIOT: A New Cultural Conversation

Days before her death on Jan. 28, 2021, Cicely Louise Tyson, one of the greatest actresses and racial barrier breakers of our time, gave a series of television interviews to promote her newly released memoir, *Just As I Am*, published on January 26. She told Gayle King a story about one of the many racist incidents she had experienced throughout her 96-year life. Tyson said a White male reporter was sent to interview her about the lead role in "Sounder," a critically acclaimed film about a poor Black family in the Deep South during the Great Depression. Tyson told King that the reporter said he felt anger rising in him when the boy in the film called his father, "Daddy." The reporter continued his line of ridiculous comments by telling Tyson he had never thought of Black men as loving, present fathers and family men. He felt only White men were fathers to their children. The privilege of his Whiteness gave him the freedom to not only to think like a racist but to openly and unapologetically express his racist views to a Black person. As racist and biased as that reporter's viewpoint was, it sent an important message: Many Whites do not see Black people as human beings but instead, essentialize them, and view them through a lens of stereotypes, bias, inferiority, and racialized fear.

Tyson's interview with that reporter took place the year "Sounder" was released, which was 1972. Some 50 years later, the sting of the exchange with him was still vividly etched in Tyson's memory. White America, we must do better, which is why the ChaRIOT Movement is indispensable to building a better and more inclusive country for every person who lives here.

If we are to take away anything from Tyson's experience, it is how deeply Americans are divided along racial lines. As a first step in the Radical Action Roadmap, we must deal with how race has always polarized this country. Even the original framers of the Constitution— men who purported to be the fathers of our country—did not have Black Americans in mind when they created the document that would shape and guide the laws of the land. The original framers did not intend for Black Americans to be part of the story. BIPOC people in America were never a component of their thoughts or consideration. As a matter of consequence, nonwhites have had to continually fight for inclusion. Even though we have seen much progress for Black people, Blacks still must slowly and gradually include themselves in the chapters of history as the American story is being written.

A change must come. We must be the change. We must be the ChaRIOTS America needs.

## The ChaRIOT Vision for a New Tomorrow

I see a rise of a new community and a new movement on the horizon, one that gives space for people who are nonblack to be a part of the effort, be a voice, be a ChaRIOT in ways that do not take away from their own identity or who they are or their communities. To my fellow Black Americans, if we do not create space for people who do not look like us to be grafted into the ChaRIOT Movement, our efforts will be ineffective. In some contexts, nonwhite people do not have the legislative reach or resources to see it through on their own. We need other persons who are non-black to help us make a difference.

The ChaRIOT Community cannot be closed off to anyone outside our community. We must let in nonwhites as allies and accomplices. Their family members could see them and say, "You know what? It makes sense as to why you are championing that call or why you are an ally for change because the state of BIPOC people in this country is not right. And I can see why it is not and why I too should become an ally."

Members of the new community must be people who have reached the zero degrees of belonging or being because they have divested themselves of their titles and degrees, their economic prowess, and dominant perspective to participate in this new community without needing to emphasize who they are, how they are honored, or the privileges they hold by virtue of the color of their skin.

The movement, the ChaRIOT Movement, will form another upsurge of the human spirit that drives people as it did in the civil rights era. I believe it is possible to build this community, and it will drive the momentum of the movement. Black Lives Matter has become, in the words of some sports figures, a lifestyle statement more than a movement. This is my vision for the community of ChaRIOTS.

The focus of the movement is deconstruction and dismantlement. I see the ChaRIOT Movement as being both a voice and a vehicle we develop on the concept of the Underground Railroad, which was constructed with a network of Black and White people—Challengers—drawn together by a shared superordinate goal. Like the Underground Railroad, the ChaRIOT Movement will be designed to get Blacks and other excluded persons in America pushed through the system to the point of equity and not just passed through the system and given small amenities to make them feel good but do not altogether eradicate inequities.

ChaRIOTS and the ChaRIOT Movement will take radical action to destroy how legislation and those aspects of the American system that drive a racist culture have manifested with Blacks still swimming upstream against a myriad of disparities and inequities. But change is coming through the Challengers that I am inviting to join me in building this movement.

Throughout this country, there are rising ChaRIOTS willing and able to take on the urgency of this moment and what follows the New Cultural Conversation on race. Those ChaRIOTS will demand a response to the questions posed on racism and injustice rather than entertain and accept the same metanarratives repeated in news cycles. The rising ChaRIOTS see that we have grown far too comfortable with just a seat at the table. It is time to pull away. There is no time or room for bargaining or compromising on the change that must come and the radical action needed to bring it to fruition. The more injustice the culture endures, the more fuel the ChaRIOT receives to go forth, without reconciliation. This is the necessary balance required for the ChaRIOT to arrive and transport the oppressed and the excluded to the point of true and lasting equity, equality, and existence.

It takes the gathering of differences, a diversity of people, to make a difference. The voice of the ChaRIOT will resound from culture to culture, seeing diversity but remaining impartial to those differences. The ChaRIOT Movement will have the ability to evoke conversations that influence perspective and demand accountability.

ChaRIOTS will bring us to a new sense of communal consciousness. This communal consciousness will require a shift in our motives that our words may be followed by radical action in support of a new way of belonging. The ChaRIOT will, yet again, force the reform of justice but this time with the goal of inclusion.

The system, as it stands now, will no longer be the standard for Black life in America. This newfound communal identity will be fuel for an awakening of the human conscience needed to drive radical action and remove the disjointedness that exists between people and replace it with connectedness and cohesion. This way, the collective voices will rise, and the muted voices of the unheard will be heard.

That is where I want ChaRIOT to live. I want this movement to take the anguished cries of slaves whose human dignity was trampled and the cries for mercy from George Floyd, Elijah McClain, Sandra Bland, and the thousands of Black men, women, and children whose lives mattered but were taken any way by members of society who did not see them as humans.

I call on the courage of people who have platforms—political, legal, cultural, or otherwise—to join this community and partner with ChaRIOTS to speak out on behalf of the Challenged and the marginalized in a way that impacts legislation and shames injustice. The grammar required for speaking out and constructing the New Cultural Conversation needed will help to generate an upsurge of the human spirit, reflecting a shift of connectivity facilitated by a shared communal consciousness. The ChaRIOT community at the zero degrees of belonging, and the fruit generated by such an upsurge of the human spirit, will subvert attempts that would create barriers to our movement to end systemic racism and inequity.

The upsurge of the human spirit among ChaRIOTS and the allies and accomplices joining them will fuel the ChaRIOT Community at the zero degrees, inspiring them to lead others who have been consumed by the disease of racism. These combined forces are not only called to share in the ChaRIOT Community, but they are also constituted as advocates of the implosion we will create to disrupt systems of inequity that continue to inflict generational harm on the dominated, conquered, exploited, and oppressed.

It is with deep humility that I, as a ChaRIOT, hope the argument of this book generates action from people who want to join me in creating a community at the zero degrees, which will navigate through the systems that are fraught with race-based inequities and inequalities occupying nearly every space in America. The contemporary and historical disregard for Black lives in America creates the space for an awakening, an equity movement that would combat the organization of power that authorizes the sentiment that Black lives have no value. This book posits that for a new community to emerge, one sympathetic to how race in America interpellates minorities and excluded persons in America, relegating them to being subjects, requires an honest polemic about these realities. Within any racially charged society, the analysis and arguments of this book can facilitate dialogues to *negotiate* the implications of race, *demonstrate* that inequalities exist, and *resist* the heavily contested spaces where people deny the racial oppression of the past is still part of our world today.

This book argues that participating in the New Cultural Conversation as part of the ChaRIOT Movement offers a blueprint for how all beings can contribute to a new humanity, and The Awakening required to completely subvert the interpellation of Black persons in America as subjects of systemic racism.

The Awakening requires a new way of thinking. The heavily contested spaces that Black people negotiate daily will not be resolved by social justice movements that seek to amplify one group's injustices without being fully reflective about injustice as a whole. The sympathy of one group for another will not be enough to interrupt the violence that racism evokes. This basic premise will empower any oppressed community to rise and not fall.

Finally, as a descendant of slaves, I acknowledge that the only way to subvert the law, the organization of power that legitimates senseless acts of violence toward Black lives and other excluded persons in America, is to answer the call of the ChaRIOT.

## Epilogue

## The Rise of a New Movement

At a busy intersection in one of the nation's most populous cities, a young White man was holding high a sign that read: "STOP KILLING BLACK PEOPLE!" It was four days after George Floyd was murdered and the crowd of peaceful, White protestors grew as the afternoon daylight faded into dusk. Throughout the evening, people of diverse races arrived and joined the robust crowd of White protesters who chanted the names of Floyd and other Black victims of police violence. That city happened to be Boston, but it was a scenario playing out in hundreds of cities around the country at the end of May.

On June 6, the Black Lives Matter protests peaked when more than 500,000 people protested in 550 locations throughout the country, making it the largest movement in American history, according to crowd-counting experts.[169]

If rearticulated rage produced an effort that attracted between 15-26 million people in the weeks after Floyd's death and resulted in an inflection point that many experts say eclipsed the civil rights movement, let us reimagine increasing that level of participation and energy: I see a new movement rising, one led by the ChaRIOT Community.

The ChaRIOT calls on the voices of those with privileged identities, as White privilege is a system in and of itself that can convert inputs into desired outputs. The ChaRIOT is aware of certain norms that can only be undone with time; these are the scars from America's legacy of racism and oppression. Privilege is indeed one. For the ChaRIOT, those with privileged identities can be used as fuel for transformative change. This equity movement will call for those

---

[169] Buchanan, Bui, and Patel. "Black Lives Matter May Be the Largest Movement in U.S. History." The New York Times. The New York Times, July 3, 2020.

with the privilege to rise and activate their advantage to become Challengers of the very systems and structures from which they inherently benefit.

As I outlined in the Radical Action Roadmap, we must first move with urgency to capture the momentum. One year after the Black Lives Matter movement peaked in June 2020, some White allies who were fired up to support racial equity were losing interest. Clearly, the passion surrounding the fight for racial equity and racial justice was waning even then, experts who study social change movements said. As we moved through summer and fall 2021, White allyship continued to trend downward.

It may seem counterintuitive given these facts, but I believe the timing for a new equity movement to rise with the power to transform could not be more opportune.

First, two years after those stunning images of Floyd's last moments and a pandemic that revealed numerous racially derived disparities topped headlines in 2020, the country is already tuned for movement building around racial inequity and injustice.

Second, some people involved in allyship and accompliship during the Black Lives Matter protest are now sitting on the sidelines, but all they need is a ChaRIOT Movement that reframes inequity and injustice to re-engage and reignite them.

Third, White allies and accomplices have played critical roles in supporting Black social justice and civil rights causes throughout America's history, from helping slaves escape to the Black Lives Matter movement. The 2020 protests showed us that galvanizing Whites to support a racial equity cause that they believe in is not only possible but achievable.

It is up to ChaRIOTS to afford allies and accomplices space to share in grammar and be a voice and use their influence. It cannot be a grammar that is unique to us or closed off to anyone outside the ChaRIOT Community. We must invite other people to be part of the New Cultural Conversation.

Making room is imperative to the mission of the Radical Action Roadmap. If we fail to make space for people who do not look like members of the BIPOC community to be welcomed into our space to help bring about change, then our efforts will be ineffective. In some contexts, we do not have the legislative reach or resources to see it through on our own. We need other persons who are non-black to help the ChaRIOT live out its purpose of making a difference the country has never experienced.

When that space at the zero degrees of belonging is opened and offered, those with privileged identities must be ready, willing, and eager to shed their titles and join the community. Concurrently, the ChaRIOT will help the marginalized divest themselves of the shame imposed upon them that does not belong to them. We will see nonwhite people and the privileged come together in a new collaboration that grows into a cultural norm. This newfound communal identity will be fuel for an awakening.

To arrive at this state, the ChaRIOT will draw upon the strength of the Challengers in history and the Challengers of today. We salute abolitionists Sojourner Truth, Frederick Douglass, John Brown, and William Lloyd Garrison. We give honor to the people who lost their lives trying to end slavery, the ugliest chapter in American history. We give reverence to the fathers and mothers of the civil rights movement and the White Challengers who marched alongside Blacks. We hold in esteem the women who saw something wrong and launched a movement that is telling the world Black people's lives count, that they matter. It is the unabashed courage and bravery of them all in challenging the colonizers and oppressors that brought us thus far. It was their risk of personal safety, compromising their incomes, endangering their lives, and in many circumstances, losing their lives, that brought us thus far.

Today, there is a need for another kind of Challenger to join this movement, one who will take the Radical Action Roadmap presented in Chapter 10 and execute it with exigency and in a way that unequivocally advocates for the Challenged, the excluded, the oppressed, and the marginalized. The time has come to disrupt and shatter the explicit acts of racism and implicit biases of our nation. The equity movement the ChaRIOT must now build and lead will disrupt the status quo and dismantle racist systems.

Somewhere, there are rising ChaRIOTS willing to take on what follows the New Cultural Conversation on race and racist ideas in America. They are just waiting for the opportunity to lead. I see the rise of a new movement composed of ChaRIOTS who possess the ability to gather the masses and disseminate a message to take radical action motivated by communal consciousness requiring a shift to a new way of belonging. The ChaRIOT will, yet again, force the reform of justice but this time from the perspective of righteousness.

In conclusion, the argument of this book has undeniable implications for me as an African-American male, and as I negotiate the heavily contested spaces occupied by descendants of slaves and slave owners. My designation as a Black intellectual does not exempt me from the senseless acts of violence directed toward my community and that are legally justified but socially unacceptable. It is not difficult to understand why many African Americans interpret these actions as a complete disregard for all Black lives. Unwarranted acts of violence, including police brutality, depict a reemergence of violence toward Black communities without fear of consequences, a depiction often supported by media portrayals and double standards, which suggest history is repeating itself.

Ten years ago, we thought the nature of Trayvon Martin's death guaranteed justice. We were disappointed. Ten years later, we have a different outcome with the murder convictions of Travis McMichael, Gregory McMichael, and William "Roddie" Bryan on Nov. 24, 2021, for killing Ahmaud Arbery. The arc of justice now connects the legacies of Arbery and Martin and offers us a new form of hope in the form of progress.

This verdict does not mean that injustice no longer exists. On the contrary, the defense attorneys' arguments echoed cries of "Make America Great Again." Moreover, the racial stereotypes defense used such as publicly protesting Black pastors' presence in the courtroom and telling the jury that Arbery had "long, dirty toenails" sought to thwart justice for Arbery's family and calls out the need to nullify White supremacists and their rhetoric.

The parents of Trayvon Martin created a pathway for the Arbery jury's decision. Fortunately, the caretakers of his legacy met with powerbrokers and politicians, and they developed strategies, contested policies, and claimed the fight for justice not as their own but one fought for our collective best interest.

What all of this means is that a ChaRIOT is on the way to manage this moment of justice and the inflection point in our country that continues to urge us to march toward progress, not just protest. Progress is the precursor to change but we must always remember that Protest is Good, but Progress is Better!

The ChaRIOT Movement is critical to ensuring this particular time in our country is not mismanaged by people who want to believe events like the verdict in the Arbery and Chauvin cases signal we are in a post-racial or colorblind society. The ChaRIOT represents what the Apostle Paul said, "Contest the patterns and prescriptions of injustice everywhere with civil disobedience."

The ChaRIOT will help us tip the balance, change metrics, drive culture, and conversations. We, Black, Indigenous, and People of Color, are the margin of victory. We alter the scales and shift political futures to ensure change is on the horizon. It is urgent that we ignite and engage in a new and critical cultural conversation about race in America and an equity movement for change, led by the ChaRIOT.

# BIBLIOGRAPHY

"16th Street Baptist Church Bombing (1963) (U.S. National Park Service)." National Parks Service. U.S. Department of the Interior, November 19, 2020. https://www.nps.gov/articles/16thstreetbaptist.htm.

AAPF. "Say Her Name." The African American Policy Forum. Accessed November 29, 2021. https://www.aapf.org/sayhername

Action, Fair Fight. "About Stacey Abrams." Fair Fight, May 13, 2021. https://fairfight.com/about-stacey-abrams/.

Adler, Margot. "Before Rosa Parks, There Was Claudette Colvin." NPR. NPR, March 15, 2009. https://www.npr.org/2009/03/15/101719889/before-rosa-parks-there-was-claudette-colvin.

Amy, Jeff. "Georgia Gov. Kemp Signs Repeal of 1863 Citizen's Arrest Law." ABC News. ABC News Network, May 10, 2021. https://abcnews.go.com/Politics/wireStory/gov-kemp-set-repeal-georgias-1863-citizens-arrest-77601118.

Andrews, Evan. "7 Famous Slave Revolts." History.com. A&E Television Networks, January 15, 2013. https://www.history.com/news/7-famous-slave-revolts.

Art Museum, Smithsonian American. "Literacy as Freedom - American Experience. https://americanexperience.si.edu/wp-content/uploads/2014/09/Literacy-as-Freedom.pdf. Accessed December 31, 2021.

Back, Les and Solomos, John, eds. *Theories of Race and Racism: A Reader*, Second edition., Routledge student readers (London; New York: Routledge, 2009), 330–331

Bates, Karen Grigsby. "Amusement Parks and Jim Crow: MLK's Son Remembers." NPR. NPR, August 11, 2013. https://www.npr.org/sections/codeswitch/2013/08/14/209877767/what-happened-to-the-children-of-civil-rights-martyrs.

Beck, Molly. "Ron Johnson Says Capitol Attackers 'Love This Country' but He Would Have Felt Unsafe If Black Lives Matter Stormed Building Instead." Milwaukee Journal Sentinel. Milwaukee Journal Sentinel, March 15, 2021. https://www.jsonline.com/story/news/politics/2021/03/12/wisconsin-senator-ron-johnson-comment-capitol-black-lives-matter-called-racist/4674016001/.

Beker, Johan Christiaan. *Paul's Apocalyptic Gospel: The Coming Triumph of God.* Minneapolis: Fortress Press, 1982.

Berman, Mark. "'I Forgive You.' Relatives of Charleston Church Shooting Victims Address Dylann Roof." The Washington Post. WP Company, October 26, 2021.

Black, Daniel. "Opinion: The Capitol Attack Was White Supremacy, Plain and Simple." CNN. Cable News Network, January 10, 2021. https://www.cnn.com/2021/01/10/opinions/capitol-attack-white-supremacy-daniel-black/index.html.

Blakemore, Erin. "How Two Centuries of Slave Revolts Shaped American History." History. National Geographic, May 3, 2021. https://www.nationalgeographic.com/history/article/two-centuries-slave-rebellions-shaped-american-history.

Boren, Cindy. "A Timeline of Colin Kaepernick's Protests against Police Brutality, Four Years after They Began." The Washington Post. WP Company, August 26, 2020. https://www.washingtonpost.com/sports/2020/06/01/colin-kaepernick-kneeling-history/.

Bortz, Daniel. "Can Blind Hiring Improve Workplace Diversity?" SHRM. SHRM, August 16, 2019.

https://www.shrm.org/hr-today/news/hr-magazine/0418/pages/can-blind-hiring-improve-workplace-diversity.aspx.

Bourne, Jenny. "Slavery in the United States." EH.net. Economic History Association. Accessed December 6, 2021. https://eh.net/encyclopedia/slavery-in-the-united-states/.

Bryan, Jami L. "Fighting for Respect: African-American Soldiers in WWI." The Campaign for the National Museum of the United States Army. Accessed December 6, 2021. https://armyhistory.org/fighting-for-respect-african-american-soldiers-in-wwi/.

Bryant, K. Edwin. *Paul and the Rise of the Slave: Death and Resurrection of the Oppressed in the Epistle to the Romans.* Leiden: Brill, 2016.

Buchanan, Larry, Quoctrung Bui, and Jugal K. Patel. "Black Lives Matter May Be the Largest Movement in U.S. History." The New York Times. The New York Times, July 3, 2020. https://www.nytimes.com/interactive/2020/07/03/us/george-floyd-protests-crowd-size.html.

Bureau, U.S. Census. "Drops in Natural Increase, Net International Migration Resulted in 0.5% Annual Growth to 328.2m." Census.gov, October 8, 2021. https://www.census.gov/library/stories/2019/12/new-estimates-show-us-population-growth-continues-to-slow.html.

Burke, Tarana J. "Me Too Movement." Me Too., October 15, 2017. https://metoomvmt.org/.

Butanis, Benjamin. "The Importance of Hela Cells." Johns Hopkins Medicine, November 8, 2021. https://www.hopkinsmedicine.org/henriettalacks/importance-of-hela-cells.html.

Cai, Jinghong. "Black Students in the Condition of Education 2020." National School Boards Association. NSBA, June

23, 2020. https://www.nsba.org/Perspectives/2020/black-students-condition-education.

Callimachi, Rukmini. "Breonna Taylor's Life Was Changing. Then the Police Came to Her Door." The New York Times. The New York Times, August 30, 2020. https://www.nytimes.com/2020/08/30/us/breonna-taylor-police-killing.html.

Chughtai, Alia. "Know Their Names: Black People Killed by the Police in the US." Al Jazeera Interactives. Al Jazeera, July 7, 2021. https://interactive.aljazeera.com/aje/2020/know-their-names/index.html.

Clark, Alexis. "How the History of Blackface Is Rooted in Racism." History.com. A&E Television Networks, February 13, 2019. https://www.history.com/news/blackface-history-racism-origins.

Clark, Alexis. "Returning from War, Returning to Racism." The New York Times. The New York Times, July 30, 2020. https://www.nytimes.com/2020/07/30/magazine/black-soldiers-wwii-racism.html.

CNN. Cable News Network. "Rep. Wilson Shouts, 'You Lie' to Obama during Speech." Accessed November 17, 2021. https://edition.cnn.com/2009/POLITICS/09/09/joe.wilson/.

Coates, Ta-Nehisi, and Photography by LaToya Ruby Frazier. "The Life Breonna Taylor Lived, in the Words of Her Mother." Vanity Fair, August 24, 2020. https://www.vanityfair.com/culture/2020/08/breonna-taylor.

Cohen, David and Quilantan, Bianca. "Trump Tells Dem Congresswomen: Go Back Where You Came From." POLITICO, July 14, 2019. https://www.politico.com/story/2019/07/14/trump-congress-go-back-where-they-came-from-1415692.

Cone, James H. Martin & Malcolm & America: A Dream or A Nightmare. New York: Orbis Books, 2005.

Connley, Courtney. "Walgreens' New CEO Roz Brewer on Bias in the C-Suite: 'When You're a Black Woman, You Get Mistaken a Lot'." CNBC. CNBC, January 27, 2021. https://www.cnbc.com/2021/01/27/walgreens-new-ceo-roz-brewer-on-dealing-with-bias-in-the-c-suite.html.

"Connor, Theophilus Eugene 'Bull.'" The Martin Luther King, Jr., Research and Education Institute, August 4, 2020. https://kinginstitute.stanford.edu/encyclopedia/connor-theophilus-eugene-bull.

Conrad, Charles R., and Marshall Scott Poole. Essay. In *Strategic Organizational Communication in a Global Economy*, 7th ed., 458. Chichester, West Sussex: Wiley-Blackwell, 2012.

Cook, Lindsey. "U.S. Education: Still Separate and Unequal | Data Mine ..." usnews.com, January 28, 2015. https://www.usnews.com/news/blogs/data-mine/2015/01/28/us-education-still-separate-and-unequal.

Coppins, McKay. "Why Romney Marched." The Atlantic. Atlantic Media Company, June 8, 2020. https://www.theatlantic.com/politics/archive/2020/06/mitt-romney-black-lives-matter/612808/.

Coqual. Formerly Center for Talent Innovation. "Diversity, Equity & Inclusion." November 16, 2021. https://coqual.org/.

Dastagir, Alia E. "The Unsung Heroes of the Civil Rights Movement Are Black Women You've Never Heard Of." USA Today. Gannett Satellite Information Network, February 18, 2018. https://www.usatoday.com/story/news/nation/2018/02/16/unsung-heroes-civil-rights-movement-black-women-youve-never-heard/905157001/.

Denchak, Melissa. "Flint Water Crisis: Everything You Need to Know." NRDC, November 8, 2018. https://www.nrdc.org/stories/flint-water-crisis-everything-you-need-know#sec-summary.

Di Corpo, Ryan. "Georgetown Reparations Plan for Slaves Sold by University Draws Criticism from Students." America Magazine, November 4, 2019. https://www.americamagazine.org/politics-society/2019/11/04/georgetown-reparations-plan-slaves-sold-university-draws-criticism.

Dorn, Emma, Bryan Hancock, Jimmy Sarakatsannis, and Ellen Viruleg. "Covid-19 and Student Learning in the United States: The Hurt Could Last A Lifetime." McKinsey & Company. McKinsey & Company, November 11, 2021. https://www.mckinsey.com/industries/public-and-social-sector/our-insights/covid-19-and-student-learning-in-the-united-states-the-hurt-could-last-a-lifetime#.

Douglass, Fredrick. "The Hutchinson Family.—Hunkerism." Douglass on minstrelsy. The North Star, September 27, 1848. http://utc.iath.virginia.edu/minstrel/miar03bt.html.

"Dr. Anthony Fauci on Health Disparities in ... - YouTube." Youtube.com, April 7, 2020. https://www.youtube.com/watch?v=Q8eDzI4MiYQ.

Driver, Julia. "The History of Utilitarianism." Stanford Encyclopedia of Philosophy. Stanford University, September 22, 2014. https://plato.stanford.edu/entries/utilitarianism-history/.

Du Bois, W. E. Burghardt. "Strivings of the Negro People." The Atlantic. Atlantic Media Company, August 1897. https://www.theatlantic.com/magazine/archive/1897/08/strivings-of-the-negro-people/305446/.

ESSENCE. "Rihanna Has a Message for Black Women | Essence News | Essence." YouTube. YouTube, September 13, 2019. https://www.youtube.com/watch?v=F3R4ypAQMIo.

Fausset, Richard. "What We Know about the Shooting Death of Ahmaud Arbery." The New York Times. The New York Times, April 28, 2020. https://www.nytimes.com/article/ahmaud-arbery-shooting-georgia.html.

Felder, Cain Hope, ed. *Stony the Road We Trod: African American Biblical Interpretation.* Minneapolis: Fortress Press, 1976.

Frey, William H. "The US Will Become 'Minority White' in 2045, Census Projects." Brookings. Brookings, September 10, 2018. https://www.brookings.edu/blog/the-avenue/2018/03/14/the-us-will-become-minority-white-in-2045-census-projects/.

Gorman, Alyx, and Josh Taylor. "CrossFit CEO Greg Glassman Resigns after Offensive George Floyd and Coronavirus Tweets." The Guardian. Guardian News and Media, June 10, 2020. http://www.theguardian.com/us-news/2020/jun/10/greg-glassman-crossfit-ceo-resigns-george-floyd-protest-coronavirus-tweets-conspiracy-theories.

Graham, Jennifer. "Could 'Patriot' Become a 4-Letter Word after the Capitol Riot and National Unrest?" Deseret News. Deseret News, January 13, 2021. https://www.deseret.com/indepth/2021/1/13/22225243/patriot-american-flag-capitol-riot-new-england-patriots-bill-belichick-donald-trump-medal-of-freedom.

Grannan, Cydney. "What Does D.C.'s Black Lives Matter Plaza Mean to Locals?" WAMU, August 6, 2021. https://wamu.org/story/20/08/27/what-does-d-c-s-black-lives-matter-plaza-mean-to-locals/.

Greensite, Gillian. "History of the Rape Crisis Movement." VALOR, November 1, 2009. https://www.valor.us/2009/11/01/history-of-the-rape-crisis-movement/.

Gura, David. "You Can Still Count the Number of Black CEOS on One Hand." NPR. NPR, May 27, 2021.

https://www.npr.org/2021/05/27/1000814249/a-year-after-floyds-death-you-can-still-count-the-number-of-black-ceos-on-one-ha.

Haidet, Ryan. "Time of Listening: Elyria Residents Invited to 'Experiences of Racism' Forum." wkyc.com. WKYC, June 2, 2020.

Harris, James Henry. *Black Suffering: Silent Pain, Hidden Hope.* Minneapolis: Fortress Press, 2020.

Hassett-Walker, Connie. Assistant Professor of Justice Studies and Sociology. "The Racist Roots of American Policing: From Slave Patrols to Traffic Stops." The Conversation, October 13, 2021. https://theconversation.com/the-racist-roots-of-american-policing-from-slave-patrols-to-traffic-stops-112816.

Hill, Evan, Ainara Tiefenthäler, Christiaan Triebert, Drew Jordan, Haley Willis, and Robin Stein. "How George Floyd Was Killed in Police Custody." The New York Times. The New York Times, June 1, 2020. https://www.nytimes.com/2020/05/31/us/george-floyd-investigation.html.

Hinchliffe, Emma. "The Female CEOS on This Year's Fortune 500 Just Broke Three All-Time Records." Fortune. Fortune, June 2, 2021. https://fortune.com/2021/06/02/female-ceos-fortune-500-2021-women-ceo-list-roz-brewer-walgreens-karen-lynch-cvs-thasunda-brown-duckett-tiaa/.

Hinchliffe, Emma. "The Number of Black Female Founders Who Have Raised More than $1 Million Has Nearly Tripled since 2018." Fortune. Fortune, December 2, 2020. https://fortune.com/2020/12/02/black-women-female-founders-venture-capital-funding-vc-2020-project-diane/.

Hinton, Elizabeth, LeShae Henderson, and Cindy Reed. "For the Record an Unjust Burden: The Disparate Treatment ..." Vera Institute of Justice, 2018. https://wildcatnyc.org/storage/2019/05/JR-Unjust-Burden-Racial-Disparities.pdf.

History.com Editors. "Black Codes." History.com. A&E Television Networks, June 1, 2010. https://www.history.com/topics/black-history/black-codes.

History.com Editors. "Brown v. Board of Education." History.com. A&E Television Networks, October 27, 2009. https://www.history.com/topics/black-history/brown-v-board-of-education-of-topeka.

History.com Editors. "Christopher Columbus." History.com. A&E Television Networks, November 9, 2009.

History.com Editors. "First Enslaved Africans Arrive in Jamestown Colony." History.com. A&E Television Networks, August 13, 2019. https://www.history.com/this-day-in-history/first-african-slave-ship-arrives-jamestown-colony.

History.com Editors. "March on Washington." History.com. A&E Television Networks, October 29, 2009. https://www.history.com/topics/black-history/march-on-washington#:~:text=The%20March%20on%20Washington%20was,challenges%20and%20inequalities%20faced%20by.

History.com Editors. "Trail of Tears." History.com. A&E Television Networks, November 9, 2009. https://www.history.com/topics/native-american-history/trail-of-tears.

History.com Editors. "Tulsa Race Massacre." History.com. A&E Television Networks, March 8, 2018. https://www.history.com/topics/roaring-twenties/tulsa-race-massacre.

Horowitz, Juliana Menasce, Kim Parker, Anna Brown, and Kiana Cox. "Amid National Reckoning, Americans Divided on Whether Increased Focus on Race Will Lead to Major Policy Change." Pew Research Center's Social & Demographic Trends Project. Pew Research Center, October 6, 2020. https://www.pewresearch.org/social-trends/2020/10/06/amid-national-reckoning-americans-divided-on-whether-increased-focus-on-race-will-lead-to-major-policy-change/.

Jack, Jack. "Lebron James' More than a Vote Launches New Campaign to Defend Voting Rights." CBS News. CBS Interactive, March 5, 2021. https://www.cbsnews.com/news/lebron-james-more-than-a-vote-voting-rights/.

Jackson, Ashawnta. "The Alpha Suffrage Club and Black Women's Fight for the Vote." JStor Daily, September 8, 2020. https://daily.jstor.org/the-alpha-suffrage-club-and-black-womens-fight-for-the-vote/.

Johnson, Katanga. "U.S. Public More Aware of Racial Inequality but Still Rejects Reparations: Reuters/Ipsos Polling." Reuters. Thomson Reuters, June 25, 2020. https://www.reuters.com/article/us-usa-economy-reparations-poll-idUSKBN23W1NG.

Kijakazi, Kilolo, Jonathan Schwabish, and Margaret Simms. "Racial Inequities Will Grow Unless We Consciously Work to Eliminate Them." Urban Institute, July 1, 2020. https://www.urban.org/urban-wire/racial-inequities-will-grow-unless-we-consciously-work-eliminate-them.

King, Dr. Martin Luther. "Letter from Birmingham Jail." Letter from Birmingham Jail, by Dr. Martin Luther King, Jr., April 16, 1963. https://letterfromjail.com/.

King, Martin Luther and Jackson Reverend Jesse L. *Why We Can't Wait*. New York, New York: New American Library, 2006.

Klein, Christopher. "How Selma's 'Bloody Sunday' Became a Turning Point in the Civil Rights Movement." History.com. A&E Television Networks, March 6, 2015. https://www.history.com/news/selma-bloody-sunday-attack-civil-rights-movement.

Kuhn, Clifford, and Gregory Mixon. "Atlanta Race Riot of 1906 - New Georgia Encyclopedia." New Georgian Encyclopedia,

September 23, 2005.
https://www.georgiaencyclopedia.org/articles/history-archaeology/atlanta-race-riot-of-1906/.

Lanum, Mackenzie. "Memphis Riot, 1866." Black Past, November 20, 2011. https://www.blackpast.org/african-american-history/memphis-riot-1866/.

Lean In. "The State of Black Women in Corporate America." 2020. https://leanin.org/research/state-of-black-women-in-corporate-america/introduction.

Lee, Trymaine. "Analysis: Trayvon Martin's Death Still Fuels a Movement Five Years Later." NBCNews.com. NBCUniversal News Group, February 27, 2017.

Little, Jon. "Behind the Song: 'Swing Low, Sweet Chariot.'" American Songwriter, December 22, 2019. https://americansongwriter.com/behind-the-song-swing-low-sweet-chariot/.

Lomax-Reese, Sara. "Essay: The Triple Weight of Being Black, American, and a Woman." WHYY. WHYY, March 22, 2018. https://whyy.org/articles/the-triple-weight-of-being-black-american-and-a-woman/

Luise, Schottroff, *Let the Oppressed Go Free: Feminist Perspectives on the New Testament* (Gender and Biblical Tradition), trans, by Annamarie S. Kidder (Louisville, KY: John Knox/Westminster Press, 1991).

Mars, Shaun Michael. "Marquette Frye (1944-1986)." April 7, 2020. https://www.blackpast.org/african-american-history/frye-marquette-1944-1986/.

"Martin Luther King, Jr. Visits Stanford (1967) - Youtube." Stanford University Libraries, September 23, 2016. https://www.youtube.com/watch?v=cYK9xGALPrU.

McCluney, Courtney L, Kathrina Robotham, Serenity Lee, Myles Durkee, and Richard Smith. "The Costs of Code-Switching."

Harvard Business Review, November 15, 2019.
https://hbr.org/2019/11/the-costs-of-codeswitching.

McGregor, Jena, and Tracy Jan. "Big Business Pledged Nearly $50 Billion for Racial Justice after George Floyd's Death. Where Did the Money Go?" The Washington Post. WP Company, August 23, 2021.
https://www.washingtonpost.com/business/interactive/2021/george-floyd-corporate-america-racial-justice/.

McGregor, Jena. "Even among Harvard MBAs, Few Black Women Ever Reach Corporate America's Top Rungs." The Washington Post. WP Company, February 20, 2018.
https://www.washingtonpost.com/news/on-leadership/wp/2018/02/20/even-among-harvard-mbas-few-black-women-ever-reach-corporate-americas-top-rungs/.

McIntosh, Peggy. "White Privilege: Unpacking The Invisible Knapsack." *Peace and Freedom Magazine*, August 0, 1989.
https://nationalseedproject.org/images/documents/Knapsack_plus_Notes-Peggy_McIntosh.pdf.

McLaverty-Robinson, Andy. "Jean Baudrillard: Hyperreality and Implosion." Ceasefire Magazine, September 7, 2012.
https://ceasefiremagazine.co.uk/in-theory-baudrillard-9/.

Michals, Debra. "Harriet Tubman Biography." National Women's History Museum, 2015.
https://www.womenshistory.org/education-resources/biographies/harriet-tubman.

Michals, Debra. "Sojourner Truth." History.com. A&E Television Networks, October 29, 2015.
https://www.history.com/topics/black-history/sojourner-truth.

Moss, Emily, Kriston McIntosh, Wendy Edelberg, and Kristen E. Broady. "The Black-White Wealth Gap Left Black Households More Vulnerable." Brookings. Brookings, December 8, 2020. https://www.brookings.edu/blog/up-front/2020/12/08/the-black-white-wealth-gap-left-black-households-more-vulnerable/.

Moss, Phelton Cortez. "Black Children Are Underserved and Undermined in School, It's Time to Change That Reality." Southern Education Foundation, October 8, 2020. https://www.southerneducation.org/resources/blog/featured/underserved-undermined/#:~:text=A%20recent%20study%20found%20that,%2454%2C000%20loss%20by%20White%20students.

Mullligan, Thomas S., and Chris Kraul. "Texaco Settles Race Bias Suit for $176 Million." Los Angeles Times. Los Angeles Times, November 16, 1996. https://www.latimes.com/archives/la-xpm-1996-11-16-mn-65290-story.html.

Mzezewa, Tariro. "The Arbery Murder Defendants Say They Were Attempting to Make a Citizen's Arrest. Is That Legal?" The New York Times. The New York Times, November 22, 2021. https://www.nytimes.com/2021/11/22/us/citizens-arrest-arbery-murder-trial.html.

Nasrallah, Laura, and Elisabeth Schüssler Fiorenza, eds. *Prejudice and Christian Beginnings: Investigating Race, Gender, and Ethnicity in Early Christian Studies*. Minneapolis: Fortress Press, 2010.

National Center For Education Statistics. "Children's Internet Access at Home." May 2021. https://nces.ed.gov/programs/coe/indicator_cch.asp.

Ngue, Pamela Nonga, Raena Saddler, Jordan Miller-Surratt, Nikki Tucker, Madison Long, Rachel E. Cooke, and Darion McCoy. "What Black Women Are up Against." Lean In, 2020. https://leanin.org/black-women-racism-discrimination-at-work.

Newkirk, Pamela. "The Diversity Business Is Booming, but What Are the Results?" Time. Time, October 10, 2019. https://time.com/5696943/diversity-business/.

Nix, Elizabeth. "Tuskegee Experiment: The Infamous Syphilis Study." History.com. A&E Television Networks, May 16, 2017. https://www.history.com/news/the-infamous-40-year-tuskegee-study.

Nodjimbadem, Katie. "Emmett Till's Open Casket Funeral Reignited the Civil Rights Movement." Smithsonian.com. Smithsonian Institution, September 2, 2015. https://www.smithsonianmag.com/smithsonian-institution/emmett-tills-open-casket-funeral-reignited-the-civil-rights-movement-180956483/.

"Notes On Interpellation." Notes on Interpellation. Longwood.edu. Accessed December 2021. http://www.longwood.edu/staff/mcgeecw/notesoninterpellation.htm.

O'Neal, Lonnae. "George Floyd's Mother Was Not There, but He Used Her as a Sacred Invocation." The Undefeated. The Undefeated, June 24, 2020. https://theundefeated.com/features/george-floyds-death-mother-was-not-there-but-he-used-her-as-a-sacred-invocation.

Olanrewaju, Adenike. "Investigations at Essence Find No Evidence of Abusive Work Culture." The New York Times. The New York Times, September 8, 2020. https://www.nytimes.com/2020/09/08/business/media/essence-magazine-harassment-investigations.html.

Patterson, Orlando. *Slavery and Social Death: A Comparative Study*. Cambridge, Mass: Harvard University Press, 2018.

Pecorin, Allison. "GOP Sen. Ron Johnson Says He Didn't Feel 'Threatened' by Capitol Marchers but May Have If BLM or Antifa Were Involved." ABC News. ABC News Network, March 13,

2021. https://abcnews.go.com/Politics/gop-sen-ron-johnson-feel-threatened-capitol-marchers/story?id=76437425.

Perry, Melissa V. Harris. *Sister Citizen: Shame, Stereotypes, and Black Women in America*. New Haven and London: Yale University Press, 2011.

Pho, Brandon. "What Does the Released Footage around OC Sheriff Deputy Killing of Kurt Reinhold Show?" Voice of OC, April 8, 2021. https://voiceofoc.org/2021/04/what-does-the-released-footage-around-oc-sheriff-deputy-killing-of-kurt-reinhold-show/.

Pickett, Carmelita. "Rosewood Massacre of 1923." Encyclopædia Britannica. Encyclopædia Britannica, inc., January 1, 2021. https://www.britannica.com/topic/Rosewood-riot-of-1923.

Potter, Gary. "The History of Policing in the United States, Part 1." EKU Online, August 20, 2021.

Press, Associated. "New Body Camera Video Shows Moments after Arbery Shooting." 90.1 FM WABE, December 16, 2020. https://www.wabe.org/new-body-camera-video-shows-moments-after-arbery-shooting/.

Quiroz-Gutierrez, Marco. "American Companies Pledged $50 Billion to Black Communities. Most of It Hasn't Materialized." Fortune. Fortune, May 6, 2021. https://fortune.com/2021/05/06/us-companies-black-communities-money-50-billion/.

Qureshi, Bilal. "From Wrong to Right: A U.S. Apology for Japanese Internment." NPR. NPR, August 9, 2013. https://www.npr.org/sections/codeswitch/2013/08/09/210138278/japanese-internment-redress.

Rabouteau, Albert J. *Canaan Land: A Religious History of African Americans*. New York: Oxford University Press, 2001.

Ray, Rashawn. "Why Are Blacks Dying at Higher Rates from Covid-19?" Brookings. Brookings, April 19, 2020. https://www.brookings.edu/blog/fixgov/2020/04/09/why-are-blacks-dying-at-higher-rates-from-covid-19/.

Reid, Maryann. "What Happens When White Women Become the Face of Diversity." Forbes. Forbes Magazine, February 21, 2020.

https://www.forbes.com/sites/maryannreid/2020/02/18/what-happens-when-white-women-become-the-face-of-diversity/?sh=5e62cb8b287d.

Resmaa, Menakem, *My Grandmother's Hands: Racialized Trauma and the Pathway to Mending Our Hearts and Bodies*, Illustrated edition. (Las Vegas, NV: Central Recovery Press, 2017).

*Roots*. United States: Wolper Productions, 1977.

Rose, Joel. "Americans Increasingly Polarized When It Comes to Racial Justice Protests, Poll Finds." NPR. NPR, September 3, 2020. https://www.npr.org/2020/09/03/908878610/americans-increasingly-polarized-when-it-comes-to-racial-justice-protests-poll-f.

Rothman, Lily. "Baltimore Protests: Behind 'A Riot Is the Language of the Unheard.'" Time. Time, April 28, 2015. https://time.com/3838515/baltimore-riots-language-unheard-quote/.

"Say Her Name." AAPF. The African American Policy Forum. Accessed November 29, 2021. https://www.aapf.org/sayhername.

Schafer, Sarah. "Coke to Pay $193 Million in Bias Suit." The Washington Post. WP Company, November 17, 2000. https://www.washingtonpost.com/archive/politics/2000/11/17/coke-to-pay-193-million-in-bias-suit/6a43c0c7-dcde-4d8c-a95f-3fe57c508c85/.

Scott, James C. Domination and the Arts of Resistance (United Kingdom: Yale University Press, 2008).

"Silence Is Not an Option." https://www.benjerry.com, June 2020. https://www.benjerry.com/about-us/media-center/dismantle-white-supremacy.

"Slavery and the Making of America. The Slave Experience: Legal Rights & Gov't" | PBS, 2004. https://www.thirteen.org/wnet/slavery/experience/legal/docs2.html.

"Slavery at Monticello FAQs- Work." Monticello. Accessed December 6, 2021. https://www.monticello.org/slavery/slavery-faqs/work/#:~:text=The%20vast%20majority%20of%20labor,he%20served%20as%20Monticell.

Southern Poverty Law Center. "The World of 'Patriots." January 1, 1999. https://www.splcenter.org/fighting-hate/intelligence-report/1999/world-patriots.

Stanislas, Breton. *A Radical Philosophy of St. Paul* (New York: Columbia University Press).

Stockley, Grif. "Elaine Massacre of 1919." Encyclopedia of Arkansas, November 18, 2020. https://encyclopediaofarkansas.net/entries/elaine-massacre-of-1919-1102/.

Swarns, Rachel L. "272 Slaves Were Sold to Save Georgetown. What Does It Owe Their Descendants?" The New York Times. The New York Times, April 16, 2016. https://www.nytimes.com/2016/04/17/us/georgetown-university-search-for-slave-descendants.html.

Tesler, Michael. "Analysis | to Many Americans, Being Patriotic Means Being White." The Washington Post. WP Company, February 14, 2018. https://www.washingtonpost.com/news/monkey-cage/wp/2017/10/13/is-white-resentment-about-the-nfl-protests-about-race-or-patriotism-or-both/.

Thernstrom, Abigail, and Stephan Thernstrom. "Black Progress: How Far We've Come, and How Far We Have to Go." Brookings. Brookings, March 1, 1998. https://www.brookings.edu/articles/black-progress-how-far-weve-come-and-how-far-we-have-to-go/.

Thomas, Evan. "Michelle Obama's 'Proud' Remarks." Newsweek. Newsweek, March 13, 2010. https://www.newsweek.com/michelle-obamas-proud-remarks-83559.

Thorpe, Isha. "Milwaukee Bucks Break Silence about Boycotting Playoff Game." REVOLT, September 7, 2021. https://www.revolt.tv/2020/8/26/21403526/milwaukee-bucks-boycotting-playoff-game-statement.

Tune, Romal. *Love Is an Inside Job: Getting Vulnerable with God*. New York, Faith Words, 2018.

Tyko, Kelly. "Aunt Jemima Brand to Be Renamed Pearl Milling Co. with New Syrup, Pancake Boxes Coming in June." USA Today. Gannett Satellite Information Network, February 10, 2021. https://www.usatoday.com/story/money/food/2021/02/09/aunt-jemima-pancake-mix-renamed-pearl-milling-company/4460628001/.

Ugwi, Gregory. "Black-Owned Businesses Received Less than 2% of PPP Loans While White-Owned Businesses Received 83%." The Business of Business. Thinknum, July 7, 2020. https://www.businessofbusiness.com/articles/black-owned-businesses-received-less-than-2-of-ppp-loans-while-whites-received-83/.

Vaughn, Jacob. "After Shingle Mountain, Floral Farms Has a Plan. Residents Say the City Isn't Listening." Dallas Observer. Dallas Observer, September 10, 2021. https://www.dallasobserver.com/news/floral-farms-community-has-plans-for-after-shingle-mountain-clean-up-but-they-say-city-isnt-listening-11988618#newsletterSignUp.

Vozzella, Laura, Jim Morrison, and Gregory S. Schneider. "Gov. Ralph Northam Admits He Was in 1984 Yearbook Photo Showing Figures in Blackface, KKK Hood." The Washington Post. WP Company, February 4, 2019. https://www.washingtonpost.com/local/virginia-politics/va-gov-northams-medical-school-yearbook-page-shows-men-in-blackface-kkk-robe/2019/02/01/517a43ee-265f-11e9-90cd-dedb0c92dc17_story.html.

Wahba, Phil. "Only 19: The Lack of Black CEOS in the History of the Fortune 500." Fortune. Fortune, February 26, 2021. https://fortune.com/longform/fortune-500-black-ceos-business-history/.

Wallace, Alicia. "Uncle Ben's Has a New Name: Ben's Original." CNN. Cable News Network, September 23, 2020. https://www.cnn.com/2020/09/23/business/uncle-bens-rice-rebrand-bens-original/index.html.

Warnick, Jennifer. "Glass Ceiling Slayer Roz Brewer Dubs Grads 'Generation Quest.'" Starbucks Stories and News, May 21, 2018. https://stories.starbucks.com/stories/2018/glass-ceiling-slayer-roz-brewer-dubs-grads/.

Washington, James M, ed. *I Have A Dream: Writings & Speeches That Changed The World*. New York: Harper One, 1992.

"We Stand in Support of H.R. 40 and Reparations for African Americans." https://www.benjerry.com, October 17, 2019. https://www.benjerry.com/about-us/media-center/reparations-statement.

Welborn, L. L. *An End to Enmity: Paul and the Wrongdoer of Second Corinthians*. Berlin: De Gruyter, 2011.

Weller, Christian E, and Lily Roberts. "Eliminating the Black-White Wealth Gap Is a Generational Challenge." Center for American Progress, March 19, 2021. https://americanprogress.org/article/eliminating-black-white-wealth-gap-generational-challenge/.

West, Cornell. *Race Matters*. New York: Vintage Books, 2001.

Williams, Kevin, Jack Healy, and Will Wright. "'A Horrendous Tragedy': The Chaotic Moments before a Police Shooting in Columbus." The New York Times. The New York

Times, April 21, 2021.
https://www.nytimes.com/2021/04/21/us/columbus-police-shooting-bryant.html.

Winter, Greg. "Coca-Cola Settles Racial Bias Case." The New York Times. The New York Times, November 17, 2000. https://www.nytimes.com/2000/11/17/business/coca-cola-settles-racial-bias-case.html.

Winters, Mary-Frances. *Black Fatigue: How Racism Erodes the Mind, Body, and Spirit*. Oakland: Berrett-Koehler Publishers, Inc., 2020.

Woolf, Steven H., Laudan Y. Aron, Lisa Dubay, Sarah M Simon, Emily Zimmerman, and Kim Luk. "How Are Income and Wealth Linked to Health and Longevity?" Urban Institute, May 4, 2020. https://www.urban.org/research/publication/how-are-income-and-wealth-linked-health-and-longevity.

"Working Together to Reduce Black Maternal Mortality." Centers for Disease Control and Prevention. Centers for Disease Control and Prevention, April 9, 2021. https://www.cdc.gov/healthequity/features/maternal-mortality/index.html.

Yuan, Jada. "Documenting John Lewis's Last Public Appearance." The Washington Post. WP Company, July 30, 2020. https://www.washingtonpost.com/lifestyle/style/documenting-john-lewiss-last-public-appearance/2020/07/30/0b1d2d04-cab3-11ea-91f1-28aca4d833a0_story.html.

Yuan, Karen. "Working While Black: Stories from Black Corporate America." Fortune. Fortune, June 16, 2020. https://fortune.com/longform/working-while-black-in-corporate-america-racism-microaggressions-stories.

Zirin, David. "Athletes Speak out for #Blacklivesmatter; New York Liberty Sets Inspiring Example for All Athletes." portside.org, July 11, 2016. https://portside.org/node/12034/printable/print.